Wiki

Topic relevant selected content from the highest rated wiki entries, typeset, printed and shipped.

Combine the advantages of up-to-date and in-depth knowledge with the convenience of printed books.

A portion of the proceeds of each book will be donated to the Wikimedia Foundation to support their mission: to empower and engage people around the world to collect and develop educational content under a free license or in the public domain, and to disseminate it effectively and globally.

Contents

Articles

References

Article Licenses

Wiki

A **wiki** is a website that uses wiki software, allowing the easy creation and editing of any number of interlinked Web pages, using a simplified markup language or a WYSIWYG text editor, within the browser.[1] [2] Wikis are often used to create collaborative websites, to power community websites, and for note taking. The collaborative encyclopedia → Wikipedia is one of the best-known wikis.[2] Wikis are used in business to provide intranet and knowledge management systems. Ward Cunningham, the developer of the first wiki software, → WikiWikiWeb, originally described it as "the simplest online database that could possibly work."[3]

"Wiki" (English pronunciation: /wiː kiː /) is a Hawaiian word for "fast".[4] "Wiki" can be expanded as "What I Know Is," but this is a backronym.[5]

History

→ WikiWikiWeb was the first site to be called a wiki.[6] Ward Cunningham started developing WikiWikiWeb in 1994, and installed it on the Internet domain c2.com [7] on March 25, 1995. It was named by Cunningham, who remembered a Honolulu International Airport counter employee telling him to take the "Wiki Wiki" shuttle bus that runs between the airport's terminals. According to Cunningham, "I chose wiki-wiki as an alliterative substitute for 'quick' and thereby avoided naming this stuff quick-web."[8] [9]

Wiki Wiki Shuttle at Honolulu International Airport.

Cunningham was in part inspired by Apple's HyperCard. Apple had designed a system allowing users to create virtual "card stacks" supporting links among the various cards. Cunningham developed Vannevar Bush's ideas by allowing users to "comment on and change one another's text".[2] [10] In the early 2000s, wikis were increasingly adopted in enterprise as collaborative software. Common uses included project communication, intranets, and documentation, initially for technical users. Today some companies use wikis as their only collaborative software and as a replacement for static intranets, and some schools and universities use wikis to enhance group learning. There may be greater use of wikis behind firewalls than on the public Internet.

On March 15, 2007, *wiki* entered the online *Oxford English Dictionary*.[11]

Characteristics

Ward Cunningham, and co-author Bo Leuf, in their book *The Wiki Way: Quick Collaboration on the Web* described the essence of the Wiki concept as follows:

- A wiki invites all users to edit any page or to create new pages within the wiki Web site, using only a plain-vanilla Web browser without any extra add-ons.
- Wiki promotes meaningful topic associations between different pages by making page link creation almost intuitively easy and showing whether an intended target page exists or not.
- A wiki is not a carefully crafted site for casual visitors. Instead, it seeks to involve the visitor in an ongoing process of creation and collaboration that constantly changes the Web site landscape.

A wiki enables documents to be written collaboratively, in a simple markup language using a web browser. A single page in a wiki website is referred to as a "wiki page", while the entire collection of pages, which are usually well interconnected by hyperlinks, is "the wiki". A wiki is essentially a database for creating, browsing, and searching through information.

A defining characteristic of wiki technology is the ease with which pages can be created and updated. Generally, there is no review before modifications are accepted. Many wikis are open to alteration by the general public without requiring them to register user accounts. Sometimes logging in for a session is recommended, to create a "wiki-signature" cookie for signing edits automatically. Many edits, however, can be made in real-time and appear almost instantly online. This can facilitate abuse of the system. Private wiki servers require user authentication to edit pages, and sometimes even to read them.

Editing wiki pages

There are many different ways in which wikis have users edit the content. Ordinarily, the structure and formatting of wiki pages are specified with a simplified markup language, sometimes known as "*wikitext*". For example, starting a line of text with an asterisk ("*") is often used to enter it in a bulleted list. The style and syntax of wikitexts can vary greatly among wiki implementations, some of which also allow HTML tags. The reason for taking this approach is that HTML, with its many cryptic tags, is not very legible, making it hard to edit. Wikis therefore favour plain text editing, with fewer and simpler conventions than HTML, for indicating style and structure. Although limiting access to HTML and cascading style sheets (CSS) of wikis limits user ability to alter the structure and formatting of wiki content, there are some benefits. Limited access to CSS promotes consistency in the look and feel and having JavaScript disabled prevents a user from implementing code, which may limit access for other users.

MediaWiki syntax	Equivalent HTML	Rendered output

"Take some more [[tea]]," the March Hare said to Alice, very earnestly."I've had nothingyet," Alice replied in an offended tone: "so I can't take more." "You mean you can't take ''less''," said the Hatter: "it'svery easy to take ''more'' than nothing."	`<p>"Take some more <a href="/wiki/Tea"title="Tea">tea</a> ," theMarch Hare said to Alice,very earnestly.</p>` `<p>"I've had nothing yet," Alice replied in an offended tone: "so I can't takemore."</p>` `<p>"You mean you can't take <i>less</i>," said the Hatter: "it's very easy to take <i>more</i> than nothing."</p>`	"Take some more tea," the March Hare said to Alice, very earnestly. "I've had nothing yet," Alice replied in an offended tone: "so I can't take more." "You mean you can't take *less*," said the Hatter: "it's very easy to take *more* than nothing."

(Quotation above from *Alice's Adventures in Wonderland* by Lewis Carroll)

Increasingly, wikis are making "WYSIWYG" ("What You See Is What You Get") editing available to users, usually by means of JavaScript or an ActiveX control that translates graphically entered formatting instructions, such as "bold" and "italics", into the corresponding HTML tags or wikitext. In those implementations, the markup of a newly edited, marked-up version of the page is generated and submitted to the server transparently, and the user is shielded from this technical detail. However, WYSIWYG controls do not always provide all of the features available in wikitext.

Most wikis keep a record of changes made to wiki pages; often every version of the page is stored. This means that authors can revert to an older version of the page, should it be necessary because a mistake has been made or the page has been vandalized. Many implementations (for example MediaWiki) allow users to supply an "edit summary" when they edit a page. This is a short piece of text (usually one line) summarizing the changes. It is not inserted into the article, but is stored along with that revision of the page, allowing users to explain what has been done and why; this is similar to a log message when committing changes to a revision control system.

Navigation

Within the text of most pages there are usually a large number of hypertext links to other pages. This form of non-linear navigation is more "native" to wiki than structured/formalized navigation schemes. That said, users can also create any number of index or table of contents pages, with hierarchical categorization or whatever form of organization they like. These may be challenging to maintain by hand, as multiple authors create and delete pages in an ad hoc manner. Wikis generally provide one or more ways to categorize or tag pages to support the maintenance of such index pages.

Most wikis have a backlink feature, which displays all pages that link to a given page.

It is typical in a wiki to create links to pages that do not yet exist, as a way to invite others to share what they know about a subject new to the wiki.

Linking and creating pages

Links are created using a specific syntax, the so-called "link pattern" (also see CURIE). Originally, most wikis used CamelCase to name pages and create links. These are produced by capitalizing words in a phrase and removing the spaces between them (the word "CamelCase" is itself an example). While CamelCase makes linking very easy, it also leads to links which are written in a form that deviates from the standard spelling. CamelCase-based wikis are instantly recognizable because they have many links with names such as "TableOfContents" and "BeginnerQuestions." It is possible for a wiki to render the visible anchor for such links "pretty" by reinserting spaces, and possibly also reverting to lower case. However, this reprocessing of the link to improve the readability of the anchor is limited by the loss of capitalization information caused by CamelCase reversal. For example, "RichardWagner" should be rendered as "Richard Wagner," whereas "PopularMusic" should be rendered as "popular music." There is no easy way to determine which capital letters should remain capitalized. As a result, many wikis now have "free linking" using brackets, and some disable CamelCase by default.

Trust and security

Controlling changes

Wikis are generally designed with the philosophy of making it easy to correct mistakes, rather than making it difficult to make them. Thus, while wikis are very open, they provide a means to verify the validity of recent additions to the body of pages. The most prominent, on almost every wiki, is the "Recent Changes" page—a specific list numbering recent edits, or a list of edits made within a given time frame.[12] Some wikis can filter the list to remove minor edits and edits made by automatic importing scripts ("bots").[13]

History comparison reports highlight the changes between two revisions of a page.

From the change log, other functions are accessible in most wikis: the revision history shows previous page versions and the diff feature highlights the changes between two revisions. Using the revision history, an editor can view and restore a previous version of the article. The diff feature can be used to decide whether or not this is necessary. A regular wiki user can view the diff of an edit listed on the "Recent Changes" page and, if it is an unacceptable edit, consult the history, restoring a previous revision; this process is more or less streamlined, depending on the wiki software used.[14]

In case unacceptable edits are missed on the "recent changes" page, some wiki engines provide additional content control. It can be monitored to ensure that a page, or a set of pages, keeps its quality. A person willing to maintain pages will be warned of modifications to the pages, allowing him or her to verify the validity of new editions quickly.[15]

Searching

Most wikis offer at least a title search, and sometimes a full-text search. The scalability of the search depends on whether the wiki engine uses a database. Indexed database access is necessary for high speed searches on large wikis. Alternatively, external search engines such as Google can sometimes be used on wikis with limited searching functions in order to obtain more precise results. However, a search engine's indexes can be very out of date (days, weeks or months) for many websites.

Software architecture

Wiki software is a type of collaborative software that runs a wiki system, allowing web pages to be created and edited using a common web browser. It is usually implemented as an application server that runs on one or more web servers. The content is stored in a file system, and changes to the content are stored in a relational database management system. Alternatively, personal wikis run as a standalone application on a single computer. For example: WikidPad.

Trustworthiness

Critics of publicly editable wiki systems argue that these systems could be easily tampered with, while proponents argue that the community of users can catch malicious content and correct it.[2] Lars Aronsson, a data systems specialist, summarizes the controversy as follows:

> Most people, when they first learn about the wiki concept, assume that a Website that can be edited by anybody would soon be rendered useless by destructive input. It sounds like offering free spray cans next to a grey concrete wall. The only likely outcome would be ugly graffiti and simple tagging, and many artistic efforts would not be long lived. Still, it seems to work very well.[6]

Security

The open philosophy of most wikis, allowing anyone to edit content, does not ensure that every editor is well-meaning. Vandalism can be a major problem. In larger wiki sites, such as those run by the → Wikimedia Foundation, vandalism can go unnoticed for a period of time. Wikis by their very nature are susceptible to intentional disruption, known as "trolling". Wikis tend to take a *soft security*[16] approach to the problem of vandalism; making damage easy to undo rather than attempting to prevent damage. Larger wikis often employ sophisticated methods, such as bots that automatically identify and revert vandalism and JavaScript enhancements that show characters that have been added in each edit. In this way vandalism can be limited to just "minor vandalism" or "sneaky vandalism", where the characters added/eliminated are so few that bots do not identify them and users do not pay much attention to them.

The amount of vandalism a wiki receives depends on how open the wiki is. For instance, some wikis allow unregistered users, identified by their IP addresses, to edit content, whilst others limit this function to just registered users. Most wikis allow anonymous editing without an account,[17] but give registered users additional editing functions; on most wikis, becoming a registered user is a short and simple process. Some wikis require an additional waiting period before gaining access to certain tools. For example, on the English

Wikipedia, registered users can only rename pages if their account is at least four days old. Other wikis such as the Portuguese Wikipedia use an editing requirement instead of a time requirement, granting extra tools after the user has made a certain number of edits to prove their trustworthiness and usefulness as an editor. Basically, "closed up" wikis are more secure and reliable but grow slowly, whilst more open wikis grow at a steady rate but result in being an easy target for vandalism. A clear example of this would be that of Wikipedia and Citizendium. The first is extremely open, allowing anyone with a computer and internet access to edit it, making it grow rapidly, whilst the latter requires the users' real name and a biography of themselves, affecting the growth of the wiki but creating an almost "vandalism-free" ambiance.

Communities

User communities

Many wiki communities are private, particularly within enterprises. They are often used as internal documentation for in-house systems and applications.

There also exist WikiNodes which are pages on wikis that describe related wikis. They are usually organized as neighbors and delegates. A *neighbor* wiki is simply a wiki that may discuss similar content or may otherwise be of interest. A *delegate* wiki is a wiki that agrees to have certain content delegated to that wiki.

One way of finding a wiki on a specific subject is to follow the wiki-node network from wiki to wiki; another is to take a Wiki "bus tour", for example: Wikipedia's Tour Bus Stop [18]. Domain names containing "wiki" are growing in popularity to support specific niches.

For those interested in creating their own wiki, there are publicly available "wiki farms", some of which can also make private, password-protected wikis. PBwiki, Socialtext, Wetpaint, and Wikia are popular examples of such services. For more information, see List of wiki farms. Note that free wiki farms generally contain advertising on every page.

The English language Wikipedia has the largest user base among wikis on the World Wide Web[19] and ranks in the top 10 among all Web sites in terms of traffic.[20] Other large wikis include the → WikiWikiWeb, → Memory Alpha, → Wikitravel, → World66 and → Susning.nu, a Swedish-language knowledge base.

Research communities

Wikis are an active topic of research. Two well-known wiki conferences are

- → The International Symposium on Wikis (WikiSym), an conference dedicated to wiki research and practice in general
- → Wikimania, a conference dedicated to research and practice of → Wikimedia Foundation projects like Wikipedia.

There are also numerous small-scale educational communities using the Wiki software or variants. Wikidot's 'Philosophical Investigations' is one of the better known.[21]

In an April 2009 article for the London Times Higher academic newspaper, the philosopher Martin Cohen predicted that this 'bottom-up' model would in due course supersede the ambitious "libraries of All Knowledge' like Wikipedia and Citizendium.[21]

See also

- → Comparison of wiki software
- → Content management system
- List of learning resources – courses, instruction videos, slides, text books, quizzes, etc, related to Wikipedia and other Wikis.
- → List of wikis
- Massively distributed collaboration
- Support wiki
- Universal Edit Button

References

[1] wiki, n. (http://dictionary.oed.com/cgi/entry/50293088) Oxford English Dictionary (draft entry, March 2007) Requires Paid Subscription

[2] " wiki (http://www.britannica.com/EBchecked/topic/1192819/wiki)". *Encyclopædia Britannica*. **1**. London: Encyclopædia Britannica, Inc. 2007. . Retrieved 2008-04-10.

[3] Cunningham, Ward (2002-06-27). " What is a Wiki (http://www.wiki.org/wiki.cgi?WhatIsWiki)". WikiWikiWeb. . Retrieved 2008-04-10.

[4] " Hawaiian Words; Hawaiian to English (http://www.mauimapp.com/moolelo/hwnwdshw.htm)". . Retrieved 2008-09-19.

[5] " The wiki principle (http://www.economist.com/surveys/displaystory.cfm?story_id=6794228)". . Retrieved 2008-08-11.

[6] (Ebersbach 2008, p. 10)

[7] http://c2.com/

[8] Cunningham, Ward (2003-11-01). " Correspondence on the Etymology of Wiki (http://c2.com/doc/etymology.html)". WikiWikiWeb.. Retrieved 2007-03-09.

[9] Cunningham, Ward (2008-02-25). " Wiki History (http://c2.com/cgi/wiki?WikiHistory)". WikiWikiWeb. . Retrieved 2007-03-09.

[10] Cunningham, Ward (2007-07-26). " Wiki Wiki Hyper Card (http://c2.com/cgi/wiki?WikiWikiHyperCard)". WikiWikiWeb. . Retrieved 2007-03-09.

[11] Diamond, Graeme (2007-03-01). " March 2007 new words, OED (http://dictionary.oed.com/news/newwords.html)". Oxford University Press. . Retrieved 2007-03-16.

[12] (Ebersbach 2008, p. 20)

[13] (Ebersbach 2008, p. 54)

[14] (Ebersbach 2008, p. 178)

[15] (Ebersbach 2008, p. 109)

[16] " Soft Security (http://www.usemod.com/cgi-bin/mb.pl?SoftSecurity)". UseModWiki. 2006-09-20. . Retrieved 2007-03-09.

[17] (Ebersbach 2008, p. 108)

[18] http://en.wikipedia.org/w/index.php?title=Wikipedia%3ATourBusStop

[19] " WikiStats by S23 (http://s23.org/wikistats/largest_html.php?sort=users_desc&th=8000&lines=500)". S23Wiki. 2008-04-03. . Retrieved 2007-04-07.

[20] " Alexa Web Search – Top 500 (http://www.alexa.com/site/ds/top_sites?ts_mode=global&lang=none)". Alexa Internet. . Retrieved 2008-04-15.

[21] 'Font of all wisdom, or not?' by Martin Cohen, Times Higher Education, 9 April 2009 (http://www.timeshighereducation.co.uk/story.asp?sectioncode=26&storycode=406100&c=1), accessed April 13, 2009.

- Ebersbach, Anja (2008), *Wiki: Web Collaboration*, Springer Science+Business Media, ISBN 3540351507

Further reading

- Mader, Stewart (2007-12-10). *Wikipatterns*. John Wiley & Sons. ISBN 0470223626.
- Tapscott, Don (2008-04-17). *Wikinomics: How Mass Collaboration Changes Everything*. Portfolio Hardcover. ISBN 1591841933.
- Leuf, Bo (2001-04-13). *The Wiki Way: Quick Collaboration on the Web*. Addison-Wesley. ISBN 020171499X.

External links

- Wikis (http://computer.howstuffworks.com/wiki.htm) at HowStuffWorks.
- WikiWikiWeb (http://c2.com/cgi/wiki?WelcomeVisitors), the first wiki
- Wikipatterns.com (http://www.wikipatterns.com/display/wikipatterns/Wikipatterns) A toolbox of patterns and anti-patterns, and a guide to major stages of wiki adoption that explores patterns to apply at each stage.
- Exploring with Wiki (http://www.artima.com/intv/wiki.html) An interview with Ward Cunningham, by Bill Verners.
- WikiMatrix (http://www.wikimatrix.org/) website for comparing wikis.

Wiki (software)

A **wiki** is a type of collaborative software program that typically allows web pages to be created and collaboratively edited using a common web browser. Websites running such programs are themselves referred to as → wikis.

A wiki system is usually an application server that runs on one or more web servers. The content is stored in a file system, and changes to the content are stored in a relational database management system.

Web-based

The first such system was created by Ward Cunningham in 1995[1], but given the relative simplicity of the wiki concept, a large number of implementations now exist, ranging from very simple "hacks" implementing only core functionality to highly sophisticated → content management systems. The primary difference between wikis and more complex types of content management systems is that wikis tend to focus on the content, at the expense of the more powerful control over layout seen in → content management systems (CMS) like Drupal, WebGUI, and Joomla! or at the expense of non-wiki features (news articles, blogs,..) like those in TikiWiki CMS/Groupware (which is a Wiki-CMS hybrid).

The software required to run a wiki might include a web server such as Apache, in addition to the wiki program itself. In some cases the web server and wiki program are bundled together as one self-contained system, which can often make them easier to install. MojoMojo, for example, requires no separate web server at all[2].

The majority of wikis are free and open source software; large engines such as PmWiki, TWiki, TikiWiki CMS/Groupware and the Wikipedia engine, MediaWiki, are developed collaboratively. Many wikis are highly modular, providing APIs which allow programmers to develop new features without requiring them to be familiar with the entire codebase.

It is hard to determine which wiki applications are the most popular, although a list of lead candidates include TWiki, MoinMoin, PmWiki, XWiki, DokuWiki and MediaWiki (Google trend history comparison [3]). TWiki, Traction TeamPage and Atlassian Confluence are popular on intranets. TikiWiki CMS/Groupware is a popular Wiki-CMS hybrid.

Personal

Some wiki applications are not intended for collaborative work, but for personal information organizing or content management. These applications are often referred to as *desktop wikis* or personal wikis.

Mobile

Mobile wiki software is an extension of web-based wikis optimized for mobile devices, especially mobile phones. This is done by providing a version of the web site with conservative HTML coding optimized for the limited function browsers on devices like the BlackBerry[4] or iPhone[5].

Offline

Various approaches to providing wiki function when the user is not on the net have been tried. One simple approach involves making a copy of the wiki database and then viewing it read only. More complex schemes for offline editing require synchronization of changes when the network is back online. One approach to doing this is using a distributed revison control system as a backend of the wiki, e.g. ikiwiki.

See also

- List of wiki software
- → Comparison of wiki software
- List of collaborative software
- → Comparison of wiki farms
- → List of wikis

External links

- WikiMatrix: Comparing Multiple Wiki Engines Side-by-Side [6]
- Comparison of different wiki software [7] (Article, November 2004)
- How to choose a Wiki [8] Cunningham & Cunningham, Inc
- Extensive list of wiki software [9] Cunningham & Cunningham, Inc
- Free tool to verify the security of a self-hosted wiki [10]
- Wikitext standard — Meta discussion on a proposed standard wikitext format

References

[1] *The Wiki Way. Quick collaboration on the Web*, Addison-Wesley (April 2001) ISBN 020171499X

[2] MojoMojo - Deployment without a web server (http://mojomojo.org/documentation/ deployment#Deployment_without_a_web_server)

[3] http://www.google.com/trends?q=TWiki%2C+MoinMoin%2C+PmWiki%2C+MediaWiki%2C+DokuWiki& ctab=0&geo=all&date=all

[4] Socialtext Optimizes Wiki for Mobile Users (http://www.cio.com/article/19955/ Socialtext_Optimizes_Wiki_for_Mobile_Users?contentId=19955&slug=&), CIO Magazine, April 5 2006, retrieved 2008-09-20

[5] W2: a little iPhone wiki (http://www.tuaw.com/2007/07/15/w2-a-little-iphone-wiki/), tuaw, July 15 2007, retrieved 2008-09-20

[6] http://www.wikimatrix.org

[7] http://www.onlamp.com/pub/a/onlamp/2004/11/04/which_wiki.html

[8] http://c2.com/cgi/wiki?ChoosingaWiki

[9] http://c2.com/cgi/wiki?WikiEngines

[10] http://sucuri.net/?page=scan

Wikipedia

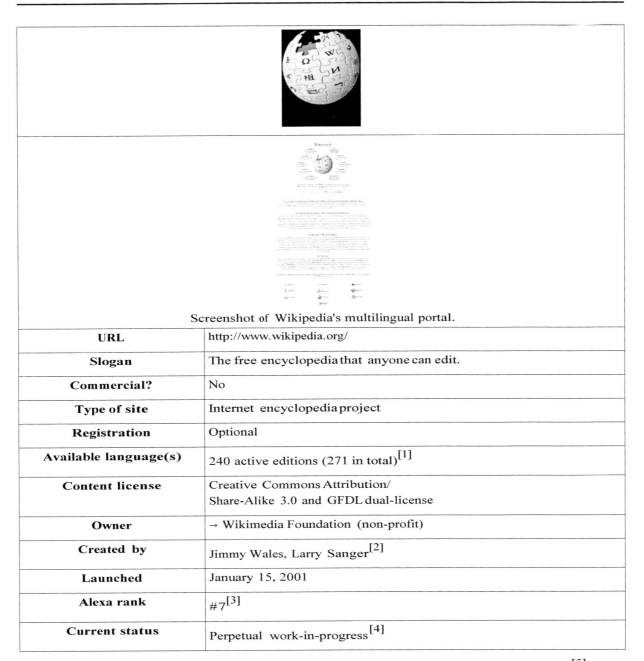

Screenshot of Wikipedia's multilingual portal.

URL	http://www.wikipedia.org/
Slogan	The free encyclopedia that anyone can edit.
Commercial?	No
Type of site	Internet encyclopedia project
Registration	Optional
Available language(s)	240 active editions (271 in total)[1]
Content license	Creative Commons Attribution/ Share-Alike 3.0 and GFDL dual-license
Owner	→ Wikimedia Foundation (non-profit)
Created by	Jimmy Wales, Larry Sanger[2]
Launched	January 15, 2001
Alexa rank	#7[3]
Current status	Perpetual work-in-progress[4]

Wikipedia (pronounced /ˌwiː kiˈ piː diə/ or /ˌwɪkiˈ piː diə/) is a free,[5] web-based and collaborative multilingual encyclopedia project supported by the non-profit → Wikimedia Foundation. Its name is a portmanteau of the words → *wiki* (a technology for creating collaborative websites, from the Hawaiian word *wiki*, meaning "quick") and *encyclopedia*. Wikipedia's 13 million articles (3 million in English) have been written collaboratively by volunteers around the world, and almost all of its articles can be edited by anyone who can access the Wikipedia website.[6] Launched in 2001 by Jimmy Wales and Larry Sanger,[7] it is currently the largest and most popular general reference work on the Internet.[3] [8] [9] [10]

Critics of Wikipedia accuse it of systemic bias and inconsistencies (including undue weight given to popular culture),[11] and allege that it favors consensus over credentials in its editorial process.[12] Wikipedia's reliability and accuracy are also an issue.[13] Other criticisms center on its susceptibility to vandalism and the addition of spurious or unverified information,[14] though scholarly work suggests that vandalism is generally short-lived.[15] [16]

Wikipedia's departure from the expert-driven style of the encyclopedia building mode and the large presence of unacademic contents have been noted several times. When *Time* magazine recognized You as its Person of the Year for 2006, acknowledging the accelerating success of online collaboration and interaction by millions of users around the world, it cited Wikipedia as one of three examples of Web 2.0 services, along with YouTube and MySpace.[17] Some noted the importance of Wikipedia not only as an encyclopedic reference but also as a frequently updated news resource because of how quickly articles about recent events appear.[18] [19]

History

Wikipedia began as a complementary project for Nupedia, a free online English-language encyclopedia project whose articles were written by experts and reviewed under a formal process. Nupedia was founded on March 9, 2000, under the ownership of Bomis, Inc, a web portal company. Its main figures were Jimmy

Wikipedia originally developed from another encyclopedia project, Nupedia.

Wales, Bomis CEO, and Larry Sanger, editor-in-chief for Nupedia and later Wikipedia. Nupedia was licensed initially under its own Nupedia Open Content License, switching to the GNU Free Documentation License before Wikipedia's founding at the urging of Richard Stallman.[20]

Larry Sanger and Jimmy Wales are the founders of Wikipedia.[21] [22] While Wales is credited with defining the goal of making a publicly editable encyclopedia,[23] [24] Sanger is usually credited with the strategy of using a → wiki to reach that goal.[25] On January 10, 2001, Larry Sanger proposed on the Nupedia mailing list to create a wiki as a "feeder" project for Nupedia.[26] Wikipedia was formally launched on January 15, 2001, as a single English-language edition at www.wikipedia.com,[27] and announced by Sanger on the Nupedia mailing list.[23] Wikipedia's policy of "neutral point-of-view"[28] was codified in its initial months, and was similar to Nupedia's earlier "nonbiased" policy. Otherwise, there were relatively few rules initially and Wikipedia operated independently of Nupedia.[23]

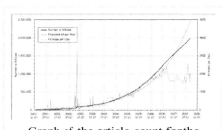

Graph of the article count for the English Wikipedia, from January 10, 2001, to September 9, 2007 (the date of the two-millionth article)

Wikipedia gained early contributors from Nupedia, Slashdot postings, and web search engine indexing. It grew to approximately 20,000 articles, and 18 language editions, by the end of 2001. By late 2002 it had reached 26 language editions, 46 by the end of 2003, and 161 by the final days of 2004.[29] Nupedia and Wikipedia coexisted until the former's servers were taken down permanently in 2003, and its text was incorporated into Wikipedia. English Wikipedia passed the 2 million-article mark on September 9, 2007, making it the largest encyclopedia ever assembled, eclipsing even the Yongle Encyclopedia (1407), which had held the record for exactly 600 years.[30]

Citing fears of commercial advertising and lack of control in a perceived English-centric Wikipedia, users of the Spanish Wikipedia Forked from Wikipedia to create the *Enciclopedia Libre* in February 2002.[31] Later that year, Wales announced that Wikipedia would not display advertisements, and its website was moved to wikipedia.org.[32] Various other projects have since forked from Wikipedia for editorial reasons. Wikinfo does not require a neutral point of view and allows original research. New Wikipedia-inspired projects — such as Citizendium, Scholarpedia, Conservapedia, and Google's Knol[33] — have been started to address perceived limitations of Wikipedia, such as its policies on peer review, original research, and commercial advertising.

Though the English Wikipedia reached 3 million articles in August 2009, the growth of the edition, in terms of the numbers of articles and of contributors, appeared to have abruptly flattened around Spring 2007.[34] In July 2007, about 2,200 articles were added daily to the encyclopedia; as of August 2009[35], that average is 1,300. A team led by Ed H Chi at the Palo Alto Research Center speculated that this is due to the increasing exclusiveness of the project. New or occasional editors have significantly higher rates of their edits reverted (removed) than an "elite" group of regular editors. This could make it more difficult for the project to recruit and retain new contributors, over the long term resulting in stagnation in article creation.

Nature of Wikipedia

Editing model

In departure from the style of traditional encyclopedias such as *Encyclopædia Britannica*, Wikipedia employs the open editing model called "wiki". Except for a few vandalism-prone pages that can be edited only by established users, or in extreme cases only by administrators, every article may be edited anonymously or with a user account, while only registered users may create a new article (only in English edition). No article is owned by its creator or any other editor, or is vetted by any recognized authority; rather, the articles are collectively owned by a community of editors. [37]

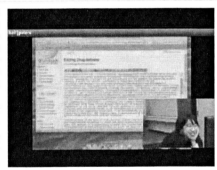

In April 2009, the → Wikimedia Foundation conducted a Wikipedia usability study, questioning users about the editing mechanism.[36]

Most importantly, when changes to an article are made, they become available immediately before undergoing any review, no matter if they contain an error, are somehow misguided or even patent nonsense. The German edition of Wikipedia is an exception to this rule: it has been testing a system of maintaining "stable versions" of articles,[38] to allow a reader to see versions of articles that have passed certain reviews. The English edition of Wikipedia plans to trial a related approach.[39] [40] Another proposal is the use of software to create "trust ratings" for individual Wikipedia contributors and using those ratings to determine which changes will be made visible immediately.[41]

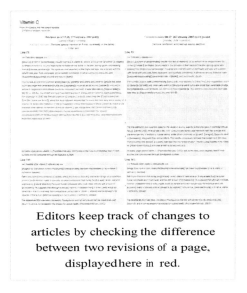

Editors keep track of changes to articles by checking the difference between two revisions of a page, displayed here in red.

Contributors, registered or not, can take advantage of features available in the software that powers Wikipedia. The "History" page attached to each article records every single past revision of the article, though a revision with libelous content, criminal threats or copyright infringements may be removed afterwards.[42] [43] This feature makes it easy to compare old and new versions, undo changes that an editor considers undesirable, or restore lost content. The "Discussion" pages associated with each article are used to coordinate work among multiple editors.[44] Regular contributors often maintain a "watchlist" of articles of interest to them, so that they can easily keep tabs on all recent changes to those articles. Computer programs called Internet bots have been used widely to remove vandalism as soon as it was made,[16] to correct common misspellings and stylistic issues, or to start articles such as geography entries in a standard format from statistical data.

Articles in Wikipedia are organized roughly in three ways: according to their development statuses, their subject matters and the access levels required for edits. The most developed state of articles is called "featured article": they are precisely ones that someday get featured in the main page of Wikipedia.[45] [46] Researcher Giacomo Poderi found that articles tend to reach the FA status via intensive works of few editors, and that the categories such as history, media, music and warfare have higher ratio of featured articles than those such as computing, mathematics, language & linguistics and philosophy & psychology, casting a doubt to the equation "more edits equal higher quality." In 2007, in preparation for producing a print version, the English-language Wikipedia introduced an assessment scale against which the quality of articles is judged;[47] other editions have also adopted this.

In 2008, two researchers theorized that the growth of Wikipedia is sustainable.[48]

Consequence of the open editing model

See also: Reliability of Wikipedia, Criticism of Wikipedia, Academic studies of Wikipedia.

The open nature of the editing model has been central to most criticism of Wikipedia. For example, at any point, a reader of an article cannot be certain whether or not the article she is reading has been vandalized. Former *Encyclopaedia Britannica* editor-in-chief Robert McHenry once described this by saying:[49]

> The user who visits Wikipedia to learn about some subject, to confirm some matter of fact, is rather in the position of a visitor to a public restroom. It may be obviously dirty, so that he knows to exercise great care, or it may seem fairly clean, so that he may be lulled into a false sense of security. What he certainly does not know is who has used the facilities before him.

and popularized the claim that Wikipedia is a "faith-based encyclopedia." Critics argue that non-expert editing undermines quality. Because contributors usually rewrite small portions of an entry rather than making full-length revisions, high- and low-quality content may be intermingled within an entry. Historian Roy Rosenzweig noted: "Overall, writing is the Achilles' heel of Wikipedia. Committees rarely write well, and Wikipedia entries often have a choppy quality that results from the stringing together of sentences or paragraphs written by different people."[50] All of these led to the question of the reliability of Wikipedia as a source of accurate information.

John Seigenthaler has described Wikipedia as "a flawed and irresponsible research tool."[51]

As a consequence of the open structure, Wikipedia "makes no guarantee of validity" of its content, since no one is ultimately responsible for any claims appearing in it.[52] Concerns have been raised regarding the lack of accountability that results from users' anonymity,[53] the insertion of spurious information, vandalism, and similar problems. In one particularly well-publicized incident, false information was introduced into the biography of American political figure John Seigenthaler and remained undetected for four months.[51] John Seigenthaler, the founding editorial director of *USA Today* and founder of the Freedom Forum First Amendment Center at Vanderbilt University, called Jimmy Wales and asked him, "...Do you ...have any way to know who wrote that?" "No, we don't", said Jimmy.[54]

Some critics claim that Wikipedia's open structure makes it an easy target for Internet trolls, spams, and those with an agenda to push.[42] [55] The addition of political spin to articles by organizations including members of the U.S. House of Representatives and special interest groups[14] has been noted,[56] and organizations such as Microsoft have offered financial incentives to work on certain articles.[57] These issues have been parodied, notably by Stephen Colbert in *The Colbert Report*.[58]

Coverage of topics

The 20 most viewed Wikipedia articles in 2009

→ Wiki
The Beatles
Michael Jackson
Favicon.ico
YouTube
→ Wikipedia
Barack Obama
Deaths in 2009
United States
Facebook
Current events portal [59]
World War II
Twitter

Transformers
Slumdog Millionaire
Lil Wayne
Adolf Hitler
India
Transformers 2
Scrubs (TV series)

See also: Notability in Wikipedia.

As an encyclopedia building project, Wikipedia seeks to create a summary of all human knowledge: all of topics covered by a conventional print encyclopedia plus any other "notable" (therefore verifiable by published sources) topics, which are permitted by unlimited disk space.[60] In particular, it contains materials that some people, including Wikipedia editors,[61] may find objectionable, offensive, or pornographic.[62] It was made clear that this policy is not up for debate, and the policy has sometimes proved controversial. For instance, in 2008, Wikipedia rejected an online petition against the inclusion of Muhammad's depictions in its English edition, citing this policy. The presence of politically sensitive materials in Wikipedia had also led the People's Republic of China to block access to parts of the site.[63] (See also: IWF block of Wikipedia)

Content in Wikipedia is subject to the laws (in particular copyright law) in Florida, where Wikipedia servers are hosted, and several editorial policies and guidelines that are intended to reinforce the notion that Wikipedia is an encyclopedia. Each entry in Wikipedia must be about a topic that is encyclopedic and thus is worthy of inclusion. A topic is deemed encyclopedic if it is "notable"[64] in the Wikipedia jargon; i.e., if it has received significant coverage in secondary reliable sources (i.e., mainstream media or major academic journals) that are independent of the subject of the topic. Second, Wikipedia must expose knowledge that is already established and recognized.[65] In other words, it must not present, for instance, new information or original works. A claim that is likely to be challenged requires a reference to reliable sources. Within the Wikipedia community, this is often phrased as "verifiability, not truth" to express the idea that the readers are left themselves to check the truthfulness of what appears in the articles and to make their own interpretations.[66] Finally, Wikipedia does not take a side.[67] All opinions and viewpoints, if attributable to external sources, must enjoy appropriate share of coverage within an article.[68] Wikipedia editors as a community write and revise those policies and guidelines[69] and enforce them by deleting, annotating with tags, or modifying article materials failing to meet them. (See also deletionism and inclusionism)[70] [71]

However, Wikipedia has been accused of exhibiting systemic bias and inconsistency;[13] critics argue that Wikipedia's open nature and a lack of proper sources for much of the information makes it unreliable.[72] Some commentators suggest that Wikipedia is generally reliable, but that the reliability of any given article is not always clear.[12] Editors of traditional reference works such as the *Encyclopædia Britannica* have questioned the project's utility and status as an encyclopedia.[73] Many university lecturers discourage students from citing any encyclopedia in academic work, preferring primary sources;[74] some specifically prohibit Wikipedia citations.[75] Co-founder Jimmy Wales stresses that encyclopedias of any type are not usually appropriate as primary sources, and should not be relied upon as authoritative.[76]

Andrew Lih, author of the 2009 book *The Wikipedia Revolution*, notes: "A wiki has all its activities happening in the open for inspection... Trust is built by observing the actions of others in the community and discovering people with like or complementary interests." [77]

Economist Tyler Cowen writes, "If I had to guess whether Wikipedia or the median refereed journal article on economics was more likely to be true, after a not so long think I would opt for Wikipedia." He comments that many traditional sources of non-fiction suffer from systemic biases. Novel results are over-reported in journal articles, and relevant information is omitted from news reports. However, he also cautions that errors are frequently found on Internet sites, and that academics and experts must be vigilant in correcting them. [78]

In February 2007, an article in *The Harvard Crimson* newspaper reported that some of the professors at Harvard University include Wikipedia in their syllabus, but that there is a split in their perception of using Wikipedia. [79] In June 2007, former president of the American Library Association Michael Gorman condemned Wikipedia, along with Google, [80] stating that academics who endorse the use of Wikipedia are "the intellectual equivalent of a dietitian who recommends a steady diet of Big Macs with everything". He also said that "a generation of intellectual sluggards incapable of moving beyond the Internet" was being produced at universities. He complains that the web-based sources are discouraging students from learning from the more rare texts which are either found only on paper or are on subscription-only web sites. In the same article Jenny Fry (a research fellow at the Oxford Internet Institute) commented on academics who cite Wikipedia, saying that: "You cannot say children are intellectually lazy because they are using the Internet when academics are using search engines in their research. The difference is that they have more experience of being critical about what is retrieved and whether it is authoritative. Children need to be told how to use the Internet in a critical and appropriate way." [80]

Wikipedia community

The Wikipedia community has established "a bureaucracy of sorts", including "a clear power structure that gives volunteer administrators the authority to exercise editorial control." [81] [82] [83] Wikipedia's community has also been described as "cult-like", [84] although not always with entirely negative connotations, [85] and criticized for failing to accommodate inexperienced users. [86] Editors in good standing in the community can run for one of many levels of volunteer stewardship; this begins with "administrator", [87] [88] a group of privileged users who have the ability to delete pages, lock articles from being changed in case of vandalism or editorial disputes, and block users from editing. Despite the name, administrators do not enjoy any special privilege in decision-making; instead they are mostly limited to making edits that have project-wide effects and thus are disallowed to ordinary editors, and to ban users making disruptive edits (such as vandalism). [89]

As Wikipedia grows with an unconventional model of encyclopedia building, "Who writes Wikipedia?" has become one of the questions frequently asked on the project, often with a reference to other Web 2.0 projects such as Digg.[90] Jimmy Wales once argued that only "a community ... a dedicated group of a few hundred volunteers" makes the bulk of contributions to Wikipedia and that the project is therefore "much like any traditional organization". Wales performed a study finding that over 50% of all the edits are done by just .7% of the users (at the time: 524 people). This method of evaluating contributions was later disputed by Aaron Swartz, who noted that several articles he sampled had

→ Wikimania, an annual conference for users of Wikipedia and other projects operated by the Wikimedia Foundation.

large portions of their content (measured by number of characters) contributed by users with low edit counts.[91] A 2007 study by researchers from Dartmouth College found that "anonymous and infrequent contributors to Wikipedia ... are as reliable a source of knowledge as those contributors who register with the site."[92] Although some contributors are authorities in their field, Wikipedia requires that even their contributions be supported by published and verifiable sources. The project's preference for consensus over credentials has been labeled "anti-elitism".[11]

In August 2007, WikiScanner, a website developed by Virgil Griffith began to trace the sources of changes made to Wikipedia by anonymous editors without Wikipedia accounts. The program revealed that many such edits were made by corporations or government agencies changing the content of articles related to them, their personnel or their work.[93]

In a 2003 study of Wikipedia as a community, economics Ph.D. student Andrea Ciffolilli argued that the low transaction costs of participating in → wiki software create a catalyst for collaborative development, and that a "creative construction" approach encourages participation.[94] In his 2008 book, *The Future of the Internet and How to Stop It*, Jonathan Zittrain of the Oxford Internet Institute and Harvard Law School' s Berkman Center for Internet & Society cites Wikipedia's success as a case study in how open collaboration has fostered innovation on the web.[95] A 2008 study found that Wikipedia users were less agreeable and open, though more conscientious, than non-Wikipedia users.[96] [97] A 2009 study suggested there was "evidence of growing resistance from the Wikipedia community to new content."[98]

The Wikipedia Signpost is the community newspaper on the English Wikipedia,[99] and was founded by Michael Snow, an administrator and the current chair of the → Wikimedia Foundation board of trustees.[100] It covers news and events from the site, as well as major events from sister projects, such as Wikimedia Commons.[101]

Operation

Wikimedia Foundation and the Wikimedia chapters

Wikipedia is hosted and funded by the → Wikimedia Foundation, a non-profit organization which also operates Wikipedia-related projects such as Wikibooks. The Wikimedia chapters, local associations of Wikipedia users, also participate in the promotion, the development, and the funding of the project.

→ Wikimedia Foundation logo

Software and hardware

The operation of Wikipedia depends on MediaWiki, a custom-made, free and open source wiki software platform written in PHP and built upon the MySQL database.[102] The software incorporates programming features such as a macro language, variables, a transclusion system for templates, and URL redirection. MediaWiki is licensed under the GNU General Public License and used by all Wikimedia projects, as well as many other wiki projects. Originally, Wikipedia ran on UseModWiki written in Perl by Clifford Adams (Phase I), which initially required CamelCase for article hyperlinks; the present double bracket style was incorporated later. Starting in January 2002 (Phase II), Wikipedia began running on a PHP wiki engine with a MySQL database; this software was custom-made for Wikipedia by Magnus Manske. The Phase II software was repeatedly modified to accommodate the exponentially increasing demand. In July 2002 (Phase III), Wikipedia shifted to the third-generation software, MediaWiki, originally written by Lee Daniel Crocker. Several MediaWiki extensions are installed[103] to extend the functionality of MediaWiki software. In April 2005 a Lucene extension[104] [105] was added to MediaWiki's built-in search and Wikipedia switched from MySQL to Lucene for searching. Currently Lucene Search 2,[106] which is written in Java and based on Lucene library 2.0,[107] is used.

Wikipedia currently runs on dedicated clusters of Linux servers (mainly Ubuntu),[108] [109] with a few OpenSolaris machines for ZFS. As of February 2008, there were 300 in Florida, 26 in Amsterdam, and 23 in Yahoo!'s Korean hosting facility in Seoul.[110] Wikipedia employed a single server until 2004, when the server setup was expanded into a distributed multitier architecture. In January 2005, the project ran on 39 dedicated servers located in Florida. This configuration included a single master database server running MySQL, multiple slave database servers, 21 web servers running the Apache HTTP Server, and seven Squid cache servers.

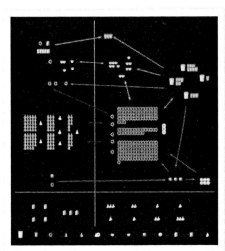

Overview of system architecture, April 2009. See server layout diagrams on Meta-Wiki.

Wikipedia receives between 25,000 and 60,000 page requests per second, depending on time of day.[111]

Page requests are first passed to a front-end layer of Squid caching servers.[112] Requests that cannot be served from the Squid cache are sent to load-balancing servers running the Linux Virtual Server software, which in turn pass the request to one of the Apache web servers for page rendering from the database. The web servers deliver pages as requested, performing page rendering for all the language editions of Wikipedia. To increase speed further, rendered pages are cached in a distributed memory cache until invalidated, allowing page rendering to be skipped entirely for most common page accesses. Two larger clusters in the Netherlands and Korea now handle much of Wikipedia's traffic load.

Delivery media

Wikipedia's original medium was for users to read and edit content using any standard web browser through a fixed internet connection. However, Wikipedia content is now also accessible through offline media, and through the mobile web.

On mobile devices access to Wikipedia from mobile phones was possible as early as 2004, through the Wireless Application Protocol (WAP), through the Wapedia service. In June 2007, Wikipedia launched en.mobile.wikipedia.org [113], an official website for wireless devices. In 2009 a newer mobile service was officially released,[114] located at en.m.wikipedia.org [115], which caters to more advanced mobile devices such as the iPhone, Android-based devices, or the Palm Pre. Several other methods of mobile access to Wikipedia have emerged (See Wikipedia:Mobile access [116]). Several devices and applications optimise or enhance the display of Wikipedia content for mobile devices, while some also incorporate additional features such as use of Wikipedia metadata (See Wikipedia:Metadata[117]), such as geoinformation.[118]

Collections of Wikipedia articles have been published on optical disks. An English version, 2006 Wikipedia CD Selection, contained about 2,000 articles.[119] [120] The Polish version contains nearly 240,000 articles.[121] There are also German versions.[122]

License and language editions

All text in Wikipedia was covered by GNU Free Documentation License (GFDL), a copyleft license permitting the redistribution, creation of derivative works, and commercial use of content while authors retain copyright of their work,[123] up until June 2009, when the site switched to Creative Commons Attribution-ShareAlike (CC-by-SA) 3.0.[124] Wikipedia had been working on the switch to Creative Commons licenses because the GFDL, initially designed for software manuals, is not suitable for online reference works and because the two licenses were incompatible.[125] In response to the Wikimedia Foundation's request, in November 2008, the Free Software Foundation (FSF) released a new version of GFDL designed specifically to allow Wikipedia to relicense its content to CC-BY-SA[126] by August 1, 2009. Wikipedia and its sister projects held a community-wide referendum to decide whether or not to make the license switch.[127] The referendum took place from April 9 to 30.[128] The results were 75.8% "Yes", 10.5% "No", and 13.7% "No opinion".[129] In consequence of the referendum, the Wikimedia Board of Trustees voted to change to the Creative Commons license, effective June 15, 2009.[129] The position that Wikipedia is merely a hosting service has been successfully used as a defense in court.[130] [131]

The handling of media files (e.g., image files) varies across language editions. Some language editions, such as the English Wikipedia, include non-free image files under fair use doctrine, while the others have opted not to. This is in part because of the difference in copyright laws between countries; for example, the notion of fair use does not exist in Japanese copyright law. Media files covered by free content licenses (e.g., Creative Commons' cc-by-sa) are shared across language editions via Wikimedia Commons repository, a project operated by the Wikimedia Foundation.

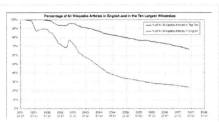

Percentage of all Wikipedia articles in English (red) and top ten largest language editions (blue). As of July 2007, less than 23% of Wikipedia articles are in English.

There are currently 262 language editions of Wikipedia; of these, 24 have over 100,000 articles and 81 have over 1,000 articles.[1] According to Alexa, the English subdomain (en.wikipedia.org; English Wikipedia) receives approximately 52% of Wikipedia's cumulative traffic, with the remaining split among the other languages (Spanish: 19%, French: 5%, Polish: 3%, German: 3%, Japanese: 3%, Portuguese: 2%).[3] As of July 2008, the five largest language editions are (in order of article count) English, German, French, Polish, and Japanese Wikipedias.[132]

Since Wikipedia is web-based and therefore worldwide, contributors of a same language edition may use different dialects or may come from different countries (as is the case for the English edition). These differences may lead to some conflicts over spelling differences, (e.g. *color* vs. *colour*)[133] or points of view.[134] Though the various language editions are held to global policies such as "neutral point of view," they diverge on some points of policy and practice, most notably on whether images that are not licensed freely may be used under a claim of fair use.[135] [136] [137]

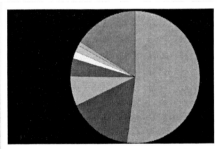

Contributors for English Wikipedia by country as of September 2006.[138]

Jimmy Wales has described Wikipedia as "an effort to create and distribute a free encyclopedia of the highest possible quality to every single person on the planet in their own language".[139] Though each language edition functions more or less independently, some efforts are made to supervise them all. They are coordinated in part by Meta-Wiki, the Wikimedia Foundation's wiki devoted to maintaining all of its projects (Wikipedia and others).[140] For instance, Meta-Wiki provides important statistics on all language editions of Wikipedia,[141] and it maintains a list of articles every Wikipedia should have.[142] The list concerns basic content by subject: biography, history, geography, society, culture, science, technology, foodstuffs, and mathematics. As for the rest, it is not rare for articles strongly related to a particular language not to have counterparts in another edition. For example, articles about small towns in the United States might only be available in English.

Translated articles represent only a small portion of articles in most editions, in part because automated translation of articles is disallowed.[143] Articles available in more than one language may offer "InterWiki" links, which link to the counterpart articles in other editions.

Cultural significance

In addition to logistic growth in the number of its articles,[145] Wikipedia has steadily gained status as a general reference website since its inception in 2001.[146] According to Alexa and comScore, Wikipedia is among the ten most visited websites worldwide.[10] [147] Of the top ten, Wikipedia is the only non-profit website. The growth of Wikipedia has been fueled by its dominant position in Google search results;[148] about 50% of search engine traffic to Wikipedia comes from Google,[149] a good portion of which is related to academic research.[150] In April 2007 the Pew Internet and American Life project found that one third of US Internet users consulted Wikipedia.[151] In October 2006, the site was estimated to have a hypothetical market value of $580 million if it ran advertisements.[152]

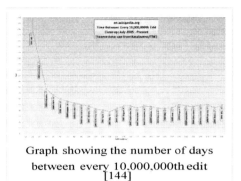

Graph showing the number of days between every 10,000,000th edit [144]

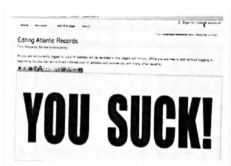

Wikipedia shown in Weird Al's music video for his song "White & Nerdy".

Wikipedia's content has also been used in academic studies, books, conferences, and court cases.[153] [154] [155] The Parliament of Canada's website refers to Wikipedia's article on same-sex marriage in the "related links" section of its "further reading" list for the Civil Marriage Act.[156] The encyclopedia's assertions are increasingly used as a source by organizations such as the U.S. Federal Courts and the World Intellectual Property Organization[157] – though mainly for *supporting information* rather than information decisive to a case.[158] Content appearing on Wikipedia has also been cited as a source and referenced in some U.S. intelligence agency reports.[159] In December 2008, the scientific journal *RNA Biology* launched a new section for descriptions of families of RNA molecules and requires authors who contribute to the section to also submit a draft article on the RNA family for publication in Wikipedia.[160]

Wikipedia has also been used as a source in journalism,[161] sometimes without attribution, and several reporters have been dismissed for plagiarizing from Wikipedia.[162] [163] [164] In July 2007, Wikipedia was the focus of a 30-minute documentary on BBC Radio 4[165] which argued that, with increased usage and awareness, the number of references to Wikipedia in popular culture is such that the term is one of a select band of 21st-century nouns that are so familiar (Google, Facebook, YouTube) that they no longer need explanation and are on a par with such 20th-century terms as Hoovering or Coca-Cola. Many parody Wikipedia's openness, with characters vandalizing or

The Onion newspaper headline "Wikipedia Celebrates 750 Years Of American Independence"

modifying the online encyclopedia project's articles. Notably, comedian Stephen Colbert has parodied or referenced Wikipedia on numerous episodes of his show *The Colbert Report* and coined the related term "wikiality".[58]

The site has created an impact upon several forms of media. Some media sources satirize Wikipedia's susceptibility to inserted inaccuracies, such as a front-page article in *The Onion* in July 2006 with the title "Wikipedia Celebrates 750 Years of American Independence".[166] Others may draw upon Wikipedia's statement that anyone can edit, such as "The Negotiation," an episode of *The Office*, where character Michael Scott said that "Wikipedia is the best thing ever. Anyone in the world can write anything they want about any subject, so you know you are getting the best possible information". Other media sources parody Wikipedia's policies, such as the *xkcd* strip named "Wikipedian Protester."

An xkcd strip entitled "Wikipedian Protester"

Dutch filmmaker IJsbrand van Veelen premiered his 45-minute television documentary *The Truth According to Wikipedia* in April, 2008.[167] Another documentary film about Wikipedia, entitled *Truth in Numbers: The Wikipedia Story*, is scheduled for a 2009 release. Shot on several continents, the film will cover the history of Wikipedia and feature interviews with Wikipedia editors around the world.[168][169]

On September 28, 2007, Italian politician Franco Grillini raised a parliamentary question with the Minister of Cultural Resources and Activities about the necessity of freedom of panorama. He said that the lack of such freedom forced Wikipedia, "the seventh most consulted website" to forbid all images of modern Italian buildings and art, and claimed this was hugely damaging to tourist revenues.[170]

On September 16, 2007, *The Washington Post* reported that Wikipedia had become a focal point in the 2008 U.S. election campaign, saying, "Type a candidate's name into Google, and among the first results is a Wikipedia page, making those entries arguably as important as any ad in defining a candidate. Already, the presidential entries are being edited, dissected and debated countless times each day."[171] An October 2007 Reuters article, entitled "Wikipedia page the latest status symbol", reported the recent phenomenon of how having a Wikipedia article vindicates one's notability.[172]

Jimmy Wales receiving the Quadriga *A Mission of Enlightenment* award

Wikipedia won two major awards in May 2004.[173] The first was a Golden Nica for Digital Communities of the annual Prix Ars Electronica contest; this came with a € 10,000 (£6,588;
$12,700) grant and an invitation to present at the PAE Cyberarts Festival in Austria later that year. The second was a Judges' Webby Award for the "community" category.[174] Wikipedia was also nominated for a "Best Practices" Webby. On January 26, 2007, Wikipedia was also awarded the fourth highest brand ranking by the readers of brandchannel.com, receiving 15% of the votes in answer to the question "Which brand had the most impact on our lives in 2006?"[175]

In September 2008, Wikipedia received Quadriga *A Mission of Enlightenment* award of Werkstatt Deutschland along with Boris Tadić, Eckart Höfling, and Peter Gabriel. The award was presented to Jimmy Wales by David Weinberger.[176]

In July 2009, BBC Radio 4 broadcast a comedy series called *Bigipedia*, which was set on a website which was a parody of Wikipedia. Some of the sketches were directly inspired by Wikipedia and its articles.[177]

Related projects

A number of interactive multimedia encyclopedias incorporating entries written by the public existed long before Wikipedia was founded. The first of these was the 1986 BBC Domesday Project, which included text (entered on BBC Micro computers) and photographs from over 1 million contributors in the UK, and covering the geography, art, and culture of the UK. This was the first interactive multimedia encyclopedia (and was also the first major multimedia document connected through internal links), with the majority of articles being accessible through an interactive map of the UK. The user-interface and part of the content of the Domesday Project have now been emulated on a website.[178] One of the most successful early online encyclopedias incorporating entries by the public was h2g2, which was created by Douglas Adams and is run by the BBC. The h2g2 encyclopedia was relatively light-hearted, focusing on articles which were both witty and informative. Both of these projects had similarities with Wikipedia, but neither gave full editorial freedom to public users. A similar non-wiki project, the GNUPedia project, co-existed with Nupedia early in its history; however, it has been retired and its creator, free software figure Richard Stallman, has lent his support to Wikipedia.[20]

Wikipedia has also spawned several sister projects, which are also run by the Wikimedia Foundation. The first, "In Memoriam: September 11 Wiki",[179] created in October 2002,[180] detailed the September 11 attacks; this project was closed in October 2006. Wiktionary, a dictionary project, was launched in December 2002;[181] Wikiquote, a collection of quotations, a week after Wikimedia launched, and Wikibooks, a collection of collaboratively written free books. Wikimedia has since started a number of other projects, including Wikiversity, a project for the creation of free learning materials and the provision of online learning activities.[182] None of these sister projects, however, has come to meet the success of Wikipedia.

Some subsets of Wikipedia's information have been developed, often with additional review for specific purposes. For example, the Wikipedia series of CDs/DVDs, produced by Wikipedians and SOS Children (aka "Wikipedia for Schools"), is a free, hand-checked, non-commercial selection from Wikipedia, targeted around the UK National Curriculum and intended to be useful for much of the English speaking world. Wikipedia for Schools is available on-line [183]: an equivalent print encyclopedia would require roughly twenty volumes. There has also been a attempt to put a select subset of Wikipedia's articles into printed book form.[184]

Other websites centered on collaborative knowledge base development have drawn inspiration from or inspired Wikipedia. Some, such as → Susning.nu, Enciclopedia Libre, and WikiZnanie likewise employ no formal review process, whereas others use more traditional peer review, such as Encyclopedia of Life, Stanford Encyclopedia of Philosophy, Scholarpedia, h2g2, and Everything2. Citizendium, an online encyclopedia, was started by Wikipedia co-founder Larry Sanger in an attempt to create an "expert-friendly"

Wikipedia.[185] [186] [187]

See also

- Academic studies about Wikipedia
- Democratization of knowledge
- List of online encyclopedias
- → List of wikis
- Open content
- USA Congressional staff edits to Wikipedia
- User-generated content
- Wikipedia Review
- Wikipedia Watch
- Wikitruth

References

Academic studies

- Nielsen, Finn (August 2007). "Scientific Citations in Wikipedia [188]". *First Monday* **12** (8). http://www.firstmonday.org/issues/issue12_8/nielsen/index.html. Retrieved 2008-02-22.
- Pfeil, Ulrike (2006). "Cultural Differences in Collaborative Authoring of Wikipedia [189]". *Journal of Computer-Mediated Communication* **12** (1): 88. doi:10.1111/j.1083-6101.2006.00316.x [190]. http://jcmc.indiana.edu./vol12/issue1/pfeil.html. Retrieved 2008-12-26.
- Priedhorsky, Reid, Jilin Chen, Shyong (Tony) K. Lam, Katherine Panciera, Loren Terveen, and John Riedl. "Creating, Destroying, and Restoring Value in Wikipedia" [191]. Proc. GROUP 2007, doi: 1316624.131663.
- Reagle, Joseph M., Jr. (2005). "Do As I Do: Leadership in the Wikipedia[192]". *Wikipedia Drafts*. http://reagle.org./joseph/2005/ethno/leadership.html. Retrieved 2008-12-26.
- Wilkinson, Dennis M. (April 2007). "Assessing the Value of Cooperation in Wikipedia [193]". *First Monday* **12** (4). http://www.firstmonday.org/issues/issue12_4/wilkinson/index.html. Retrieved 2008-02-22.

Books

- Phoebe Ayers, Charles Matthews, and Ben Yates (September 2008). *How Wikipedia Works: And How You Can Be a Part of It*. San Francisco: No Starch Press. ISBN 978-1-59327-176-3.
- Broughton, John (2008). *Wikipedia - The Missing Manual*. O'Reilly Media. ISBN 0-596-51516-2. (See book rev. by Baker, as listed below.)
- Broughton, John (2008). *Wikipedia Reader's Guide*. Sebastopol: Pogue Press. ISBN 059652174X.
- Lih, Andrew (2009). *The Wikipedia Revolution*. New York: Hyperion. ISBN 1401303714.

Book reviews and other articles

- Crovitz, L. Gordon. "Wikipedia's Old-Fashioned Revolution: The online encyclopedia is fast becoming the best." [194] (Originally published in *Wall Street Journal* online - April 6, 2009, 8:34 A.M. ET)

- Baker, Nicholson. "The Charms of Wikipedia" [195]. *The New York Review of Books*, March 20, 2008. Accessed December 17, 2008. (Book rev. of *The Missing Manual*, by John Broughton, as listed above.)
- Rosenzweig, Roy. Can History be Open Source? Wikipedia and the Future of the Past [196]. (Originally published in *Journal of American History* 93.1 (June 2006): 117-46.)

Learning resources

- Wikiversity list of learning resources. (Includes related courses, Web-based seminars, slides, lecture notes, text books, quizzes, glossaries, etc.)

Media debate

- "Thought Leader: Wikipedia vs. Encyclopedia [197]". *Delta-Sky, The Official Inflight Magazine of Delta Air Lines*. December 2008. http://www.delta-sky.com/sections/ index.php/lifestyle/wikipedia_vs_encyclopedia/. Retrieved 2009-01-14. "(Earlier this year, [Andrew] Keen and [Jimmy] Wales appeared at Inforum, a division of the Commonwealth Club of California, which is the largest and oldest public forum in the United States. Following is a portion of their discussion, moderated by National Public Radio's David Ewing Duncan.)"

Other media coverage

- Dee, Jonathan (2007-07-01). "All the News That's Fit to Print Out [198]". *The New York Times Magazine* (The New York Times Company). http://www.nytimes.com/2007/07/ 01/magazine/01WIKIPEDIA-t.html?_r=1&ref=magazine&oref=slogin. Retrieved 2008-02-22.
- "For Music Fans: Wikipedia; MySpace [199]". *Houston Chronicle (Blog)*. March 2008. http://blogs.chron.com/brokenrecord/2008/03/for_music_fans_wikipedia_myspa. html. Retrieved 2008-12-17.
- Freeman, Sarah (2007-08-16). "Can We Really Trust Wikipedia? [200]". *Yorkshire Post* (yorkshirepost.co.uk). http://www.yorkshirepost.co.uk/highlights?articleid=3115718. Retrieved 2008-09-20.
- Giles, Jim (2007-09-20). "Wikipedia 2.0 - Now with Added Trust [201]". *New Scientist*. http://www.newscientist.com/article/mg19526226.200. Retrieved 2008-01-14.
- Miliard, Mike (2007-12-02). "Wikipedia Rules [202]". The Phoenix. http://thephoenix. com/Boston/Life/52864-Wikipedia-rules/. Retrieved 2008-02-22.
- Poe, Marshall (September 2006). "The Hive [203]". *The Atlantic Monthly*. http://www. theatlantic.com/doc/200609/wikipedia. Retrieved 2008-03-22.
- Taylor, Chris (2005-05-29). "It's a Wiki, Wiki World [204]". *Time* (Time, Inc). http://www. time.com/time/magazine/article/0,9171,1066904-1,00.html. Retrieved 2008-02-22.
- "Technological Quarterly: Brain Scan: The Free-knowledge Fundamentalist [205]". *The Economist Web and Print*. 2008-06-05. http://www.economist.com/science/tq/ displaystory.cfm?story_id=11484062. Retrieved 2008-06-05. "Jimmy Wales changed the world with Wikipedia, the hugely popular online encyclopedia that anyone can edit. What will he do next? [leader]."
- "Hoaxers force Wiki to weigh pre-checks Wikipedia [206]". *Metro Boston edition*. 2009-01-28. http://www.metrobostonnews.com/us/article/2009/01/28/03/4644-72/ index.xml.
- Is Wikipedia Cracking Up?, The Independent, February 3, 2009 [207]
- The Wiki-snobs Are Taking Over, The Sunday Times, timesonline.co.uk, February 8, 2009 [208]

- Runciman, David (2009-05-28). "Like Boiling a Frog [209]". *London Review of Books*. http://www.lrb.co.uk/v31/n10/runc01_.html. Retrieved 2009-06-03.

External links

- Wikipedia [210] – multilingual portal (contains links to all language editions of the project)
- Version for mobile phones [211] – 15 languages
- Press coverage of Wikipedia [212]
- Wikipedia [213] at the Open Directory Project
- CBC News: I, editor [214]
- Help Edit Wikipedia [215] – wikiHow article
- Class assignment: Write an original Wikipedia article [216]
- #Wikipedia [217] on freenode
- Video of TED Talk by Jimmy Wales on the birth of Wikipedia [218]
- Audio of interview with Jimmy Wales about Wikipedia in general [219] on the EconTalk podcast
- Wikipedia and why it matters [220] – Larry Sanger's 2002 talk at Stanford University about Wikipedia. video archive [221] and transcript of the talk
- "Intelligence in Wikipedia" Google TechTalk [222] at YouTube (Adobe Flash video), describing an intelligence project utilizing Wikipedia, and how Wikipedia articles could be auto-generated from web content

ace:Wikipèdia mwl:Biquipédia pnb:ايڈيا وکی ckb:ويكيپيديا وي ک ي پ يدي

References

[1] " Statistics (http://en.wikipedia.org/wiki/Special:Statistics)". English Wikipedia. . Retrieved 2008-06-21.

[2] Jonathan Sidener. " Everyone's Encyclopedia (http://www.signonsandiego.com/uniontrib/20041206/news_mz1b6encyclo.html)". *The San Diego Union-Tribune*. . Retrieved 2006-10-15.

[3] " Five-year Traffic Statistics for Wikipedia.org (http://www.alexa.com/data/details/traffic_details/wikipedia.org?range=5y&size=large&y=t)". Alexa Internet. . Retrieved 2008-07-15.

[4] " Wikipedia:Wikipedia is a work in progress (http://en.wikipedia.org/wiki/Wikipedia:Wikipedia_is_a_work_in_progress)". Wikipedia. . Retrieved 2008-07-03.

[5] Some versions, such as the English language version, contain non-free content.

[6] In some parts of the world, the access to Wikipedia has (or had) been blocked.

[7] Mike Miliard (2008-03-01). " Wikipediots: Who Are These Devoted, Even Obsessive Contributors to Wikipedia? (http://www.cityweekly.net/utah/article-5129-feature-wikipediots-who-are-these-devoted-even-obsessive-contributors-to-wikipedia.html)". *Salt Lake City Weekly*. . Retrieved 2008-12-18.

[8] Bill Tancer (2007-05-01). " Look Who's Using Wikipedia (http://www.time.com/time/business/article/0,8599,1595184,00.html)". *Time*. . Retrieved 2007-12-01. "The sheer volume of content [...] is partly responsible for the site's dominance as an online reference. When compared to the top 3,200 educational reference sites in the U.S., Wikipedia is #1, capturing 24.3% of all visits to the category" Cf. Bill Tancer (Global Manager, Hitwise), "Wikipedia, Search and School Homework" (http://weblogs.hitwise.com/bill-tancer/2007/03/wikipedia_search_and_school_ho.html), *Hitwise*: An Experian Company (Blog), March 1, 2007. Retrieved December 18, 2008.

[9] Alex Woodson (2007-07-08). " Wikipedia remains go-to site for online news (http://www.reuters.com/article/internetNews/idUSN0819429120070708)". *Reuters*. . Retrieved 2007-12-16. "Online encyclopedia Wikipedia has added about 20 million unique monthly visitors in the past year, making it the top online news and information destination, according to Nielsen//NetRatings."

[10] " Top 500 (http://www.alexa.com/site/ds/top_sites?ts_mode=global&lang=none)". Alexa. . Retrieved 2007-12-04.

[11] Larry Sanger, Why Wikipedia Must Jettison Its Anti-Elitism (http://www.kuro5hin.org/story/2004/12/30/142458/25), Kuro5hin, December 31, 2004.

[12] Danah Boyd (2005-01-04). " Academia and Wikipedia (http://many.corante.com/archives/2005/01/04/ academia_and_wikipedia.php)". *Many 2 Many: A Group Weblog on Social Software.* Corante. . Retrieved 2008-12-18. "[The author, Danah Boyd, describes herself as] an expert on social media[,] ... a doctoral student in the School of Information at the University of California, Berkeley [,] and a fellow at the Harvard University Berkman Center for Internet & Society [at Harvard Law School.]"

[13] Simon Waldman (2004-10-26). " Who knows? (http://www.guardian.co.uk/technology/2004/oct/26/g2. onlinesupplement)". *Guardian.co.uk.* . Retrieved 2007-02-11.

[14] Ahrens, Frank (2006-07-09). " Death by Wikipedia: The Kenneth Lay Chronicles (http://www. washingtonpost.com/wp-dyn/content/article/2006/07/08/AR2006070800135.html)". The Washington Post. . Retrieved 2006-11-01.

[15] Fernanda B. Viégas, Martin Wattenberg, and Kushal Dave (2004). " Studying Cooperation and Conflict between Authors with History Flow Visualizations (http://alumni.media.mit.edu/~fviegas/papers/ history_flow.pdf)" (PDF). *Proceedings of the ACM Conference on Human Factors in Computing Systems (CHI)* (Vienna, Austria: ACM SIGCHI): 575 – 582. doi: 10.1145/985921.985953 (http://dx.doi.org/10.1145/985921. 985953). ISBN 1-58113-702-8. . Retrieved 2007-01-24.

[16] Reid Priedhorsky, Jilin Chen, Shyong (Tony) K. Lam, Katherine Panciera, Loren Terveen, and John Riedl (GroupLens Research, Department of Computer Science and Engineering, University of Minnesota) (2007-11-04). " Creating, Destroying, and Restoring Value in Wikipedia (http://www-users.cs.umn.edu/ ~reid/papers/group282-priedhorsky.pdf)" (PDF). *Association for Computing Machinery GROUP '07 conference proceedings* (Sanibel Island, Florida). . Retrieved 2007-10-13.

[17] " Time's Person of the Year: You (http://www.time.com/time/magazine/article/0,9171,1569514,00.html)". *TIME* (Time, Inc). 2006-12-13. . Retrieved 2008-12-26.

[18] Jonathan Dee (2007-07-01). " All the News That's Fit to Print Out (http://www.nytimes.com/2007/07/01/ magazine/01WIKIPEDIA-t.html)". The New York Times Magazine. . Retrieved 2007-12-01.

[19] Andrew Lih (2004-04-16). " Wikipedia as Participatory Journalism: Reliable Sources? Metrics for Evaluating Collaborative Media as a News Resource (http://jmsc.hku.hk/faculty/alih/publications/ utaustin-2004-wikipedia-rc2.pdf)" (PDF). *5th International Symposium on Online Journalism* (University of Texas at Austin). . Retrieved 2007-10-13.

[20] Richard M. Stallman (2007-06-20). " The Free Encyclopedia Project (http://www.gnu.org/encyclopedia/ encyclopedia.html)". Free Software Foundation. . Retrieved 2008-01-04.

[21] Jonathan Sidener (2004-12-06). " Everyone's Encyclopedia (http://www.signonsandiego.com/uniontrib/ 20041206/news_mz1b6encyclo.html)". *The San Diego Union-Tribune.* . Retrieved 2006-10-15.

[22] Meyers, Peter (2001-09-20). " Fact-Driven? Collegial? This Site Wants You (http://query.nytimes.com/gst/ fullpage.html?res=9800E5D6123BF933A1575AC0A9679C8B63&n=Top/Reference/Times Topics/Subjects/C/ Computer Software)". *New York Times* (The New York Times Company). . Retrieved 2007-11-22. " 'I can start an article that will consist of one paragraph, and then a real expert will come along and add three paragraphs and clean up my one paragraph,' said Larry Sanger of Las Vegas, who founded Wikipedia with Mr. Wales."

[23] Sanger, Larry (April 18, 2005). " The Early History of Nupedia and Wikipedia: A Memoir (http://features. slashdot.org/features/05/04/18/164213.shtml)". *Slashdot.* . Retrieved 2008-12-26.

[24] Sanger, Larry (January 17, 2001). " Wikipedia Is Up! (http://web.archive.org/web/20010506042824/www. nupedia.com/pipermail/nupedia-l/2001-January/000684.html)". Internet Archive. . Retrieved 2008-12-26.

[25] " Wikipedia-l: LinkBacks? (http://lists.wikimedia.org/pipermail/wikipedia-l/2001-October/000671.html)". . Retrieved 2007-02-20.

[26] Sanger, Larry (2001-01-10). " Let's Make a Wiki (http://web.archive.org/web/20030414014355/http:// www.nupedia.com/pipermail/nupedia-l/2001-January/000676.html)". Internet Archive. Archived from the original (http://www.nupedia.com/pipermail/nupedia-l/2001-January/000676.html) on 2003-04-14. . Retrieved 2008-12-26.

[27] " Wikipedia: HomePage (http://web.archive.org/web/20010331173908/http://www.wikipedia.com/)". Archived from the original (http://www.wikipedia.com/) on 2001-03-31. . Retrieved 2001-03-31.

[28] " Wikipedia: Neutral point of view (http://en.wikipedia.org/w/index. php?title=Wikipedia:Neutral_point_of_view&oldid=102236018), Wikipedia (January 21, 2007)

[29] "" statistics Multilingual statistics (http://en.wikipedia.org/wiki/Wikipedia:Multilingual)". *Wikipedia.* March 30, 2005. statistics. Retrieved 2008-12-26.

[30] "Encyclopedias and Dictionaries". *Encyclopædia Britannica, 15th ed..* **18**. Encyclopædia Britannica. 2007. pp. 257– 286.

[31] " [long] Enciclopedia Libre: msg#00008 (http://osdir.com/ml/science.linguistics.wikipedia.international/ 2003-03/msg00008.html)". *Osdir.* . Retrieved 2008-12-26.

[32] Clay Shirky (February 28, 2008). *Here Comes Everybody: The Power of Organizing Without Organizations* (http://www.amazon.com/gp/reader/1594201536/ref=sib_dp_srch_pop?v=search-inside&

keywords=spanish&go.x=0&go.y=0&go=Go!). The Penguin Press via Amazon Online Reader. p. 273. ISBN 1-594201-53-6.. Retrieved 2008-12-26.

[33] BBC News (http://news.bbc.co.uk/2/hi/technology/7144970.stm)

[34] Bobbie Johnson. " Wikipedia approaches its limits (http://www.guardian.co.uk/technology/2009/aug/12/ wikipedia-deletionist-inclusionist)". .

[35] http://en.wikipedia.org/wiki/Wikipedia

[36] http://usability.wikimedia.org/wiki/UX_and_Usability_Study

[37] Wikipedia:Ownership of articles

[38] Birken, P. (2008-12-14). " Bericht Gesichtete Versionen (http://lists.wikimedia.org/pipermail/wikide-l/ 2008-December/021594.html)" (in German). *Wikide-l mailing list*. Wikimedia Foundation. . Retrieved 2009-02-15.

[39] Cohen, Noam (2009-08-25). " Wikipedia to Limit Changes to Articles on People (http://www.nytimes.com/ 2009/08/25/technology/internet/25wikipedia.html)". *The New York Times*. ISSN 0362-4331 (http:// worldcat.org/issn/0362-4331). . Retrieved 2009-08-25.

[40] " Wikipedia:Flagged protection and patrolled revisions - Wikipedia, the free encyclopedia (http://en. wikipedia.org/wiki/Wikipedia:Flagged_protection_and_patrolled_revisions#cite_ref-7)". . Retrieved 2009-08-25.

[41] Giles, Jim (2007-09-20). " Wikipedia 2.0 - now with added trust (http://www.newscientist.com/article/ mg19526226.200-wikipedia-20--now-with-added-trust.html)". NewScientist.com news service. . Retrieved 2008-12-26.

[42] Kleinz, Torsten (February, 2005). " World of Knowledge (http://w3.linux-magazine.com/issue/51/ Wikipedia_Encyclopedia.pdf)" (PDF). *The Wikipedia Project* (Linux Magazine). . Retrieved 2007-07-13. "The Wikipedia's open structure makes it a target for trolls and vandals who malevolently add incorrect information to articles, get other people tied up in endless discussions, and generally do everything to draw attention to themselves."

[43] The Japanese Wikipedia, for example, is known for deleting every mention of real names of victims of certain high-profile crimes, even though they may still be noted in other language editions.

[44] Fernanda B. Viégas, Martin Wattenberg, Jesse Kriss, Frank van Ham (2007-01-03) (PDF). *Talk Before You Type: Coordination in Wikipedia* (http://www.research.ibm.com/visual/papers/wikipedia_coordination_final. pdf). Visual Communication Lab, IBM Research. . Retrieved 2008-06-27.

[45] First Monday (http://firstmonday.org/htbin/cgiwrap/bin/ojs/index.php/fm/article/view/2365/2182)

[46] Fernanda B. Viégas, Martin Wattenberg, and Matthew M. McKeon (2007-07-22) (PDF). *The Hidden Order of Wikipedia* (http://www.research.ibm.com/visual/papers/hidden_order_wikipedia.pdf). Visual Communication Lab, IBM Research. . Retrieved 2007-10-30.

[47] " Wikipedia:Version 1.0 Editorial Team/Assessment (http://en.wikipedia.org/wiki/Wikipedia:Version_1. 0_Editorial_Team/Assessment)". . Retrieved 2007-10-28.

[48] Diomidis Spinellis and Panagiotis Louridas (2008): The collaborative organization of knowledge (http://www. dmst.aueb.gr/dds/pubs/jrnl/2008-CACM-Wikipedia/html/SL08.pdf). In Communications of the ACM, August 2008, Vol 51, No 8, Pages 68 - 73. DOI:10.1145/1378704.1378720. Quote: "Most new articles are created shortly after a corresponding reference to them is entered into the system". See also: Inflationary hypothesis of Wikipedia growth

[49] http://www.caslon.com.au/wikiprofile1.htm

[50] Roy Rosenzweig. " Can History be Open Source? Wikipedia and the Future of the Past (http://chnm.gmu. edu/resources/essays/d/42)". The Journal of American History Volume 93, Number 1 (June, 2006): 117-46. . Retrieved 2007-10-29.

[51] Seigenthaler, John (2005-11-29). " A False Wikipedia 'biography' (http://www.usatoday.com/news/opinion/ editorials/2005-11-29-wikipedia-edit_x.htm)". USA Today. . Retrieved 2008-12-26.

[52] " Wikipedia:General disclaimer (http://en.wikipedia.org/wiki/Wikipedia:General_disclaimer)". English Wikipedia. . Retrieved 2008-04-22.

[53] Public Information Research – Wikipedia Watch. Retrieved on 2007-01-28.

[54] Thomas L. Friedman *The World is Flat*, p. 124, Farrar, Straus & Giroux, 2007 ISBN 978-0374292782

[55] " Toward a New Compendium of Knowledge (longer version) (http://www.citizendium.org/essay.html)". *Citizendium.org*. . Retrieved 2006-10-10.

[56] Kane, Margaret (2006-01-30). " Politicians notice Wikipedia (http://news.cnet.com/ 8301-10784_3-6032713-7.html)". CNET. . Retrieved 2007-01-28.

[57] Bergstein, Brian (2007-01-23). " Microsoft offers cash for Wikipedia edit (http://www.msnbc.msn.com/id/ 16775981/)". MSNBC. . Retrieved 2007-02-01.

[58] Stephen Colbert (2006-07-30). " Wikiality (http://www.colbertnation.com/the-colbert-report-videos/72347/ july-31-2006/the-word---wikiality)". Comedycentral.com. . Retrieved 2008-12-26.

[59] http://en.wikipedia.org/wiki/Portal:Current_events

[60] Wikipedia:PAPER

[61] Schliebs, Mark (2008-09-09). " Wikipedia users divided over sexual material (http://www.news.com.au/ technology/story/0,25642,24318423-5014239,00.html)". news.com.au. . Retrieved 2008-12-26.

[62] " Wikipedia is not censored (http://en.wikipedia.org/wiki/ Wikipedia:Wikipedia_is_not#Wikipedia_is_not_censored)". Wikipedia. . Retrieved 2008-04-30.

[63] Sophie Taylor (2008-04-05). " China allows access to English Wikipedia (http://in.reuters.com/article/ technologyNews/idINIndia-32865420080405)". *Reuters*. . Retrieved 2008-07-29.

[64] " Wikipedia:Notability (http://en.wikipedia.org/wiki/Wikipedia:Notability)". . Retrieved 2008-02-13. "A topic is presumed to be notable if it has received significant coverage in reliable secondary sources that are independent of the subject."

[65] " Wikipedia:No original research (http://en.wikipedia.org/wiki/Wikipedia:No_original_research)". . Retrieved 2008-02-13. "Wikipedia does not publish original thought"

[66] " Wikipedia:Verifiability (http://en.wikipedia.org/wiki/Wikipedia:Verifiability)". . Retrieved 2008-02-13. "Material challenged or likely to be challenged, and all quotations, must be attributed to a reliable, published source."

[67] " Wikipedia:Neutral_point_of_view (http://en.wikipedia.org/wiki/Wikipedia:Neutral_point_of_view)". . Retrieved 2008-02-13. "All Wikipedia articles and other encyclopedic content must be written from a neutral point of view, representing significant views fairly, proportionately and without bias."

[68] Eric Haas (2007-10-26). " Will Unethical Editing Destroy Wikipedia's Credibility? (http://www.alternet.org/ story/61365/?page=entire)". AlterNet.org. . Retrieved 2008-12-26.

[69] " Who's behind Wikipedia? (http://www.pcworld.idg.com.au/index.php/id;1866322157;fp;2;fpid;2)". PC World. 2008-02-06. . Retrieved 2008-02-07.

[70] " The battle for Wikipedia's soul (http://www.economist.com/printedition/displaystory. cfm?story_id=10789354)". The Economist. 2008-03-06. . Retrieved 2008-03-07.

[71] " Wikipedia: an online encyclopedia torn apart (http://www.telegraph.co.uk/connected/main.jhtml?xml=/ connected/2007/10/11/dlwiki11.xml)". Daily Telegraph. 2007-11-10. . Retrieved 2008-03-11.

[72] Stacy Schiff (2006-07-31). "Know It All". *The New Yorker*.

[73] Robert McHenry, " The Faith-Based Encyclopedia (http://www.techcentralstation.com/111504A.html)", Tech Central Station, November 15, 2004.

[74] " Wide World of Wikipedia (http://www.emorywheel.com/detail.php?n=17902)". The Emory Wheel. April 21, 2006. . Retrieved 2007-10-17.

[75] Jaschik, Scott (2007-01-26). " A Stand Against Wikipedia (http://www.insidehighered.com/news/2007/01/ 26/wiki)". Inside Higher Ed. . Retrieved 2007-01-27.

[76] Helm, Burt (2005-12-14). " Wikipedia: "A Work in Progress" (http://www.businessweek.com/technology/ content/dec2005/tc20051214_441708.htm)". BusinessWeek. . Retrieved 2007-01-29.

[77] Noam Cohen (2009-03-29). " Wikipedia: Exploring Fact City (http://www.nytimes.com/2009/03/29/ weekinreview/29cohen.html?_r=1&ref=weekinreview&pagewanted=print)". The New York Times. . Retrieved 2009-03-29.

[78] Tyler Cowen (2008-03-14). " Cooked Books (http://www.tnr.com/story. html?id=82eb5d70-13bd-4086-9ec0-cb0e9e8411b3)". The New Republic. . Retrieved 2008-12-26.

[79] Child, Maxwell L., "Professors Split on Wiki Debate" (http://www.thecrimson.com/article. aspx?ref=517305), The Harvard Crimson, Monday, February 26, 2007.

[80] Chloe Stothart, Web threatens learning ethos (http://www.timeshighereducation.co.uk/story. asp?sectioncode=26&storycode=209408), *The Times Higher Education Supplement*, 2007, **1799** (June 22), page 2

[81] Hafner, Kate (June 17, 2006). " Growing Wikipedia Refines Its 'Anyone Can Edit' Policy (http://www. nytimes.com/2006/06/17/technology/17wiki.html?scp=8&sq=wikipedia&st=cse)". New York Times. . Retrieved 2009-07-12.

[82] Corner, Stuart (June 18, 2006). " What's all the fuss about Wikipedia? (http://www.itwire.com/content/ view/4666/127/)". iT Wire. . Retrieved 2007-03-25.

[83] Wilson, Chris (2008-02-22). " The Wisdom of the Chaperones (http://www.slate.com/id/2184487)". Slate. . Retrieved 2008-03-04.

[84] Arthur, Charles (2005-12-15). " Log on and join in, but beware the web cults (http://www.guardian.co.uk/ technology/2005/dec/15/wikipedia.web20)". Guardian. . Retrieved 2008-12-26.

[85] Lu Stout, Kristie (2003-08-04). " Wikipedia: The know-it-all Web site (http://www.cnn.com/2003/TECH/ internet/08/03/wikipedia/index.html)". CNN. . Retrieved 2008-12-26.

[86] "Wikinfo (2005-03-30). " Critical views of Wikipedia (http://wikinfo.org/index.php/ Critical_views_of_Wikipedia)". . Retrieved 2007-01-29.

[87] Wikipedia:Administrators (http://en.wikipedia.org/w/index.php?title=Wikipedia:Administrators)

[88] Mehegan, David (February 13, 2006). " Many contributors, common cause (http://www.boston.com/business/technology/articles/2006/02/13/many_contributors_common_cause/)". The Boston Globe. . Retrieved 2007-03-25.

[89] " Wikipedia:Administrators (http://en.wikipedia.org/wiki/Wikipedia:Administrators#Administrator_conduct)". . Retrieved 2009-07-12.

[90] Kittur, Aniket. " Power of the Few vs. Wisdom of the Crowd: Wikipedia and the Rise of the Bourgeoisie (http://www.viktoria.se/altchi/submissions/submission_edchi_1.pdf)" (PDF). . Retrieved 2008-02-23.

[91] Swartz, Aaron (2006-09-04). " Raw Thought: Who Writes Wikipedia? (http://www.aaronsw.com/weblog/whowriteswikipedia)". . Retrieved 2008-02-23.

[92] " Wikipedia "Good Samaritans *Are on the Money* (http://www.sciam.com/article.cfm?id=good-samaritans-are-on-the-money)". Scientific American. 2007-10-19. . Retrieved 2008-12-26.

[93] Hafner, Katie (2007-08-19). " Seeing Corporate Fingerprints From the Editing of Wikipedia (http://www.nytimes.com/2007/08/19/technology/19wikipedia.html)". New York Times. . Retrieved 2008-12-26.

[94] Andrea Ciffolilli, " Phantom authority, self-selective recruitment and retention of members in virtual communities: The case of Wikipedia (http://firstmonday.org/issues/issue8_12/ciffolilli/index.html)", *First Monday* December 2003.

[95] Zittrain, Jonathan (2008). *The Future of the Internet and How to Stop It — Chapter 6: The Lessons of Wikipedia* (http://yupnet.org/zittrain/archives/16). Yale University Press. ISBN 978-0300124873. . Retrieved 2008-12-26.

[96] Yair Amichai– Hamburger, Naama Lamdan, Rinat Madiel, Tsahi Hayat Personality Characteristics of Wikipedia Members (http://www.liebertonline.com/doi/abs/10.1089/cpb.2007.0225) *CyberPsychology & Behavior* December 1, 2008, 11(6): 679-681. doi:10.1089/cpb.2007.0225

[97] Wikipedians are 'closed' and 'disagreeable' (http://www.newscientist.com/article/mg20126883.900-wikipedians-are-closed-and-disagreeable.html)

[98] Jim Giles After the boom, is Wikipedia heading for bust? (http://www.newscientist.com/article/dn17554-after-the-boom-is-wikipedia-heading-for-bust.html) *New Scientist* 04 August 2009

[99] " *The Wikipedia Signpost* (http://en.wikipedia.org/wiki/Wikipedia:Wikipedia_Signpost)". Wikipedia. . Retrieved 2009-03-24.

[100] Cohen, Noam (2007-03-05). " A Contributor to Wikipedia Has His Fictional Side (http://www.nytimes.com/2007/03/05/technology/05wikipedia.html?pagewanted=2&_r=1)". *The New York Times*. . Retrieved 2008-10-18.

[101] Rubel, Steve (2005-12-19). " Ten More Wikipedia Hacks (http://www.webpronews.com/blogtalk/2005/12/19/ten-more-wikipedia-hacks)". *WebProNews*. . Retrieved 2008-10-18.

[102] Mark Bergman. " Wikimedia Architecture (http://www.nedworks.org/~mark/presentations/san/Wikimedia architecture.pdf)" (PDF). Wikimedia Foundation Inc.. . Retrieved 2008-06-27.

[103] " Version: Installed extensions (http://en.wikipedia.org/wiki/Special:Version#Installed_extensions)". .

[104] Michael Snow. " Lucene search: Internal search function returns to service (http://en.wikipedia.org/wiki/Wikipedia:Wikipedia_Signpost/2005-04-18/Lucene_search)". Wikimedia Foundation Inc.. . Retrieved 2009-02-26.

[105] Brion Vibber. " [Wikitech-l] Lucene search (http://lists.wikimedia.org/pipermail/wikitech-l/2005-April/016297.html)". . Retrieved 2009-02-26.

[106] " Extension:Lucene-search (http://www.mediawiki.org/wiki/Extension:Lucene-search)". Wikimedia Foundation Inc.. . Retrieved 2009-02-26.

[107] " Lucene Search 2: extension for MediaWiki (http://svn.wikimedia.org/svnroot/mediawiki/trunk/lucene-search-2/README.txt)". Wikimedia Foundation Inc.. . Retrieved 2009-02-26.

[108] Todd R. Weiss (October 9, 2008 (Computerworld)). " Wikipedia simplifies IT infrastructure by moving to one Linux vendor (http://www.computerworld.com/action/article.do?command=viewArticleBasic&taxonomyName=Servers+and+Data+Center&articleId=9116787&taxonomyId=154&pageNumber=1)". Computerworld.com. . Retrieved 2008-11-01.

[109] " Wikipedia adopts Ubuntu for its server infrastructure (http://arstechnica.com/news.ars/post/20081009-wikipedia-adopts-ubuntu-for-its-server-infrastructure.html)". Arstechnica.com. . Retrieved 2008-11-01.

[110] " Wikimedia servers at wikimedia.org (http://meta.wikimedia.org/wiki/Wikimedia_servers)". . Retrieved 2008-02-16.

[111] "Monthly request statistics", Wikimedia. Retrieved on 2008-10-31.

[112] Domas Mituzas. " Wikipedia: Site internals, configuration, code examples and management issues (http://dammit.lt/uc/workbook2007.pdf)" (PDF). MySQL Users Conference 2007. . Retrieved 2008-06-27.

[113] http://en.mobile.wikipedia.org/

[114] " Wikimedia Mobile is Officially Launched (http://techblog.wikimedia.org/2009/06/ wikimedia-mobile-launch/)". *Wikimedia Technical Blog*. 2009-06-30. . Retrieved 2009-07-22.

[115] http://en.m.wikipedia.org/

[116] http://en.wikipedia.org/w/index.php?title=Wikipedia%3AMobile+access

[117] http://en.wikipedia.org/w/index.php?title=Wikipedia%3AMetadata

[118] " iPhone Gems: Wikipedia Apps (http://www.ilounge.com/index.php/articles/comments/15802/)". 30 Nov 2008. . Retrieved 22 July 2008.

[119] " Wikipedia on DVD (http://www.wikipediaondvd.com/)". Linterweb. Accessed June 1, 2007. "Linterweb is authorized to make a commercial use of the Wikipedia trademark restricted to the selling of the Encyclopedia CDs and DVDs."

[120] " Wikipedia 0.5 Available on a CD-ROM (http://www.wikipediaondvd.com/site.php?temp=buy)". *Wikipedia on DVD*. Linterweb. Accessed June 1, 2007. "The DVD or CD-ROM version 0.5 was commercially available for purchase."

[121] " Polish Wikipedia on DVD (http://meta.wikimedia.org/wiki/Polska_Wikipedia_na_DVD_(z_Helionem)/ en)". . Retrieved 2008-12-26.

[122] " Wikipedia:DVD (http://de.wikipedia.org/wiki/Wikipedia:Wikipedia-Distribution)". . Retrieved 2008-12-26.

[123] " Wikipedia:Copyrights (http://en.wikipedia.org/wiki/Wikipedia:Copyrights)". English Wikipedia. . Retrieved 2008-04-22.

[124] " Wikimedia community approves license migration (http://blog.wikimedia.org/2009/05/21/ wikimedia-community-approves-license-migration/)". *Wikimedia Foundation*. Wikimedia Foundation. . Retrieved 2009-05-21.

[125] Walter Vermeir (2007). " Resolution:License update (http://wikimediafoundation.org/wiki/ Resolution:License_update)". Wikizine. . Retrieved 2007-12-04.

[126] http://en.wikipedia.org/w/index.php?title=Wikipedia%3ATransition+to+Creative+Commons+ licensing

[127] " Licensing update/Questions and Answers (http://meta.wikimedia.org/wiki/Licensing_update/ Questions_and_Answers)". *Wikimedia Meta*. Wikimedia Foundation. . Retrieved 2009-02-15.

[128] " Licensing_update/Timeline (http://meta.wikimedia.org/wiki/Licensing_update/Timeline)". *Wikimedia Meta*. Wikimedia Foundation. . Retrieved 2009-04-05.

[129] http://meta.wikimedia.org/wiki/Licensing_update/Result

[130] " Wikipedia cleared in French defamation case (http://www.reuters.com/article/internetNews/ idUSL0280486220071102?feedType=RSS&feedName=internetNews)". Reuters. 2007-11-02. . Retrieved 2007-11-02.

[131] Anderson, Nate (2008-05-02). " Dumb idea: suing Wikipedia for calling you "dumb" (http://arstechnica. com/news.ars/post/20080502-dumb-idea-suing-wikipedia-for-calling-you-dumb.html)". Ars Technica. . Retrieved 2008-05-04.

[132] " Wikipedia:Multilingual statistics (http://en.wikipedia.org/wiki/Wikipedia:Multilingual_statistics)". English Wikipedia. . Retrieved 2007-12-23.

[133] " spelling (http://en.wikipedia.org/wiki/Wikipedia:Spelling)". *Manual of Style*. Wikipedia. . Retrieved 2007-05-19.

[134] " Countering systemic bias (http://en.wikipedia.org/wiki/ Wikipedia:WikiProject_Countering_systemic_bias)". . Retrieved 2007-05-19.

[135] " Fair use (http://meta.wikimedia.org/wiki/Fair_use)". Meta wiki. . Retrieved 2007-07-14.

[136] " Images on Wikipedia (http://meta.wikimedia.org/wiki/Images_on_Wikipedia)". . Retrieved 2007-07-14.

[137] Fernanda B. Viégas (2007-01-03) (PDF). *The Visual Side of Wikipedia* (http://www.research.ibm.com/ visual/papers/viegas_hicss_visual_wikipedia.pdf). Visual Communication Lab, IBM Research. . Retrieved 2007-10-30.

[138] " Edits by project and country of origin (http://meta.wikimedia.org/wiki/ Edits_by_project_and_country_of_origin)". 2006-09-04. . Retrieved 2007-10-25.

[139] Jimmy Wales, " Wikipedia is an encyclopedia (http://lists.wikimedia.org/pipermail/wikipedia-l/ 2005-March/020469.html)", March 8, 2005, <Wikipedia-l@wikimedia.org>

[140] " Meta-Wiki (http://meta.wikimedia.org/)". Wikimedia Foundation. . Retrieved 2009-03-24.

[141] " Meta-Wiki Statistics (http://meta.wikimedia.org/wiki/Statistics)". Wikimedia Foundation. . Retrieved 2008-03-24.

[142] " List of articles every Wikipedia should have (http://meta.wikimedia.org/wiki/ List_of_articles_every_Wikipedia_should_have)". Wikimedia Foundation. . Retrieved 2008-03-24.

[143] " Wikipedia: Translation (http://en.wikipedia.org/wiki/Wikipedia:Translations)". *English Wikipedia*. . Retrieved 2007-02-03.

[144] http://en.wikipedia.org/w/index.php?title=User%3AKatalaveno%2FTBE

[145] " Wikipedia:Modelling Wikipedia's growth (http://en.wikipedia.org/wiki/ Wikipedia:Modelling_Wikipedia's_growth)". . Retrieved 2007-12-22.

[146] " 694 Million People Currently Use the Internet Worldwide According To comScore Networks (http://www. comscore.com/press/release.asp?press=849)". comScore. . Retrieved 2007-12-16. "Wikipedia has emerged as a site that continues to increase in popularity, both globally and in the U.S."

[147] " comScore Data Center (http://www.comscore.com/press/data.asp)". October 2007. . Retrieved 2008-01-19.

[148] Petrilli, Michael J. " Wikipedia or Wickedpedia? (http://www.hoover.org/publications/ednext/16111162. html)". *Hoover Institution* **8** (2). . Retrieved 2008-03-21.

[149] " Google Traffic To Wikipedia up 166% Year over Year (http://weblogs.hitwise.com/leeann-prescott/2007/ 02/wikipedia_traffic_sources.html)". Hitwise. 2007-02-16. . Retrieved 2007-12-22.

[150] " Wikipedia and Academic Research (http://weblogs.hitwise.com/leeann-prescott/2006/10/ wikipedia_and_academic_researc.html)". Hitwise. 2006-10-17. . Retrieved 2008-02-06.

[151] Rainie, Lee (2007-12-15). " Wikipedia users (http://web.archive.org/web/20080306031354/http://www. pewinternet.org/pdfs/PIP_Wikipedia07.pdf)" (PDF). *Pew Internet & American Life Project*. Pew Research Center. Archived from the original (http://www.pewinternet.org/pdfs/PIP_Wikipedia07.pdf) on 2008-03-06. . Retrieved 2007-12-15. "36% of online American adults consult Wikipedia. It is particularly popular with the well-educated and current college-age students."

[152] Karbasfrooshan, Ashkan (2006-10-26). " What is Wikipedia.org's Valuation? (http://www.watchmojo.com/ web/blog/?p=626)". . Retrieved 2007-12-01.

[153] " in the media Wikipedia:Wikipedia in the media (http://en.wikipedia.org/wiki/Wikipedia:Wikipedia)". *Wikipedia*. in the media. Retrieved 2008-12-26.

[154] " Bourgeois *et al.* v. Peters *et al.* (http://www.ca11.uscourts.gov/opinions/ops/200216886.pdf)" (PDF). . Retrieved 2007-02-06.

[155] " Wikipedian Justice (http://papers.ssrn.com/sol3/Delivery.cfm/SSRN_ID1346311_code835394. pdf?abstractid=1346311)" (PDF). . Retrieved 2009-06-09.

[156] C-38 Government of Canada Site | Site du gouvernement du Canada (http://www.parl.gc.ca/LEGISINFO/ index.asp?Session=13&query=4381&List=ot#2), LEGISINFO (March 28, 2005)

[157] Arias, Martha L. (2007-01-29). " Wikipedia: The Free Online Encyclopedia and its Use as Court Source (http://www.ibls.com/internet_law_news_portal_view.aspx?s=latestnews&id=1668)". *Internet Business Law Services*. . Retrieved 2008-12-26. (the name "*World Intellectual Property Office*" should however read "*World Intellectual Property Organization*" in this source)

[158] Cohen, Noam (2007-01-29). " Courts Turn to Wikipedia, but Selectively (http://www.nytimes.com/2007/ 01/29/technology/29wikipedia.html)". *New York Times*. . Retrieved 2008-12-26.

[159] Aftergood, Steven (2007-03-21). " The Wikipedia Factor in U.S. Intelligence (http://www.fas.org/blog/ secrecy/2007/03/the_wikipedia_factor_in_us_int.html)". Federation of American Scientists Project on Government Secrecy. . Retrieved 2007-04-14.

[160] Butler, Declan (December 16, 2008). "Publish in Wikipedia or perish". *Nature News*. doi: 10.1038/news.2008.1312 (http://dx.doi.org/10.1038/news.2008.1312).

[161] Shaw, Donna (February/March 2008). " Wikipedia in the Newsroom (http://www.ajr.org/Article. asp?id=4461)". American Journalism Review. . Retrieved 2008-02-11.

[162] Shizuoka newspaper plagiarized Wikipedia article, *Japan News Review*, July 5, 2007

[163] " Express-News staffer resigns after plagiarism in column is discovered (http://web.archive.org/web/ 20071015045010/http://www.mysanantonio.com/news/metro/stories/MYSA010307.02A.richter.132c153. html)", *San Antonio Express-News*, January 9, 2007.

[164] " Inquiry prompts reporter's dismissal (http://archives.starbulletin.com/2006/01/13/news/story03. html)", *Honolulu Star-Bulletin*, January 13, 2007.

[165] " Radio 4 Documentary (http://www.bbc.co.uk/radio4/factual/pip/efv21/)". . Retrieved 2008-12-26. [166] " Wikipedia Celebrates 750 Years Of American Independence (http://www.theonion.com/content/node/ 50902)". *The Onion*. 2006. . Retrieved October 15 2006.

[167] Schonfeld, Erick (April 8, 2008). " The Truth According to Wikipedia (http://www.techcrunch.com/2008/ 04/08/the-truth-according-to-wikipedia/)". TechCruch.com. . Retrieved 2009-05-30.

[168] " Truth in Numbers: The Wikipedia Story (http://wikidocumentary.wikia.com/wiki/Main_Page)". Wikidocumentary.wikia.com. . Retrieved 2008-11-01.

[169] Hart, Hugh (March 11, 2007). " Industry Buzz (http://www.sfgate.com/cgi-bin/article.cgi?f=/c/a/2007/ 03/11/PKGRJN87UI1.DTL)". SFGate.com. . Retrieved 2008-12-26.

[170] " Comunicato stampa. On. Franco Grillini. Wikipedia. Interrogazione a Rutelli. Con "diritto di panorama" promuovere arte e architettura contemporanea italiana. Rivedere con urgenza legge copyright (http://www.

grillini.it/show.php?4885)". October 12, 2007. . Retrieved 2008-12-26.

[171] Jose Antonio Vargas (2007-09-17). " On Wikipedia, Debating 2008 Hopefuls' Every Facet (http://www. washingtonpost.com/wp-dyn/content/article/2007/09/16/AR2007091601699_pf.html)". The Washington Post. . Retrieved 2008-12-26.

[172] Jennifer Ablan (2007-10-22). " Wikipedia page the latest status symbol (http://www.reuters.com/article/ domesticNews/idUSN2232893820071022?sp=true)". Reuters. . Retrieved 2007-10-24.

[173] "Trophy Box", Meta-Wiki (March 28, 2005).

[174] " Webby Awards 2004 (http://www.webbyawards.com/webbys/winners-2004.php)". The International Academy of Digital Arts and Sciences. 2004. . Retrieved 2007-06-19.

[175] Zumpano, Anthony (2007-01-29). " Similar Search Results: Google Wins (http://www.brandchannel.com/ features_effect.asp?pf_id=352)". Interbrand. . Retrieved 2007-01-28.

[176] " Die Quadriga — Award 2008 (http://loomarea.com/die_quadriga/e/index.php?title=Award_2008)". . Retrieved 2008-12-26.

[177] " Interview With Nick Doody and Matt Kirshen (http://www.comedy.org.uk/guide/radio/bigipedia/ interview/)". British Comedy Guide. . Retrieved 31 July, 2009.

[178] Web-based emulator of the Domesday Project User Interface (http://web.archive.org/web/ 20070115135325/http://www.domesday1986.com/) and data from the Community Disc (contributions from the general public) -- most articles can be accessed using the interactive map

[179] " In Memoriam: September 11, 2001 (http://www.sep11memories.org/wiki/In_Memoriam)". . Retrieved 2007-02-06.

[180] First edit to the wiki (http://www.sep11memories.org/index.php?title=In_Memoriam&oldid=1502) In Memoriam: September 11 wiki (October 28, 2002),

[181] " Announcement of Wiktionary's creation (http://meta.wikimedia.org/w/index. php?title=Wikimedia_News&diff=prev&oldid=4133)", December 12, 2002. Retrieved on 2007-02-02.

[182] " Our projects (http://wikimediafoundation.org/wiki/Our_projects)", Wikimedia Foundation. Retrieved on 2007-01-24

[183] http://schools-wikipedia.org/

[184] Telegraph.co.uk (http://www.telegraph.co.uk/news/newstopics/howaboutthat/5549589/ Wikipedia-turned-into-book.html)

[185] Frith, Holden (March 26, 2007,). " Wikipedia founder launches rival online encyclopedia (http://technology. timesonline.co.uk/tol/news/tech_and_web/the_web/article1571519.ece)". The Times. . Retrieved 2007-06-27. "Wikipedia's de facto leader, Jimmy Wales, stood by the site's format. – Holden Frith."

[186] Orlowski, Andrew (September 18, 2006). " Wikipedia founder forks Wikipedia, More experts, less fiddling? (http://www.theregister.co.uk/2006/09/18/sanger_forks_wikipedia/)". The Register. . Retrieved 2007-06-27. "Larry Sanger describes the Citizendium project as a "progressive or gradual fork", with the major difference that experts have the final say over edits." – Andrew Orlowski.

[187] Lyman, Jay (September 20, 2006). " Wikipedia Co-Founder Planning New Expert-Authored Site (http:// www.crmbuyer.com/story/53137.html)". LinuxInsider. . Retrieved 2007-06-27.

[188] http://www.firstmonday.org/issues/issue12_8/nielsen/index.html

[189] http://jcmc.indiana.edu./vol12/issue1/pfeil.html

[190] http://dx.doi.org/10.1111%2Fj.1083-6101.2006.00316.x

[191] http://portal.acm.org/citation.cfm?doid=1316624.1316663

[192] http://reagle.org./joseph/2005/ethno/leadership.html

[193] http://www.firstmonday.org/issues/issue12_4/wilkinson/index.html

[194] http://online.wsj.com/article/SB123897399273491031.html

[195] http://www.nybooks.com/articles/21131

[196] http://chnm.gmu.edu/resources/essays/d/42

[197] http://www.delta-sky.com/sections/index.php/lifestyle/wikipedia_vs_encyclopedia/

[198] http://www.nytimes.com/2007/07/01/magazine/01WIKIPEDIA-t.html?_r=1&ref=magazine& oref=slogin

[199] http://blogs.chron.com/brokenrecord/2008/03/for_music_fans_wikipedia_myspa.html

[200] http://www.yorkshirepost.co.uk/highlights?articleid=3115718

[201] http://www.newscientist.com/article/mg19526226.200

[202] http://thephoenix.com/Boston/Life/52864-Wikipedia-rules/

[203] http://www.theatlantic.com/doc/200609/wikipedia

[204] http://www.time.com/time/magazine/article/0,9171,1066904-1,00.html [205] http://www.economist.com/science/tq/displaystory.cfm?story_id=11484062 [206] http://www.metrobostonnews.com/us/article/2009/01/28/03/4644-72/index.xml

[207] http://www.independent.co.uk/life-style/gadgets-and-tech/features/is-wikipedia-cracking-up-1543527. html

[208] http://technology.timesonline.co.uk/tol/news/tech_and_web/the_web/article5682896.ece

[209] http://www.lrb.co.uk/v31/n10/runc01_.html

[210] http://www.wikipedia.org/

[211] http://mobile.wikipedia.org/

[212] http://en.wikipedia.org/wiki/Wikipedia:Press_coverage

[213] http://www.dmoz.org/Computers/Open_Source/Open_Content/Encyclopedias/Wikipedia/

[214] http://www.cbc.ca/news/background/tech/wikipedia.html

[215] http://www.wikihow.com/Contribute-to-Wikipedia

[216] http://www.neowin.net/news/main/07/11/02/class-assignment-write-an-original-wikipedia-article

[217] irc://irc.freenode.net/Wikipedia

[218] http://www.ted.com/index.php/talks/jimmy_wales_on_the_birth_of_wikipedia.html

[219] http://www.econtalk.org/archives/2009/03/wales_on_wikipe.html

[220] http://www.stanford.edu/class/ee380/Abstracts/020116.html

[221] http://stanford-online.stanford.edu/courses/ee380/020116-ee380-100.asx

[222] http://www.youtube.com/watch?v=cqOHbihYbhE

WikiWikiWeb

WikiWikiWeb (also known as **WardsWiki**) was the first wiki application ever written. It was developed in 1994 by Ward Cunningham in order to make the exchange of ideas between programmers easier and was based on the ideas developed in HyperCard stacks that he built in the late 1980s.[1] [2] [3] He installed the WikiWikiWeb on his company's (Cunningham & Cunningham) website, c2.com, on March 25, 1995. Cunningham named it WikiWikiWeb because he remembered a Honolulu International Airport counter employee who told him to take the Wiki Wiki Shuttle, a shuttle bus line that runs between the airport's terminals. "Wiki Wiki" is a reduplication of "wiki," a Hawaiian language word for *fast*. Cunningham's idea was to make WikiWikiWeb's pages quickly editable by its users, so he initially thought about calling it "QuickWeb," but later changed his mind and dubbed it "WikiWikiWeb." The WikiWikiWeb's *WelcomeVisitors* page contains the following description:

> *Our site's primary focus is PeopleProjectsAndPatterns in SoftwareDevelopment. Nevertheless, it is much more than just an InformalHistoryOfProgrammingIdeas. It has a culture and DramaticIdentity of its own. In particular, all Wiki content is WorkInProgress and this will always be a forum where people share new ideas. WardsWiki changes as people come and go. Much of the information that remains is subjective or dated. If you are looking for a dedicated reference site, try WikiPedia.*

Some words are written in CamelCase because this is the markup used to create inter-page links by → WikiWikiWeb's software, WikiBase [4].

WikiWikiWeb and its designated sister sites

Site	Pages	Founder
WikiWikiWeb	34084 [5]	Ward Cunningham
WhyClublet	4777 [6]	Richard Drake
MeatBallWiki	4885 [7]	Clifford Adams, Sunir Shah
GreenCheese	(dead)	Peter Merel

TheReformSociety	(dead)	Peter Merel
The Adjunct	719 [8]	Earle Martin
WikiBase	359 [9]	Ward Cunningham
FitWiki	225 [10]	Ward Cunningham

WikiWikiWeb as a precursor to other online communities

The WikiWikiWeb played an important historical role in the World Wide Web and the Internet because of its influence on other online communities. Its focus on specialized programming made its content relatively unintelligible to people outside the programming sphere; however, editors (so-called wiki citizens, or wikizens), visitors, and readers of the WikiWikiWeb took up the basic idea of making pages user-modifiable and created their own new wiki engines (programs that run wikis) and wikis outside of the WikiWikiWeb.

Wiki communities outside the WikiWikiWeb implemented their wiki engines to create wikis focused on content other than programming. The versatility of wikis and their multiple applications is what subsequently made them popular in the Internet's communities.

A notable example of the WikiWikiWeb's legacy is → Wikipedia. A WikiWikiWeb user, programmer Ben Kovitz of San Diego, California, introduced the WikiWikiWeb to Larry Sanger of Internet company Bomis on the evening of January 2, 2001. At the time, Bomis was working on the online encyclopedia Nupedia; but that project failed, so Sanger suggested running an open encyclopedia on UseModWiki, an indirect clone of WikiWikiWeb's engine. Sanger presented the idea to Jimmy Wales, then head of Bomis, and he agreed. The UseModWiki-based encyclopedia eventually came to be known as "Wikipedia."

Other popular websites have since come to embrace the wiki method, such as Amazon.com, which in 2007 launched its own *Amapedia* after two years of trialing wiki technology for customer reviews for items.

See also

- → Wiki
- → History of wikis

External links

- WikiWikiWeb [11]
- WikiWikiWeb:WikiHistory, including comments by Ward Cunningham
- WikiWikiWeb:WelcomeVisitors
- WikiWikiWeb:WikiDesignPrinciples
- WikiWikiWeb:WikiBase — the Wiki Base software
- Correspondence on the Etymology of Wiki [12] — Ward Cunningham

References

[1] WikiHistory (http://c2.com/cgi/wiki?WikiHistory) on c2.com

[2] Interview: Wikinewsie Kim Bruning discusses Wikimania (http://en.wikinews.org/wiki/
     Interview:_Wikinewsie_Kim_Bruning_discusses_Wikimania) on WikiNews

[3] Interview with Ward Cunningham (http://video.google.com/videoplay?docid=-7739076742312910146) on
     Google Video

[4] http://c2.com/cgi/wiki?WikiBase

[5] http://c2.com/cgi/wikiPages

[6] http://clublet.com/c/c/why?FindPage

[7] http://www.usemod.com/cgi-bin/mb.pl?action=index

[8] http://grault.net/adjunct/

[9] http://c2.com/w4/wikibase/search.cgi

[10] http://fit.c2.com/search.cgi

[11] http://c2.com/cgi/wiki

[12] http://c2.com/doc/etymology.html

History of wikis

There were several **historical** antecedents to the **wikis**, which is the name used to refer to a website with pages that can be edited by any visitor. One of the earliest precursors was Vannevar Bush's vision of a microfilm hypertext system which he called the "memex" (1945). Other precursors were an early collaborative hypertext database called the ZOG (1972), and the Apple Computer hypertext system called HyperCard (1987).

However, the creation of the first wiki website only became possible with the development of the hypertext protocol of the World Wide Web (1991) and graphical web browsers such as the Netscape Navigator (1994). In order to facilitate communication between software developers, and also to experiment with the new hypertext capabilities, Ward Cunningham created the first wiki, which he called → WikiWikiWeb (using the Hawaiian word "wiki" in place of "quick"). Cunningham went public with the first wiki in early 1995, inviting a selected group of programmers to participate in the experiment.

Ward Cunningham's first wiki met with immediate success, and quickly spawned "wiki clones," alternative versions of the wiki software. The use of wiki websites was rapidly adopted by communities of free software developers, but at first remained confined to these specialised groups. In the meantime the WikiWikiWeb evolved rapidly as features were added to the software and as the growing body of users developed a unique "wiki culture." By 2000 the number of contributors to Ward Cunningham's website had grown so large that conflicts developed between those who wanted to restrict the discussion to computer programming and those who wanted to discuss issues relating to the functioning of the wiki itself. The conflict was resolved by the creation of the "SisterSites" MeatballWiki and WhyClublet as separate forums for discussion.

Wikis remained largely unknown outside of circles of software developers until around 2001, when the success of the free content encyclopedia → Wikipedia introduced wikis to the general public. After 2001 the number of wiki websites and the varieties of wiki engines (software implementations) increased exponentially. There now exist thousands of wiki websites and hundreds of wiki engines.

Pre-1994

Historical antecedents of the wiki concept

A distant precursor of the wiki concept was Vannevar Bush's vision of the "memex," a microfilm reader which would create automated links between documents. In an article for the journal Atlantic Monthly from the year 1945 titled *As we may think*, Vannevar Bush described how he imaged the future experience of the user: "Before him are the two items to be joined, projected onto adjacent viewing positions... The user taps a single key, and the items are permanently joined.... Thereafter, at any time, when one of these items is in view, the other can be instantly recalled merely by tapping a button below the corresponding code space. Moreover, when numerous items have been thus joined together to form a trail, they can be reviewed in turn..." This vision clearly foresees the hypertext mechanism, which will be taken advantage of by all wikis. However, hypertext is a general feature of all World Wide Web applications, rather than a feature that is specific to wikis.[1]

Another precursor of the wiki concept was the ZOG multi-user database system, developed in 1972 by researchers at Carnegie-Mellon University. The ZOG interface consisted of text-only frames, each containing a title, a description, a line with standard ZOG commands, and a set of selections (hypertext links) leading to other frames.

Two members of the ZOG team, Donald McCracken and Robert Akscyn, spun off a company from CMU in 1981 and developed an improved version of ZOG called Knowledge Management System (KMS). KMS was a collaborative tool based on direct manipulation, permitting users to modify the contents of frames, freely intermixing text, graphics and images, any of which could be linked to other frames. Because the database was distributed and accessible from any workstation on a network, changes became visible immediately to other users, enabling them to work concurrently on shared structures (documents, programs, ...). [2]

The "ZOG" system was the model for Janet Walker's Document Examiner, created in 1985 for the operation manuals of Symbolics computers. Document Examiner was in turn the model for the Note Cards system, released by Xerox in 1985. Note Cards is a hypertext system that features scrolling windows for each note card, combined with a separate browser and navigator window. Note Cards was the inspiration for Bill Atkinson's WildCard, which was later called HyperCard. [2] Ward Cunningham traces the wiki idea back to a HyperCard stack that he wrote in the late 1980s. [3]

The influence of HyperCard on wiki inventor Ward Cunningham

Ward Cunningham was introduced to HyperCard (then called WildCard) by Kent Beck, who obtained access to it after joining Apple Computer. Cunningham used HyperCard to make a stack with three kinds of cards:

- cards for ideas,
- cards for people who hold ideas,
- cards for projects where people share ideas.

(One can recognise here the Patterns, People and Projects that are mentioned on the Front Page of Cunningham's original wiki, the WikiWikiWeb.) Cunningham made a single card that would serve for all uses. It had three fields: Name, Description and Links. The fields in HyperCard were WYSIWYG editors, but linking was a pain that involved moving between both cards. Cunningham abandoned regular stack links and used search-on-demand instead. Normally one would type links into the Links field. When using the card, each link had a button that would take you to the card if it existed, or beep otherwise. If you held the button down, it would relent and go make the card for you. (One can recognise here the traditional wiki feature by which a new page is opened for editing whenever one clicks on any new word formed in camel-case. In Wikipedia the equivalent feature is called "red links".) [4]

The World Wide Web sets the stage for the first wiki

Ward Cunningham's first wiki was made possible by the hypertext capabilities of the World Wide Web. In 1990 Tim Berners-Lee of CERN built the first hypertext client, which he called World Wide Web (it was also a Web editor), and the first hypertext server (info.cern.ch). In 1991 he posted a short summary of the World Wide Web project on the alt.hypertext newsgroup, marking the debut of the Web as a publicly available service on the Internet.

Early adopters of the World Wide Web were primarily university-based scientific departments or physics laboratories. In May 1992 appeared ViolaWWW, a graphical browser providing features such as embedded graphics, scripting, and animation. However, the turning point for the World Wide Web was the introduction of the Mosaic graphical browser in 1993, which gained wide popularity due to its strong support of integrated multimedia and the authors' rapid response to user bug reports and recommendations for new features. Its creators formed Mosaic Communications Corporation, which changed its name to Netscape in April 1994, and the browser was developed further as Netscape Navigator. That same month CERN agreed that anyone could use the Web protocol and code for free. The stage was set for the appearance of Ward Cunningham's WikiWikiWeb.

Post-WikiWikiWeb (1994-2001)

The creation of WikiWikiWeb, the first wiki

Ward Cunningham started developing the → WikiWikiWeb in 1994 as a supplement to the Portland Pattern Repository, a website containing documentation about Design Patterns, a particular approach to object-oriented programming. [3]

The WikiWikiWeb was intended as a collaborative database, dedicated to People, Projects and Patterns, [3] in order to make the exchange of ideas between programmers easier. Cunningham wrote the software to run it using the Perl programming language. He named it using the alliterative Hawaiian word wiki-wiki, which means "quick-quick," to avoid calling it "quick-web". [3]

Cunningham installed a prototype of the software on his company Cunningham & Cunningham's website c2.com. In a surviving email received by Ward Cunningham on 6 November 1994, the server administrator Randy Bush wrote: "You will find the web stuff started and running, but rather content-free. It is in the directory /usr/local/etc/httpd/htdocs. You can send folk to ... http://c2.com." Cunningham replied: "Actually, a higher priority for me is completing a first cut at my repository."[5]

A few months later, when the Repository was functioning, Cunningham sent to a colleague the following email, dated March 16, 1995:

> Steve -- I've put up a new database on my web server and I'd like you to take a look. It's a web of people, projects and patterns accessed through a cgi-bin script. It has a

forms based authoring capability that doesn't require familiarity with html. I'd be very pleased if you would get on and at least enter your name in RecentVisitors. I'm asking you because I think you might also add some interesting content. I'm going to advertise this a little more widely in a week or so. The URL is http://c2.com/cgi-bin/ wiki.Thanks and best regards. – Ward [5]

Cunningham dates the official start of WikiWikiWeb as March 25, 1995. [3] On May 1, 1995 he sent to a number of programmers an InvitationToThePatternsList , which caused an increase in participation. [3] This note was posted to the " Patterns" listserv, a group of software developers gathered under the name "Hillside Group" to develop Erich Gamma's use of object-oriented patterns (inspired by Christopher Alexander's use of patterns in architecture). Cunningham had noticed that the older contents of the listserv tended to get buried under the more recent posts, and he proposed instead to collect ideas in a set of pages which would be collectively edited. Cunningham' s post stated: " The plan is to have interested parties write web pages about the People, Projects and Patterns that have changed the way they program." He added: "Think of it as a moderated list where anyone can be moderator and everything is archived. It's not quite a chat, still, conversation is possible."[6]

The site was immediately popular within the pattern community, due to both the newness of the World Wide Web and the good slate of invited authors. [3]

Initial WikiWiki software clones

Clones of the → WikiWikiWeb software were soon developed. PatrickMueller wrote probably the first WikiWikiClone, using the RexxLanguage. [3] Ward Cunningham wrote a version of wiki that could host its own source code, called Wiki Base, and announced WikiWikiGoesPublic. The announcement said: "WikiWikiWeb is almost public. Actually, a pretty good clone of it is public at: http://c2.com/cgi/wikibase.I've translated almost all of the actual wiki script into HyperPerl, a wiki-literate programming system that I think you will like." Visitors were requested to register on the wiki before they took the Wiki Base code. [3] . Cunningham expected users to fold changes back into his editable version, but those who implemented changes generally chose to distribute the modified versions on their own sites. [3]

One of the early clones of Wiki Base was CvWiki, developed in 1997 by Peter Merel. CvWiki was the first Wiki Base clone to have functioning transclusion and backlinks. It was fully integrated with Concurrent Version System (CVS) software, thereby providing unlimited undo and no edit collisions.[7]

Initial wiki websites for software development

Inspired by the example of the WikiWikiWeb, programmers soon started several other wikis to build knowledge bases about programming topics. Wikis became popular in the free and open-source software (FOSS) community, where they were ideal for collaboratively discussing and documenting software, particularly given the loose structure of the projects. However, being used only by specialists, these early software-focused wikis failed to attract widespread public attention.[8]

Growth and innovations in WikiWikiWeb from 1995 to 2000

The → WikiWikiWeb grew steadily from 1995 to 1998, and then snowballed between 1998 and 2000. Ward Cunningham's statistics about disk-usage show the following progression in the number of 1k blocks consumed by WikiWikiWeb pages: [3]

- Nov 29 1994: -
- Dec 15 1995: 2426
- Dec 1 1996: 5134
- Dec 31 1997: 10600
- Mar 25 1998: 14554
- Dec 2 2000: 62919

Some of the major innovations within WikiWikiWeb from 1995 to 2000, many of which were proposed by the community of users, were: [3]

- 1995 RecentVisitors, PeopleIndex: pages to help users know who was contributing
- 1995 NotSoRecentChanges: excess lines from the RecentChanges page were (manually) copied to a file of "ChangesIn<Month>"
- 1996 EditCopy: offers the possibility to edit the backup copy of a page (this was replaced in 2002 with Page History)
- 1996 ThreadMode: the form of a page where community members hold a discussion, each signing their own contribution
- 1996 WikiCategories: categories can be added as an automatic index to pages
- 1997 RoadMaps: proposed lists of pages to consult about specific topics, such as the Algorithms RoadMap or the Leadership RoadMap
- 1999 ChangeSummary: an aid to telling which changes added interesting new content and which were only minor
- 2000 UserName: the Wiki will accept a cookie that specifies a User Name to be used in place of the host name (IP identity) in the RecentChanges log

"ThreadMode" is defined as "a form of discussion where our community holds a conversation." It consists of a series of signed comments added down the page in chronological order. Ward Cunningham generally frowned on ThreadMode, writing: "Chronological is only one of many possible organizations of technical writing and rarely the best one at that." [9]

Cunningham encouraged contributors to "refactor" (rewrite) the ThreadMode discussions into DocumentMode discourse. In practice many pages started out at the top in DocumentMode and degenerated into ThreadMode further down. When ThreadMode becomes incomprehensible the result is called ThreadMess. [10] (On Wikipedia the conflict between these two modes has been resolved by putting all document text on the main page of an article, and all discussion text on the Talk page.)

The Categories were proposed by Stan Silver on August 27, 1996. [11] His initial post suggested: "If everyone adds a category and topic to their page, then the category and topic pages themselves can be used as automatic indexes into the pages." [12]

Ward Cunningham had originally created Wiki with the capability to click on the title of a page to see which pages pointed to it. Stan Silver used this reverse index technology to provide lists of the categories: [11] "Go to the CategoryCategory page and press its title to see all categories." [12]

Initially Stan Silver had proposed both categories and topics: categories denoted what the page was about (a book, a person, a pattern), while topics denoted the contents of the page (Java, extreme programming, Smalltalk). However, people ignored this separation, and so the topics were collapsed into the categories. [11]

The ChangeSummary began as an aid to telling which changes added interesting new content, and which were just minor adjustments of spelling, punctuation, or correction of web links. It started when some users began taking the RecentChanges page, annotating each line with a brief description of each change, and posting the result to the ChangeSummary page. This practice was highly time-consuming and rapidly petered out, but was replaced by the "MinorEdit/RecentEdits" feature, designed to reduce the RecentChanges clutter. (The ChangeSummary is the ancestor of the Wikipedia feature whereby an editor can enter a line of descriptive text when saving changes to a page.) [3]

Tensions within WikiWikiWeb and the creation of SisterSites

Between early 1998 and the end of 2000 participation in → WikiWikiWeb snowballed, and the disk space consumed by wiki pages more than quadrupled. With increased participation tensions began to appear.

In 1998 proponents of Extreme Programming showed up on the WikiWikiWeb and started posting comments about ExtremeProgramming on most of the pages related to software development. This annoyed a number people who wanted to talk about patterns, leading to the tag "XpFreeZone," which was put onto pages as a request not to talk about ExtremeProgramming on that page. Eventually most of the DesignPatterns people left to discuss patterns on their own wikis, and WikiWikiWeb was referred to as WardsWiki instead of the PortlandPatternRepository. [3]

Around the summer of 1999 a Wiki user known as SamGentile posted the comment "I'm through here" on his user page, and began systematically removing his text from all pages on WikiWikiWeb that he had contributed to. Sam Gentile worked at Microsoft and had been hurt by what he perceived as anti-Microsoft bias on WikiWikiWeb. His deletions led to controversy about whether he had the right to remove his own material, and whether others had the right to put it back in (which some began to do). This event became referred to as the WikiMindWipe, a term which would come to denote a general type of action, which in this particular case had taken the form of WikiSuicide. It was the first case of massive deliberate deletions of text on the WikiWikiWeb. It would be followed by another. [13]

On the morning of Friday 14 April 2008 four Europeans, Richard Drake, Keith Braithwaite, Stephan Houben, and Manfred Schaefer, starting independently, tried to reduce the amount of text on Wiki by a large number of deletions. [14] They mainly attacked the "soft target" of WikiOnWiki material, which is defined as "Wiki pages devoted to Wiki, its nature, form and postulated future development." [15] They considered this material to be dead weight, and would have preferred to see it all replaced by concise guidance to newcomers. The primary focus of WikiWikiWeb was supposed to be on computer programming design patterns, and users who strayed too far from the focus were considered by some to be WikiSquatting [16], which meant developing their own separate community within the WikiWikiWeb.

The group that made the deletions became known as the WikiReductionists. The term has come to represent a general approach to Wiki editing, those advocating a contrary approach being called WikiConstructionists. [14] (On Wikipedia the equivalent terms are inclusionist and exclusionist, or deletionist.)[17] [18]

Contributors who were outraged by the deletions of the WikiReductions began copying all of the deleted text back in again. A vote was taken of where the Wiki users stood on this issue. It was proposed that any "reductions" should be pre-announced, with an opportunity for response before action is taken. [14] (This was a distant precursor of the Wikipedia deletion policy, which requires announcement, discussion and voting before any controversial deletion of an article.)

Critics of the WikiReductionists accused them of escalating a flame war to the level of a ForestFire [19]. [20] The longer-term result of the attack was the formation of WikiWikiWeb Sister Sites. In an amicable resolution to the conflict, Sunir Shah created MeatballWiki and invited all those who were interested in WikiOnWiki discussions to post their comments there. A few months later, Richard Drake created the WhyClublet (or "Why?") wiki to host discussion of Christian issues. Many pages were moved from WikiWikiWeb to these alternative sites, with a stub of the moved page left on the WikiWikiWeb, containing a link to the new page and the message: "This page exists only on SisterSites." The implementation of SisterSites at the level of changes to the Wiki script dates from 2001. [3]

In 2001 → WikiWikiWeb founder Ward Cunningham and user Bo Leuf published a book, *The Wiki Way*, which distilled the lessons learned during the collective experience of the first → wiki.[21]

Post-Wikipedia (2001-present)

The creation of Wikipedia

Until 2001 wikis were virtually unknown outside of the restricted circles of computer programmers. Wikis were introduced to the general public by the success of Wikipedia, a free content encyclopedia that can be edited by anyone.

Wikipedia was originally conceived as a complement to Nupedia, a free on-line encyclopedia founded by Jimmy Wales, with articles written by highly qualified contributors and evaluated by an elaborate peer review process. The writing of content for Nupedia proved to be extremely slow, with only 12 articles completed during the first year, despite a mailing-list of interested editors and the presence of a full-time editor-in-chief recruited by Wales, Larry Sanger. Learning of the wiki concept, Wales and Sanger decided to try creating a collaborative website to provide an additional source of rapidly-produced draft articles that could be polished for use on Nupedia.

Nupedia's editors and reviewers resisted the idea of associating Nupedia with a wiki-style website, so Wikipedia was launched on its own domain, wikipedia.com, on January 15 2001. It initially ran on UseModWiki software, with the original text stored in flat-files rather than in a database, and with articles named using the CamelCase convention UseModWiki was replaced by a PHP wiki engine in January 2002 and by MediaWiki in July 2002.

Wikipedia attracted new participants after being mentioned on Slashdot as well as in an article on the community-edited website Kuro5hin. It quickly overtook Nupedia. In the first year of its existence, over 20,000 encyclopedia entries were created, and the rate of growth has generally increased steadily since the inception of the project. As of 2008, Wikipedia includes several million freely-usable articles and pages in hundreds of languages worldwide, and content from millions of contributors. It is one of the most popular web sites and extensively used reference sites worldwide.

Development of wiki software to the end of 2002

Clones of the → WikiWikiWeb software began to be developed as soon as Ward Cunningham made the Wiki Base software available online. One of the early clones was CvWiki, developed in 1997 by Peter Merel, which was the first Wiki clone to have functioning transclusion, backlinks, and WayBackMode.

Another early wiki engine was JosWiki, developed by an international group of Java programmers who were trying to create a free and open Java Operating System (JOS). [22]

TWiki was created in Perl by Peter Thoeny in 1998, based on JosWiki. Twiki was aimed at large corporate Intranets. It used flat-files, which means that the data is stored in plain text files instead of in a database. (Flat-files allow a more rapid system than does the more complicated storage of pages in a database, but a database system can have more capabilities than a flat-file system.)[23] [24]

PikiPiki was created by Martin Pool in 1999 as a rewrite of WikiWikiWeb in Python Language. It was made to be a small program, using flat files and doing away with versioning (Martin Pool felt that a wiki is not meant to be a document-management system). [25] [26]

PhpWiki, created by Steve Wainstead in 1999 was the first wiki software written in PHP language. The initial version was a feature-for-feature reimplementation of the original WikiWikiWeb at c2.com. Subsequent versions adopted many features from UseModWiki.[24]

Swiki was written in Squeak by Mark Guzdial and Jochen Rick in 1999. It is used at the Georgia Institute of Technology for collaborative group web pages. One installation of a swiki allows a large number of virtual wikis to be created through the administrative interface using any web browser. A Swiki has its own web server and consists of the Virtual Machine (VM) file, an image file, and a set of files and folders with templates and the virtual wikis. [23]

Zwiki, written in Python in 1999, is based on the Zope web application server (it can also co-exist with the Plone content management system). It was developed by Simon Michael, Joyful Systems and contributors from around the world. It uses a ZODB Object Database.

UseModWiki was developed from 1999 to 2000 by Clifford Adams. UseModWiki is a flat-file wiki written in Perl. It was based on Markus Denker's AtisWiki, which was in turn based on Peter Merel's CvWiki. It introduced the square bracket syntax for linking words that was later adopted by many other wiki engines, such as Wikipedia's own MediaWiki.[27]

MoinMoin, created in Python by Jürgen Hermann and Thomas Waldmann in mid-2000, was initially based on PikiPiki. It is a flat-file wiki with a simple code base but many possible extensions, which makes it often the wiki of choice for many open source projects and corporate wikis. MoinMoin uses the idea of separating the parsers (for parsing the wiki syntax) from the formatters (for outputting HTML code), with an interface between them, so that new output formatters can be written, and all parsers using the interface will be automatically supported.[23]

JSPWiki, created by Janne Jalkanen in 2001, is flat-file wiki software built around JavaServer Pages (JSP). JSPWiki adapted and extended the Php wiki markup. It is primarily used for company and university intranets as a project wiki or a knowledge management application. Sun Microsystems has integrated JSPWiki into their portal server software. Due to its easy installation, many people also use it as a Personal Information Manager (PIM). The MediaWiki program was written for Wikipedia in 2002 by Lee Daniel Crocker, based on the user interface design of an earlier PHP wiki engine developed by Magnus Manske. Manske's PHP-based software suffered load problems due to increased use, so Crocker re-wrote the software with a more scalable MySQL database backend. As Wikipedia grew to one of the world's largest websites, achieving scalability through multiple layers of caching and database replication became a major concern for the developers. Internationalization has also received significant attention by MediaWiki developers (the user interface has been translated into more than 70 languages). One of the earliest differences between MediaWiki and other wiki engines was the use of freely formatted links instead of links in CamelCase. MediaWiki provides specialized syntax to support rich content, such as rendering mathematical formulas using LaTeX, graphical plotting, image galleries and thumbnails, and Exif metadata. MediaWiki lacks native WYSIWYG support, but comes with a graphical toolbar to simplify editing. One innovation for structuring content is "namespaces." Namespaces allow each article to contain multiple sheets with different standard names: one sheet presents the encyclopedic content, another contains the discussions surrounding it, and so on. While new namespaces can be added, the number of namespaces in a wiki typically remains low.

PmWiki was created in Php language by Patrick Michaud in 2002. It is a flat-file wiki engine that was designed to be easy to install and customize as an engine for creating professional web sites with one or many content authors. PmWiki offers a template scheme that makes it possible to change the look and feel of the wiki. Customization is made easy through a wide selection of custom extensions, known as "recipes" available from the PmWiki Cookbook.

TikiWiki was created in Php language by Luis Argerich in 2002. It is designed as a CMS and Groupware application enabling websites on the Internet and on intranets. TikiWiki is modular with components that can be individually enabled and customized by the TikiWiki administrator, and extending customization to the user with selectable skins and themes. TikiWiki is an international project, providing translations of the interface in several languages. Though developed primarily in Php, TikiWiki has some JavaScript code. It will run on any server and supports several possible databases. Its components incorporate several other open source projects and applications.

coWiki was developed by Daniel T. Gorski in 2002. It was one of the largest projects being developed under Php5 when that language was still in early development. coWiki used a markup language similar to that of TWiki. It suffered from a mysterious bug called the "bad magic" bug, and became inactive in 2006.

EditMe was developed by the EditMe company in 2002. It was built on Java (hosted) elements, with a MySQL database. Unlike most other early wikis, EditMe was proprietary. [23]

Development of wiki software after 2002

After 2002 the number of wiki engines continued to grow exponentially, as new commercial products were introduced, and as new open-source projects continually forked off of existing ones. For example, the small, easy-to-modify open source wiki engine named WakkaWiki, while having itself been discontinued 2004, has spawned at least five forks: CitiWiki, UniWakka, WackoWiki, WikiNi and WikkaWiki.

As they developed, wikis incorporated many of the features used on other websites and blogs, including:

- support for various wiki markup styles
- editing of pages with a GUI editor, wysiwyg HTML, specific applications such as LaTeX
- optional use of external editors
- support for plugins and custom extensions
- use of RSS feeds
- integrated email discussion
- precise access control
- spam protection

Around 2005 wikis began to be massively confronted with wiki spam, produced by spammers who enter website addresses onto wikis in order to improve the ranking of the displayed websites by search engines. Various strategies have been developed to counter wikispam. [28]

Development of wiki websites to the end of 2003

After the creation of the first wiki website → WikiWikiWeb in 1995, the usage of wikis was rapidly adopted by free software development groups. However, for several years participation in wikis was restricted to these specialised programming communities.

While many early wiki websites were devoted to the development of open source software, one early wiki was created by the FoxPro company, sellers of proprietary software. FoxPro Wiki was founded in 1999 by Steven Black and evolved into a popular site with many pages. [29]

→ World66 was a Dutch company which tried to transform the open content idea into a profitable business. The website was founded in 1999 by Richard and Douwe Osinga. It contains travel-related articles covering destinations around the world. All of the articles are licensed under the Creative Commons Attribution-ShareAlike Licence.

A wiki forum was created in 1999 for discussion of newly-created PhpWiki software. This became one of larger software-related wikis. In 2000 Arno Hollosi contributed heavily to development of PhpWiki because he was interested in running a wiki for the game Go (he created Sensei's wiki in 2002, as described below).

Clifford Adams began running a wiki for his Usemod Project in 1999 using AtisWiki. Late in 1999 he began running test versions of his own UseModWiki engine, and in 2000 he created the UseModWiki as forum to discuss the UseModWiki software. In April 2000 Adams invited Sunir Shah to install the MeatballWiki on the usemod.com website, using the same UseModWiki software. MeatballWiki was a friendly fork from the WikiWikiWeb, dedicated to online communities, Around the same time, the WhyClublet (or "Why?") wiki was forked from WikiWikiWeb to host discussion of Christian issues.

MeatballWiki rapidly became a popular wiki for discussions of online communities and WikiOnWiki topics. [27] MeatballWiki provided key contributions to a series of innovations in the linking together of wikis which included: [30] [31]

- InterWikiMap on WikiWikiWeb provided a simple InterWiki linking system (2000) [32]
- MetaWiki, the idea of a wiki that helps people find other wikis [33]
- TourBus project (summer 2002)
- OneBigWiki (2002), the idea of having one wiki distributed across several servers [34]

- SwitchWiki (2003): the idea of having one site where one can switch between wikis [35]
- WikiIndex, an actual wiki listing other wikis, thereby implementing the MetaWiki and SwitchWiki ideas [35]
- WikiNode, another way to implement InterWiki

Sensei's Library, a wiki, dedicated to discussion of the game of Go, was created by Morten G. Pahle and Arno Hollosi in October 2000. It is one of the largest and most active wikis on the internet outside of the Wikipedia project.

→ Wikipedia's English edition was launched on January 15, 2001 (see separate section above).

→ Susning.nu is a Swedish language wiki, created in October 2001 by Lars Aronsson. It has become one of the largest wikis. Aronsson's aim for Susning is "to make it into what the users want it to be." Susning is an encyclopedia, a dictionary, and a discussion forum about any concept of interest to its users. It is in direct competition with the Swedish Wikipedia. Unlike Wikipedia, Susning places advertisements on practically all its articles. It has no license agreement, and contributions remain copyrighted by their submitters (the right to modify is said to be implicit in the site's function). Third parties, such as Wikipedia contributors, cannot legally use Susning materials contributed by others without permission.

The Enciclopedia Libre was founded by a group of contributors to the Spanish-language Wikipedia, led by Edgar Enyedy, who left Wikipedia on February 26, 2002 to start an independent project. Their stated reasons for the split were that they rejected censorship and were against a proposal to put advertising on the wiki. They seeded the new website with the freely licensed articles of the Spanish-language Wikipedia.

SourceWatch (formerly Disinfopedia) is the wiki website of the Center for Media and Democracy (CMD). It was launched by Sheldon Rampton in March 2003. It aims to produce a directory of public relations firms and industry-funded organizations that influence public opinion and public policy on behalf of corporations, governments and special interests. The content of Sourcewatch is licensed under the GNU Free Documentation License.

Javapedia is a project openly inspired by Wikipedia. The project was launched in June 2003 during the JavaOne developer conference. It is part of the java.net wiki, which is promoted by Sun Microsystems as the central meeting place for the Java community. The Project aims at creating an online encyclopedia covering all aspects of the Java platform.

Wikinfo (formerly Internet-Encyclopedia) is a fork of the English Wikipedia initiated by Fred Bauder in July 2003. Rather than adopting Wikipedia's neutral point of view editorial policy, Wikinfo's policy is to edit for either a sympathetic point of view or a critical point of view. Thus Wikinfo can host a set of articles about a particular topic, each presenting a particular point of view, and linked to the others at the top of the article.[36]

→ Wikitravel was started in July 2003 by Evan Prodromou and Michele Ann Jenkins. Wikitravel was inspired in part by Wikipedia, but is not a Wikimedia project. Since it uses the Creative Commons Attribution ShareAlike license, rather than the GNU Free Documentation License used by Wikipedia, it is easier for individuals and tourism agencies to make free reprints of individual pages. While Wikipedia and Wikitravel are both free content resources, content cannot be freely copied between them because of the incompatible licenses.

WikiZnanie is a Russian language encyclopedia (znanie is Russian for knowledge) created in 2003 by Andrey Vovk. WikiZnanie differs from the Russian Wikipedia project by licensing under the FreeBSD Documentation License (instead of GFDL) and by displaying commercial ads on article pages. It also allows original research, which Wikipedia prohibits.

→ Memory Alpha is a wiki devoted to the Star Trek fictional universe. It was launched by Harry Doddema and Dan Carlson in December 2003. It has become one of the largest wiki projects.

Other wiki websites created in 2003 include: [26]

- CommunityWiki
- CraoWiki
- EmacsWiki
- FractalWiki
- GründerWiki

Development of wiki websites after 2003

Since 2003 the number of wiki websites has grown at an exponential rate. In addition to an ever-increasing number of new wiki websites on the Internet, covering an enormous range of topics, there has been increasing use of corporate wikis on intranets behind firewalls.

Many wikis created after 2003, especially on pop cultural topics, are hosted by Wikia.

See also

- → Comparison of wiki software
- History of Wikipedia
- List of wiki software
- → List of wikis
- meta:List of largest wikis
- → Wiki
- → WikiWikiWeb

External links

- WikiHistory page on WikiWikiWeb [37]
- WikiMindWipe discussion on WikiWikiWeb [38]
- WikiReductionist story on WikiWikiWeb [39]
- WikiHistory page on MeatballWiki [40]
- WikInfo [41]
- Cunningham's note suggesting creation of WhyClublet [42]
- Canonical list of wiki engines on WikiWikiWeb [9]
- Wiki engine Hall of Fame on WikiWikiWeb [43]

References

[1] Vannevar Bush, "As we may think", 1945. (http://www.theatlantic.com/doc/194507/bush)

[2] Wiki Wiki Origin (http://c2.com/cgi/wiki?WikiWikiOrigin)

[3] Wiki History (http://c2.com/cgi/wiki?WikiHistory)

[4] Wiki Wiki Hypercard (http://c2.com/cgi/wiki?WikiWikiHypercard)

[5] http://c2.com/wiki/mail-history.txt

[6] Robert E. Cummings, What Was a Wiki, and Why Do I Care? A Short and Usable History of Wikis (http://www.
     wildwiki.net/mediawiki/index.
     php?title=â□□WhatWas_a_Wiki,_and_Why_Do_I_Care?_A_Short_and_Usable_History_of_Wikisâ□□)

[7] http://www.123exp-technology.com/t/03881190874

[8] Andy Szybalski, Why it's not a wiki world (yet), 14 March
2005 [9] Thread Mode (http://c2.com/cgi/wiki?ThreadMode)

[10] Thread Mess (http://c2.com/cgi/wiki?ThreadMess)

[11] History Of Categories (http://c2.com/cgi/wiki?HistoryOfCategories)

[12] AboutCategoriesAndTopics (http://web.archive.org/web/19961129234150/c2.com/cgi/
     wiki?AboutCategoriesAndTopics)

[13] Wiki Mind Wipe Discussion (http://c2.com/cgi/wiki?WikiMindWipeDiscussion)

[14] Wiki Reductionists (http://c2.com/cgi/wiki?WikiReductionists)

[15] Wiki On Wiki (http://c2.com/cgi/wiki?WikiOnWiki)

[16] http://c2.com/cgi/wiki?WikiSquatting

[17] http://meta.wikimedia.org/wiki/Transwiki:Constructionism_and_reductionism_%28wiki%29

[18] *Marked for Deletion*, National Public Radio, http://weekendamerica.publicradio.org/programs/2007/01/
     20/marked_for_deletion.html

[19] http://www.usemod.com/cgi-bin/mb.pl?ForestFire

[20] Meatball Wiki: ForestFire (http://www.usemod.com/cgi-bin/mb.pl?ForestFire)

[21] Ward Cunningham and Bo Leuf, The Wiki Way, 2001

[22] Jos Wiki (http://c2.com/cgi/wiki?JosWiki)

[23] Comparison of wiki software

[24] Top Ten Wiki Engines (http://c2.com/cgi/wiki?TopTenWikiEngines)

[25] Piki Piki (http://c2.com/cgi/wiki?PikiPiki)

[26] Meatball Wiki: WikiHistory (http://www.usemod.com/cgi-bin/mb.pl?WikiHistory)

[27] UseModWiki

[28] chongqed.org wiki: WikiHome (http://wiki.chongqed.org)

[29] Wiki FAQ - Visual FoxPro Wiki (http://fox.wikis.com/wc.dll?Wiki~WikiFAQ~Wiki)

[30] ProgressionOfWikiOrganization - WikiNodes (http://wikinodes.wiki.taoriver.net/moin.cgi/
     ProgressionOfWikiOrganization)

[31] Inter Wiki (http://c2.com/cgi/wiki?InterWiki)

[32] Inter Wiki Map (http://c2.com/cgi/wiki?InterWikiMap)

[33] Meatball Wiki: MetaWiki (http://usemod.com/cgi-bin/mb.pl?MetaWiki)

[34] Meatball Wiki: OneBigWiki (http://usemod.com/cgi-bin/mb.pl?OneBigWiki)

[35] Switch Wiki (http://c2.com/cgi/wiki?SwitchWiki)

[36] Jane E. Klobas, Angela Beesley. *Wikis: tools for information work and collaboration*, Chandos, 2006, ISBN
     1843341794 p. 46

[37] http://c2.com/cgi/wiki?WikiHistory

[38] http://c2.com/cgi/wiki?WikiMindWipeDiscussion

[39] http://c2.com/cgi/wiki?WikiReductionists

[40] http://www.usemod.com/cgi-bin/mb.pl?WikiHistory

[41] http://www.wikinfo.org/index.php/Main_Page

[42] http://clublet.com/c/c/why?WhyWouldOneBother

[43] http://c2.com/cgi/wiki?WikiEngineHallOfFame

Memory Alpha

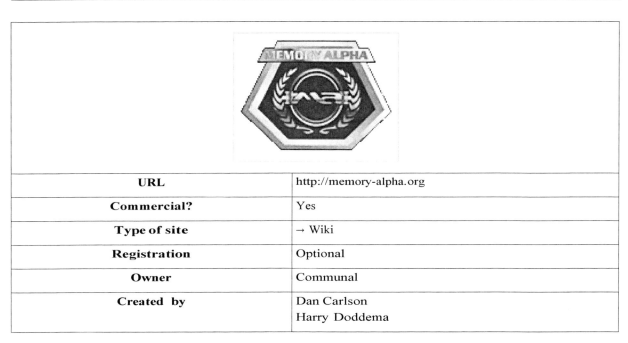

URL	http://memory-alpha.org
Commercial?	Yes
Type of site	→ Wiki
Registration	Optional
Owner	Communal
Created by	Dan Carlson Harry Doddema

Memory Alpha (often abbreviated to **MA**) is a → wiki that is an encyclopedic reference for topics related to the *Star Trek* fictional universe.[1] [2] [3] [4] Conceived by Harry Doddema and Dan Carlson in September 2003 and officially launched on December 5 of that year, it uses the → wiki model and is hosted by Wikia, Inc. on the MediaWiki software. According to Jane Klobas, the site is a large and vibrant resource.[5] Memory Alpha contains over 30,000 articles in its English edition alone as of June 2009[6], making it one of the → largest wiki projects. The site is also available in several other languages,[7] including Bulgarian, Chinese, Czech, Dutch, Esperanto, French, German, Italian, Japanese, Polish, Portuguese, Russian, Serbian, Spanish and Swedish. There is also a "Mirror Universe" Memory Alpha.

The contents of Memory Alpha are licensed under the Creative Commons Attribution-Non-Commercial license. Because this license does not allow commercial reuse, it is incompatible with the GNU Free Documentation License (GFDL), and material from the site cannot be copied into projects that use the GFDL.[8] This distinction makes Memory Alpha a "sister project" of the GFDL-based Wikia project. Memory Alpha is cited as a source by academic journals, scholarly studies and books as well as *Star Trek*-universe novels and reference works.[9] [10] [11] [12] [13] [14] [15] [16]

History

Memory Alpha aims to create a comprehensive database for all fans, but was not conceived as a wiki.[17] Two concerns spurred its creation: many *Star Trek* references of the time were incomplete, and the most promising would shut down regularly, like the site TrekPulse, which closed inexplicably in late 2005 to be reborn the next year as TrekCore. Doddema and Carlson christened their project Memory Alpha, after the Federation's largest information archive, from the original series episode "The Lights of Zetar".

The two decided on a wiki format, which allowed for more collaboration than other formats available. As Carlson said in the Charlotte Observer, "The idea I latched onto with the wiki concept is you can spread the work around. Everyone can pitch in and go in on their own special interest." After experimenting with TikiWiki software, they switched to the MediaWiki platform, finding it less cumbersome. The platform of choice for Wikimedia proved to be, in their opinion, more stable and efficient, and they brought a testsite online on November 11 2003. Memory Alpha officially launched on December 5 that year.

The site gained momentum in the following months, aided by a mention on the *Star Trek* fan site "TrekNation" on December 23. Memory Alpha reached 1,000 articles by January 12 2004, but on March 23, the site's database was accidentally erased during an upgrade of the MediaWiki software. Although this caused six weeks of work to be lost, the project expanded to include Dutch and German versions on April 10 and May 14 respectively. It remained stable until the following year, when the fees associated with hosting the site became more than the founders could afford.

In February 2005, Memory Alpha switched hosting servers and joined Wikia, a free for-profit wiki-hosting company started by → Wikimedia Foundation board members Jimmy Wales and Angela Beesley. The site remained stable on Wikia, opening a Swedish site on May 5 and a French one on November 5. It also received several distinctions that year, such as the *Ex Astris Excellentia* award from Ex Astris Scientia, a *Star Trek* reference site, in September 2005, and it was featured as the SciFi Channel's Site of the Week for October 10, 2005.[18] *Star Trek: Voyager* and *Star Trek: Enterprise* writer/producer Mike Sussman joined the community that year as well.[19]

Technical issues led the MediaWiki software to believe Memory Alpha was started on November 23, 2004, and despite the inaccuracy, this date was adopted *ex post facto* as Memory Alpha's "birthday". To celebrate the occasion, Uncyclopedia (which is also hosted by Wikia) altered its main page to be a parody of Memory Alpha on November 23, 2005. The spoof page was retained under the namespace "tlh:", for *tlhIngan Hol* (the Klingon name for the Klingon language), modeled after the way wikis link to pages in other languages.[20]

The latter part of 2005 and early 2006 saw several new features added to the site. Among these was a peer review process, implemented on September 21, 2005 in response to questions about the process by which articles become featured.[21] On November 20 of that year, Memory Alpha began a "Babel" program, inspired by and modeled after that of the Wikimedia Commons, to help users who speak the same language. Other recent innovations include an area for user projects, sometimes referred to as WikiProjects on other wikis, and coverage of fan films.

The site has remained popular since its inception, although its growth has slowed in recent times. For instance, it was the largest project on Wikia[22] until October 2005, when its article count was surpassed by Wookieepedia and Uncyclopedia. Today, it has approximately 1300 registered users (80 of whom are active) and upwards of 17 million page views since its move to Wikia. As of February 2006[6], it receives on average, slightly more visitors and page views per day than the official *Star Trek* website according to Alexa.[23]

Memory Alpha has influenced the design of other wikicities dedicated to information about television franchises, including The X-Files Wiki [24] and the 24 Wiki [25]. It is a resource used by mainstream journalists for information on *Star Trek* related issues.[26] Influential edublogger Will Richardson hailed the site in his 2006 book *Blogs, Wikis, Podcasts, and Other Powerful Web Tools for Classrooms* as "one of the most impressive [wikis] out there".[27]

On June 12, 2007, Memory Alpha reached a milestone of 25,000 articles with the creation of the article Robert Iscove. [28]

Entertainment Weekly named Memory Alpha one of the 25 Essential Fansites in 2007. In comparing it to other *Star Trek* sites, the reviewer wrote, "Memory Alpha wins out for its handsome, intuitive presentation and its overwhelming mass".[29]

Structure

Several aspects of Memory Alpha set it apart from other reference works, such as its method of citing sources. All information must be cited from a valid source (see Canon section below), but rather than a "Works Cited" or "References" list, Memory Alpha prefers stand-alone inline citations, which are placed in parentheses after the sentence or section in question. For television episodes, this consists of an abbreviation for the series from which the information came (e.g. DS9 for *Star Trek: Deep Space Nine*), followed by the name of the episode in double quotation marks. So, in order to cite information from the *Star Trek: The Next Generation* (TNG) pilot "Encounter at Farpoint", one would add: (TNG: "Encounter at Farpoint"). The same rule applies for films, sans the series prefix and with italics in place of quotation marks. The same method of notation is also used in the printed *Star Trek Encyclopedia*, which is unrelated to the Memory Alpha wiki.

Articles on Memory Alpha are written from two points of view: "in-universe", which are written as if the reader is a part of the *Star Trek* universe, and "production", which speak from a real-world perspective. For "in-universe" articles, behind-the-scenes information is not included in the main body of the article; rather, it is placed in a separate background section or included indented and italicized to separate it from the in-universe perspective. The latter method is used in cases where either the information is particularly important (such as conflicting information from two canon sources) or there is not enough background to justify a separate section. In most cases, the background method is preferred and italics are used sparingly.

Like many wikis, Memory Alpha has a section for "featured articles", those believed to represent the best the community has to offer.[18] The criteria for this distinction are that an article must be well-written, comprehensive (which includes citing sources), accurate and undisputed – criteria any article could hypothetically fulfill. This has caused some conflict over the criteria involved (see Current issues section). To be featured, an article must be nominated by a user and unanimously supported by at least five other users; any objections must be fixable and may be invalidated if deemed irrational or unreasonable. Each week, one of the site's featured articles becomes the "Article of the Week" to be displayed on the project home page.

Several methods of communication are available beyond conventional talk pages. The "community portal" section of the website is named after Ten Forward, a locale frequented by characters on *The Next Generation*. Issues discussed there range from disputes between users to new ideas on how to improve the site to upcoming projects. A separate area, the reference desk, exists for discussions and questions related to what is considered canon, discrepancies between sources, and other such topics. However, "meta-Trek" topics (a term used for *Star Trek*-related topics that do not pertain in any way to Memory Alpha) are not discussed on the wiki; a separate IRC chatroom exists for these discussions.

Canon policy

The question of Star Trek canon is a complex one and has plagued fans since *Star Trek* began in 1966. The general policy of Paramount Pictures is that anything outside live-action television episodes and movies is apocryphal, or non-canon.[30] However, grey areas in this policy, especially in relation to the canonical status of *Star Trek: The Animated Series* (TAS), further complicate the matter and have led to many debates among fans. In light of this, Memory Alpha crafted its own unique definition of canon in relation to what may be used as a "valid resource". *The Animated Series* is included as valid, or canonical, for a number of reasons, such as the fact that *Star Trek* creator Gene Roddenberry and most of the cast of the original series were involved with it and the existence of several references to TAS events in later series.

Information taken from the *Star Trek Encyclopedia* and *Star Trek Chronology* is mostly accepted on Memory Alpha as well, to the extent that it does not break from established on-screen facts. Content from these sources is an acknowledged grey area of Memory Alpha's canon policy and is disregarded if deemed speculative or contradictory. Thus, in some ways they hold the same weight as novels and other publications do for Star Wars canon: a "second tier" of canonicity, which is subservient to primary (on-screen) sources.

Other sources such as books and computer games are not included as canon, but are covered by Memory Alpha in a way which sets it apart from other *Trek* resources: books, comics, and other products are included as articles about the products (i.e. from a "production point of view"), but "in-universe" information unique or new to them is covered on the product page. For example, in the *Star Trek: New Frontier* line of books, a new host of characters is introduced to the Trek universe, and their vessel is known as the USS *Excalibur*. The characters, ships and information from *New Frontier* books do not receive pages of their own, but they are covered on the pages about the books. In this way, Memory Alpha remains all-inclusive while attempting to distinguish canon from apocrypha.

Non-canon characters and topics are instead covered on the Memory Beta encyclopedia, and fan-films are included on Memory Gamma.

Issues

Several issues face the Memory Alpha community, one of which is the question of which articles should be given "featured" status. Under Memory Alpha's current policies, both major and minor topics are eligible; however, the question has been raised of whether the criteria for featuring should be more subjective, i.e., if a topic is not significant enough, it should not be featured regardless of how comprehensive its article is.[31] There is currently no consensus in the Memory Alpha community about the topic, although there has been no change in featuring policy.

The question of what content Memory Alpha should cover has plagued the project since its creation. On the project's home page, it describes itself as "a collaborative project to create the most definitive, accurate, and accessible encyclopedia and reference for everything related to *Star Trek*", but fans often have different interpretations of what "everything" means. In some cases, one or more users may add content about a subject – such as a website, fan club or parody – that does not fit existing pages, necessitating a community decision about whether to keep the content and, if so, what to do with it. Such incidents led to the creation of an article on *Star Trek* parodies after several questions were raised about where to put information related to, but not a part of, the *Star Trek* franchise. An example of the reverse case is "The Sunspots", a musical group consisting of Patrick Stewart, Jonathan Frakes, LeVar Burton and Michael Dorn. Although the actors involved were all prominent parts of *Star Trek: The Next Generation*, several articles on the group have been deleted because the community deemed the topic not directly related to the franchise. As of 2006[6], information about The Sunspots can be found on the different actors' pages rather than a single, separate article.

Perhaps the most heated issue on Memory Alpha in recent years is the controversy surrounding their canon policy. Aside from issues of length and excessive use of legalese, this policy has been put into question by several of the site's regular users because of its rule that articles and information which were not seen on-screen but were derived from official production sources are not considered canon on Memory Alpha. The site's archivists are divided as to exactly whether such information should be allowed as canon; some want only to allow what was seen on-screen while others wish to include that which was originally intended to be used on-screen but never made it, such as information from deleted scenes, early script drafts, etc. The latter archivists believe that such information can be included so long as it does not contradict what was seen on-screen and so long as it states where the source of the information comes from. As of July 2006, this debate has died down significantly, with most having accepted the terms of the new policy.[32]

Despite early concern about how to incorporate information from the 2009 movie *Star Trek*, which is considered a semi-reboot of the original series, Memory Alpha members found a solution to the issue. All information from this film is recorded as separate articles, which are titled according to their subject with the term "alternate reality" included in the title. For example, the article *Nyota Uhura* discusses the character as portrayed by Nichelle Nichols, while the article *Nyota Uhura (alternate reality)* discusses the character as played by Zoë Saldana.

See also

- List of online encyclopedias

References

- Barnett, Cynthia (September 1, 2005). "Wikimania". *Florida Trend*, Vol. 48, No. 5; Pg. 62; ISSN: 0015-4326. [33]
- Lee, Ellen (January 1, 2006). "The world's gone wild for everything wiki-wise". *The Charlotte Observer*, p. 4E.

External links

- Memory Alpha's home page

References

[1] Barron, James (July 6, 2006). " It's an Auction, Jim, but Not as We Know It (http://www.nytimes.com/2006/ 07/06/nyregion/06trek.html?ex=1152849600&en=bb5649b7462124bc&ei=5070&emc=eta1)". *The New York Times* (The New York Times Company). .

[2] Tossell, Ivor (January 12, 2007). " It's a wiki world (http://www.theglobeandmail.com/servlet/story/RTGAM. 20070112.gtweb12/BNStory/Technology/?page=rss&id=RTGAM.20070112.gtweb12)". *The Globe and Mail.* .

[3] Lee, Ellen (December 25, 2005). "The (mostly) wonderful world of Wikis.". *Contra Costa Times.* Knight-Ridder/Tribune News Service.

[4] no byline (October 14, 2006). "Webwatch: Star Trek sites abound", *The Record*, p. F1

[5] Klobas, Jane (2005). *Wikis: Tools for Information Work and Collaboration: Tools for Information Work and Collaboration.* City: Chandos Publishing (Oxford) Ltd. p. 25. ISBN 1843341794.

[6] http://en.wikipedia.org/wiki/Memory_alpha

[7] Crockett, Christine (September 17, 2006). "A 40-year 'Trek'", *Sun Journal*, p. B1.

[8] Peter Black, Hayden Delaney; Fitzgerald, Brian (2007), " Legal Issues for Wikis: the Challenge of User-generated and Peer-Produced Knowledge, Content and Culture (https://elaw.murdoch.edu.au/issues/ 2007/1/eLaw_legal issues for wikis.pdf)", *Murdoch University Electronic Journal of Law* **14** (1): 245,

[9] Ochoa et al.. " A Game Board Implementing Data Mining and Cultural Algorithms (http://revistaseletronicas. pucrs.br/ojs/index.php/hifen/article/view/3893/2959)". *Uruguaiana* **31** (59/60 year=). .

[10] Edited By Emilio Corchado, Juan M. Corchado; Abraham, Ajith (2007), *Innovations in hybrid intelligent systems*, Berlin: Springer, p. 490, ISBN 978-3540749714

[11] Conley, Tim (2006). *Encyclopedia of Fictional and Fantastic Languages.* Westport: Greenwood Press. ISBN 031333188X.

[12] Firsing, Scott T. (2007), *Disturbing times : the state of the planet and its possible future*, New York: Pocket, ISBN 1416527419

[13] Jill Sherwin et al. (2001). *The Definitive Star Trek Trivia Book.* Simon & Schuster. ISBN 0743406710.

[14] A. Decandido, Keith R.; David, Peter; Shaw, Sarah (2007), *Star Trek : mirror universe : obsidian alliances*, New York: Pocket Books, ISBN 1416524711

[15] Lajoie, John (2007), *Enterprising Endeavour: Scorpius Rising*, p. 309, ISBN 0557007941

[16] Sennewald, Nadja (2007), *Alien gender : die Inszenierung von Geschlecht in Science-Fiction-Serien*, Bielefeld: Transcript, p. 65, ISBN 3899428056

[17] Ebersbach, Anja (2008). *Wiki: Web Collaboration.* Berlin: Springer. p. 33. ISBN 3540351507.

[18] Newquist, Ken (October 10, 2005). " Sci-Fi Site of the Week (http://www.scifi.com/sfw/issue442/site. html)". *SciFi.com.* .

[19] Some (but not all) of Memory Alpha's distinctions can be found on Memory Alpha's announcements page. Among the announcements are links to the Ex Astris Excellentia award (http://www.ex-astris-scientia.org/ our_award.htm) and SciFi newsletter (http://www.scifi.com/sfw/issue442/site.html). Mr. Sussman's identity on Memory Alpha has been verified as authentic; see his talk page for more details.

[20] "Happy Birthday, Memory Alpha!" page from the Uncyclopedia website.

[21] The issue at hand was originally raised by user AJHalliwell on July 15 of that year, and a subsequent discussion (http://memory-alpha.org/en/wiki/Memory_Alpha_talk:Featured_article_nomination_policy#.22.. .community.27s_work....22) resulted in the creation of Memory Alpha's Peer Review section. According to the page history (http://memory-alpha.org/en/index.php?title=Memory_Alpha:Peer_review&action=history) of the Peer Review page, it was created by user Cid Highwind at 22:53, 21 September 2005 UTC.

[22] Barnett, Cynthia (September 1, 2005). "Wiki, mania", *Florida Trend* **48** (5): 62.

[23] Any user count on Memory Alpha should be treated as prone to error because Memory Alpha's users are pooled with those of other Wikia sites. A full list of editors can be found on Memory Alpha's maintenance page, but the estimate of 80 users is based on a voluntary listing of users (who call themselves "archivists"). Page views, which are easier to gauge, can be found on the statistics page. The Alexa claim is based on a page view comparison (http://www.alexa.com/data/details/traffic_details?&compare_sites=startrek.com&y=p&q=& url=memory-alpha.org) on February 6, 2005.

[24] http://x-files.wikia.com/wiki/X-Files_Wiki:About

[25] http://24.wikia.com/wiki/Wiki_24:About

[26] Barron, James "It's an Auction, Jim, But Not as We Know It." New York Times. (Late Edition (East Coast)). New York, N.Y.: Jul 6, 2006. pg. B.3

[27] Richardson, Will (2006). *Blogs, Wikis, Podcasts, and Other Powerful Web Tools for Classrooms*. Thousand Oaks: Corwin Press. p. 62. ISBN 1412927676.

[28] Forum:MA Press Release - Memory Alpha, the Star Trek Wiki (http://memory-alpha.org/en/index.php?title=Forum:MA_Press_Release&t=20070613163046)

[29] Vary, Adam B. (December 28, 2007). " 25 Essential Fansites (http://www.ew.com/ew/article/0,,20165619_20165621_20167049_15,00.html)", *Entertainment Weekly* 971: T9.

[30] Startrek.com states in an FAQ (http://www.startrek.com/startrek/view/help/faqs/faq/676.html) dated 10 September 2003, "Story lines, characters, events, stardates, etc. that take place within the fictional novels, the Animated Adventures, and the various comic lines are not canon." However, even the FAQ acknowledges certain facts outside this rule have become canon. It should also be noted that the FAQ is meant as a rule of thumb and is not an official rule.

[31] Hippocrates Noah's archived nomination for featured status can be found on Memory Alpha. There was an unprecedented level of debate associated with the nomination.

[32] Memory Alpha:Canon policy - Memory Alpha, the Star Trek Wiki (http://memory-alpha.org/en/wiki/Memory_Alpha:Canon_policy)

[33] http://www.floridatrend.com/issue/default.asp?a=5617&s=1&d=9/1/2005

Comparison of wiki farms

A **wiki farm** is a server or an array of servers that offer users tools to simplify the creation and development of individual, independent → wikis.

Prior to wiki farms, the administrator of multiple wikis had to install each wiki independently. Deployment of redundant code and configurations on the server wasted administrative time and server storage. With a wiki farm the administrator installs the core wiki code once and establishes unique space on the server(s) for the content of each individual wiki with the shared core code executing the functions of each wiki. The wiki farm approach has fostered the development of publicly-available wiki hosting services which relieve users of the need to install a wiki server, configure it, connect it to the Internet and maintain it. This has greatly increased the availability of wiki technology for users who want to share information on-line through their own wiki.

Both non-commercial and commercial wiki farms are available for users and online communities. While most of the wiki farms allow anyone to open their own wiki, some impose restrictions. Many wiki farm companies generate revenue through the insertion of advertisements, but often allow payment of a monthly fee as an alternative to accepting ads.

A server running a single wiki instance with groups of pages dedicated for specific topics is not a wiki farm.

General

The following tables compare general information for several wiki farms; however, more than 100 wiki farms have been created.[1] Further information can be found at the websites themselves, or in the linked article for some of the more notable ones. This article is not all-inclusive or necessarily up to date. It does not review or endorse any wiki farm, nor does it include any advertising hyperbole. The Alexa traffic rankings are not accurate for those wiki farms that allow some of their hosted wikis to have separate domain names. In those cases there may be some additional Alexa rankings listed below for some of the larger individual wikis in a wiki farm. The wikis are normally provided with a standard layout, or a choice of layouts, usually known as skins. Some wiki farms allow the layout to be customised using cascading style sheets (css).

Wiki farm	Alexa rank as of August 2009[2] (lower = higher traffic)[3]	Cost?	Ad?	Content license
@wiki	96000 [4] as of June 4, 2009.	Free	Yes	
BrainKeeper	630000 [5] as of June 4, 2009.	Nonfree	?	
BusinessWiki	550000 [6] as of June 4, 2009.	Free (3 users) / Paid (14 days trial)	No	GPL
Central Desktop	17000 [7] as of August 3, 2009.	Nonfree	?	
ClearWiki	500000 [8] as of August 18, 2009.	Free/Paid	?	
Confluence Hosted	15000 [9] as of August 3, 2009.	Nonfree[10]	?	
CustomerVision BizWiki	2400000 [11] as of June 6, 2009.	Nonfree	?	
EditMe	95000 [12] as of June 10, 2009.	Nonfree	?	
EditThis.info	150000 [13] as of June 10, 2009.	Free	Yes	
eTouch SamePage	630000 [14] as of June 10, 2009.	Nonfree	?	
GROU.PS SuperWiki	5600 [15] as of August 3, 2009.	Free	No	Any
HelpingStudents.org	15000000 [16] as of June 10, 2009.	Free/paid	?	Creative Commons[17]
Hive Wiki	2100000 [18] as of June 10, 2009.	Free	?	
HOAwiki	3900000 [19] as of June 10, 2009.	Nonfree	No	Users Choice
Intodit	360000 [20] as of June 10, 2009.	Free	AS	
MyFreeWiki (en, fr)	3300000 [21] as of June 10, 2009.	Free	No	User Choice
Netcipia	300000 [22] as of August 18, 2009.	Free[23]	No	
nexdo (formerly Partnertext)	3900000 [24] as of June 10, 2009.	Nonfree	?	

Oddwiki	736381 [25] as of July 12, 2009.	Free	?	
OpenTeams	2000000 [26] as of June 11, 2009.	Nonfree[27]	?	
Ourproject.org	350000 [28] as of June 11, 2009.	Free	No	Copyleft (choice of Creative Commons, GNU FDL, other licenses)
PAUX	no data [29] as of June 11, 2009.	Free/paid	?	Copyleft license
PBworks	3100 [30] as of August 3, 2009.	Free/paid	No	
PicoWiki	1500000 [31]	Free/donationware - for personal wikis optimized for iPhone and smartphones	No	user choice
ProjectForum	750000 [32]	Nonfree	?	
ProjectLocker	161000 [33]	Nonfree	?	
Referata	405000 [34] as of August 18, 2009.	Free/paid	No	User choice (via site settings), default is Creative Commons by-sa[35]
Russian wiki community	1540000 [36]	negotiable	?	negotiable
SeedWiki	492000 [37]	Free/paid	No	Closing as a free site Sept. 1, 2009
SnoutHold Cospire	2217000 [38]	Free	?	
Socialtext Workspace Hosted	49000 [39]	Nonfree[40]	No	Wiki creators can set their own.
Swirrl	921000 [41]	Nonfree	No	[42]
Wetpaint	1800 [43]	Free/Paid	AS	Creative Commons
Wik.is	50000 [44]	Free/paid	?	
Wikia	264 [45]	Free	Yes	Creative Commons
Wikidot	4100 [46]	Free/paid	Yes/No	By default Creative Commons, GNU FDL, other licenses as requested
Wikihost.org	481000 [47]	Free	Yes	By default Creative Commons, others as needed
Wiki-site.com	207000 [48]	Free/paid	AS	Wiki creators can set their own
Wikispaces	3800 [49]	Free/paid	Yes/No	Choice of Creative Commons, GNU FDL, other licenses

Wiki farm	Alexa. Approximative rank according to Alexa Internet. Click on the rank to get the last figures.	Cost?	Ad?	Content license
Wiki Spot	238000 [50], 96000 [51]	Free[52]	No	User choice, default Creative Commons Attribution
WikiZones.com	462711 [53]	Free	No	
Wikkii	2536000 [54]	Free	Yes	
WikyBlog.com	360000 [55]	Free	?	Any, integrated Creative Commons licenses
XWiki	390000 [56]	Free/paid	No	Any
YourWiki	732808 [57]	Free	AS	User choice

Technical

WARNING: Table could not be rendered - ouputting plain text.

Potential causes of the problem are: (a) table contains a cell with content that does not fit on a single page (b) nested tables (c) table is too wide

Wiki farm WYSIWYG editing Features Base wiki engine Multilingual support Syntax support @wiki Yes Selectable edit-mode (WikiText or WYSIWYG or text), access control, file uploads, importing, full-text search, and RSS abilities. [?] (custom) English, Chinese, Korean and others Some HTML,JavaScript,Math formulas BrainKeeper Yes Access control, full-text search, calendaring, single sign-on to multiple projects, project templates, RSS enabled. [?] (custom) Some HTML,no scriptNo formulas BusinessWiki Yes Visual editing, Folders and tags, Easy PDF document creating, Backups mechanisms, Multiple feeds allowing to track information and notify about changes (RSS, mail, mobile web), Comprehensive user guide, Compatibility with MediaWIki (database standard, wiki-text) and Open-source version for your safety. Each site gets a subdomain on .onbusinesswiki.com. MediaWiki English WikiText, HTML Central Desktop Yes Access control, full-text search, calendaring, single sign-on to multiple projects, project templates, RSS enabled. [?] (custom) HTML,CSS/templatingNo formulas ClearWiki Yes Private secure wikis (with sub-domains) - each wiki has own physical database. File storage, version control, full text search (incl docs/files), to-do lists, RSS enabled, blogs, discussions, image galleries (with thumbnailing), meta-tagging (labelling), content starring, teams/groups. [?] (custom) English only Some HTML,WYSIWYG editConfluence (software)Confluence Hosted Yes Wiki markup language, plugins, SSL, file storage, permissioning, WebDAV. HTML pluginscript pluginNo formulas CustomerVision BizWiki Yes Access control, page templates, domain mapping, solution templates include Sales Support, and Learning Support. [?] (custom) EditMe Subscription-based, SSL Encryption, and Custom Domain

Support. Java (programming language)Java-based (custom) All HTML,JavaScript,No formulas EditThis.info? Unlimited pages and users (but no longer upload of photos" ConstantSun: Image upload issues". Constantsun.blogspot.com. 2008-07-06. . Retrieved 2009-06-10.), wiki spam protection, 25MB of file upload space, and RSS feeds. Apparently allows free wikis to profit from Google AdSense.This is visible from the Control PanelMediaWiki 1.5.5 Some HTML,JavaScript,No formulas eTouch SamePage Yes Project management, permissioning, administration and support for multiple domains. eTouch CMS (custom, powered by) GROU.PS SuperWiki Yes Secure SSL encrypted login, Advanced Privacy and Moderation Settings, Revisions, Real-Time Chat (optional), RSS & Email Alerts for your group members, Categories (Subfolders), Wiki Comments (optional), Multilingual; all texts customizable, Unlimited file upload space, Domain masking, Customizable templates. [?] (custom) English, French, Greek, Turkish, Hebrew, Swedish and extensible All HTML HelpingStudents.org Yes Java server pages, scripts and plugin wiki options for school administrators and teachers that provide parental information resources WikiText and HTML editing, metasearch, factoring, permissioning, SSL Encryption, Private Intranet implementation with public integration administration and support. JSPWikiHive Wiki? WikiText and HTML editing, metasearch, factoring, permissioning, administration and support for multiple domains and publicly creatable subdomains .NET Framework.NET-based (custom) HOAwiki Yes Hosted and supported TikiWiki CMS/groupware.Archiving Work Orders and Violation Reports, layered permissions, dynamic content, online forms, articles, blogs, slideshow, RSS/Atom, directory, classifieds, mail-in, mobile, newsletters.TikiWikiTikiWiki CMS/groupware 2.2 (last stable) Multilingual to 30 languages HTML, Smarty code, javascript Intodit Yes WYSIWYG editing only, custom page hierarchies, Comment and Reply forums, group rating, layout templates, keyword search, tags, skins, RSS, profiles, activity report, No changes preview. Supported browsers: Internet Explorer, Firefox, Safari. [?] (custom) No HTML,Unknown scriptNo formulas MyFreeWiki Yes Easy and Fast, plaintext editors available. Integrated photo gallery. Enzym (custom) English and French All HTML, Javascript Netcipia Yes Blog, public and private wikiswiki, 2GB per wiki created, no time limit, right management XWiki English only All HTML,JavaScript,No math nexdo (formerly Partnertext) Yes WYSIWYG HTML editing [?] (custom) All HTML,unknown scriptNo formulas Oddwiki?OddmuseOpenTeams Yes 3-pane drag-and-drop Ajax (programming)Ajax-based interface similar to email and newsfeed readers, private secure wiki spaces (including invitation-only and a domain security option based on validated email domains, i.e. "Everybody with email@domain.com"), Tag (metadata)tags, blog, bliki, "What's New" views, draft autosaving, discussion, attachments with version history, SSL, unlimited spaces, pages, edits, versions, storage, and bandwidth. [?] (custom) Ourproject.org Yes It offers freely a wide collection of services for multi-purpose free/libre projects (not only free software: free knowledge), including wikis, mailing lists, forums, FTP, subdomains, hosting, ddbb, email alias, backups, CVS/SVN, Task management... MoinMoin Supports English, Spanish, French, and many other languages. PAUX Password-protected wikis on .dreusicke-verlag.de. No page limits, Transport Layer SecuritySSL, picture gallery included. [?] (custom) Some HTML,unknown scriptMath formulas PBworks Private or public wikis on .pbworks.com subdomain (higher-level paid plans allow use of a custom domain). No page limits, SSL, RSS & Atom, ZIP backups, diffs, colour schemes, email notifications, file management, page access settings. Over 800,000 workspaces hosted. One level of folders used to organize pages.

Folder- and page-level access controls available to paying customers and business users. Free accounts limited to 2 GB, paying accounts get up to unlimited storage. [?] (custom) All HTML,JavaScript,LaTeX formulas ProjectForum [?] (custom) Optional HTML,unknown scriptNo formulasProjectLocker Focused on providing software development tools as a service. Wiki features include Unlimited document storage, Custom access profiles for partners, customers, and managers, Support for attachments on documents, Privacy Commitment - Your Data is Yours Alone, Secure access via SSL, RAID 1 redundant storage of all data, Nightly backups, 24/7 Server Monitoring [?] (custom) Referata No A semantic wiki hosting site. Uses MediaWiki, along with Semantic MediaWiki and related extensions, to enable wikis to serve as collaborative databases, with custom forms, result tables, calendars, maps, etc. Free wikis are limited to 5 MB of uploaded file storage; there is no limit on the size of the wiki text. Every wiki gets a subdomain of referata.com, although some paid service levels also allow for custom domains." Features". Referata. 2008-11-25. . Retrieved 2009-06-10.MediaWiki 1.15 Dozens of languages, although help pages are mostly in English Standard MediaWiki scripting, math formulas Riters.com Line document collaboration service and Wiki farm MoinMoinRussian wiki community negotiable MediaWiki 1.5.8 UTF-8/Russian Some HTML,JavaScript,Math formulas SeedWiki Yes cross-platform WYSIWYG editing, stylesheets, subdomains.seedwiki.com, wiki-mode, subscriptions; paid option for having one's own domain that the wiki-owner can tag on to his wiki [?] (custom) All HTML,JavaScript and Seedwiki widgetsPlugin formulas SnoutHold Cospire Yes Permissions, public/private security models, ratings, feedback mechanisms, search engine, category organizer, profiles [?] (custom) Socialtext Workspace Yes Enterprise Wiki. Supports text, rich text, embedded images, video, and attachments (including from email). Derived from Kwiki Swirrl Yes Text pages, data sets (with spreadsheet-like user interface), permissions, public/private pages, versioning, searching, tags Custom Enter content in many languages, user interface in English ViaWiki Yes Free version is ad-supported, paid version has option of using own domain, attach files, no limit on number of pages and backups, max 5GB (paid version)" viawiki.com". viawiki.com. . Retrieved 2009-06-10.Deki WikiWetpaint Yes WYSIWYG editing only, custom page hierarchies, Comment and Reply forums with comment ratings, access control, keyword search, tags, tag filtering, skins, RSS, page locking, profiles, site activity report, page and comment watching. No page permission settings. No changes preview. Supported browsers: Internet Explorer, Firefox. Java (programming language)Java-based (custom) No HTML,Unknown scriptNo formulas MindTouchWik.is Yes Access control, full-text search (including file attachments), document management, light project management, database, project templates, RSS enabled, stores in XML, Deki Wiki a full featured engine (a MediaWiki fork). Free account 50 MB. Paid account ($99/yr) 1 GB. Deki WikiWikia Yes Wiki hosting service created in 2004, formerly known as Wikicities. All wikis have common login and preferences. Single sign-on to multiple projects. Database download available. No means to close an inactive wiki, even if the community has moved elsewhere. Wikia domains, names, and identifiers owned by Wikia Inc, not the respective communities; in a recent change of policies, all communities are being migrated to .wikia.com subdomains. Will configure Semantic MediaWiki on request." wikia.com, Help:Semantic MediaWiki". wikia.com. . Retrieved 2009-07-22.MediaWiki 1.15.1 All languages Wikipedia exists for (and some more); Community Support in English, Chinese, German, Japanese, Spanish and Portuguese. Some HTML,JavaScript,Math formulas Wikidot Each site gets a subdomain on .wikidot.com (like mywiki.wikidot.com). Also there is possibility to map a custom domain (like mywiki.com -- if previously registered by the wiki owner) for free. One can optionally allow Wikidot to display ads on their wiki and get 80% of revenue. RSS (file format)RSS import/export, private RSS feeds for Users (notifications and watched items), RSS for page changes and forum, customizable themes (every item can be styled with CSS), advanced forum for each Site. Custom page hierarchies, searching, advanced page (full/section/append) edit locking, blocking users and IP addresses. Private messages between users. Uses Ajax (programming)Ajax for clean and fast (no browser page-reload) interface. SEO-friendly. No limits on site size. Public and private wikis. Lots of widgets, that allow to embed a video from YouTube, GoogleVideo, photos from Flickr, chats from Meebo and many more). Each user can create up to 20 wiki sites and be a member of an unlimited number of wikis. Modified Text_Wiki engine English, Polish, Russian and Community support in French, German, ... more to come. No HTML,CSS stylingLaTeX math formulas Wikihost.org 100 MB space, File and Image upload, User authentication, Private wikis, Subdomains for wikis larger than 30 pages, RSS, Edit locking, Fulltext search, Email notifications, Complete wiki export, Unlimited pages, Unlimited Revisions, Diff function, Revert of old revisions GeboGebo Wiki-site.com Yes Wiki farm with unlimited pages and users, wiki spam protection, user rights control for paid accounts. Interface in 150 languages. A free *.wiki-site.com domain is offered. Google text-ads added to the right sidebar for free accounts. MediaWiki 1.11.0 English, French, Spanish, Italian, German and over 70 other languages. Some HTML,JavaScript,Math formulas Wikispaces Yes Clean easy to use interface, users get a subdomain on wikispaces.com. Free version supported by Google ads - Wikispaces ads can be turned off for a fee. No limits on numbers of pages, spaces, or members. Full RSS (file format)RSS support; easy space backups in ZIP (file format)zip and Tar (file format)tgz. Blog import function/ integration with Blogger.com and Typepad. Themes and stylesheets can be customized. Private label service available. [?] (custom) Optional HTML,Unknown scriptMath formulas Wiki Spot No advertising, user accounts work on all wikis, use bookmarks and track changes across multiple wikis. Customizable CSS by wiki and user CSS. Simple, intuitive syntax. No limits on pages/disk space. RSS feeds available on all pages. Easy to create a wiki and configure settings. Sycamore Wikkii.com Features complete back-end control with full FTP and Cpanel access. Initially 1GB storage and 10GB bandwidth. Install any wiki script. Add unlimited custom templates, add-ons, and plugins. Free domain names for popular wikis. MediaWiki or User Chosen WikyBlog.com No advertising on user accounts, unlimited custom skins, AJAX enhanced tabbed interface WikyBlog (custom) UTF-8 with English, Arabic, Russian, Turkish, Spanish and Korean Some HTML,No scriptNo math WikiZones.com Free, one sub-domain per wiki (yourwiki.wikizones.com), full-text search, standard wiki markup language (MediaWiki compatible) Java-based (custom) All languages (UTF-8), interface in English Wikitext (MediaWiki compatible) XWiki custom skin, unlimited users XWiki All HTML,velocity/groovyNo formulas YourWiki Yes Founded in 2008, YourWiki provides users with their own yourwiki.net sub domain and will support custom domains. There are no limits on quantity of pages, users, traffic, images etc. Low profile adsense advertising only (can be removed for a small fee). Supports custom extensions, skins, css and JavaScript. Also Supports single user login (SUL / SSO / Global Accounts), OpenID, Google Login, Live Journal, Yahoo, AOL and more. Private and Public wikis with access to content dumps (by request). Can close an inactive wiki. Supports migration to and from other wiki hosts. Provides users with WYSIWYG, HTML and wiki syntax editing. Supports images from

Wikimedia Commons and Flickr seamlessly as well as videos from most popular video sharing sites (YouTube, GoogleVideo etc). Choose your own free content licence (GFDL, CC, PD etc). Full RSS support. YourWiki also has a Toolserver for hosting scripts and bots. Automated wiki creation has been announced. Will configure Semantic MediaWiki on request. MediaWiki 1.15 Support for the vast majority of languages, Technical Support in English. Most HTML,JavaScript,Math formulas Wiki farm WYSIWYG editing Features Wiki engine Multilingual support Syntax support

See also

- Collaborative real-time editor
- Collaborative software
- → Comparison of wiki software
- List of collaborative software
- List of wiki software
- → List of wikis
- Wiki software

External links

- Wiki farms [65] at the Open Directory Project
- Wikimatrix, with interactive selection of wikifarms based on user preference [66]

References

[1] "WikiMatrix - Compare them all" (selectable table), WikiMatrix, 2007, webpage: wikimatrix-org-main (http://www.wikimatrix.org/).

[2] http://en.wikipedia.org/wiki/Comparison_of_wiki_farms

[3] Approximative rank according to Alexa Internet. Click on the rank to get the last figures.

[4] atwiki (http://www.alexa.com/data/details/traffic_details/atwiki.com) traffic rank

[5] Brainkeeper (http://www.alexa.com/data/details/traffic_details/brainkeeper.com) traffic rank

[6] BusinessWiki (http://www.alexa.com/data/details/traffic_details/onbusinesswiki.com) traffic rank

[7] Central Desktop (http://www.alexa.com/data/details/traffic_details/centraldesktop.com) traffic rank

[8] ClearWiki (http://www.alexa.com/data/details/traffic_details/clearwiki.com) traffic rank

[9] Confluence Hosted (http://www.alexa.com/data/details/traffic_details/atlassian.com) traffic rank

[10] Free for charitable nonprofits and open source projects

[11] CustomerVision BizWiki (http://www.alexa.com/data/details/traffic_details/customervision.com) traffic rank

[12] EditMe (http://www.alexa.com/data/details/traffic_details/editme.com) traffic rank

[13] EditThis (http://www.alexa.com/data/details/traffic_details/editthis.info) traffic rank

[14] eTouch SamePage (http://www.alexa.com/data/details/traffic_details/etouch.net) traffic rank

[15] GROU.PS SuperWiki (http://www.alexa.com/data/details/traffic_details/grou.ps) traffic rank

[16] HelpingStudents (http://www.alexa.com/data/details/traffic_details/helpingstudents.org) traffic rank

[17] (http://helpingstudents.org/JSPWiki/Wiki.jsp?page=License)

[18] Hive Wiki (http://www.alexa.com/data/details/traffic_details/hivewiki.com) traffic rank

[19] HOAwiki (http://www.alexa.com/data/details/traffic_details/hoawiki.com) traffic rank

[20] Intodit (http://www.alexa.com/data/details/traffic_details/intodit.com) traffic rank

[21] MyFreeWiki (http://www.alexa.com/data/details/traffic_details/myfreewiki.net) traffic rank

[22] Netcipia (http://www.alexa.com/data/details/traffic_details/netcipia.com) traffic rank

[23] paid for dedicated servers

[24] nexdo (http://www.alexa.com/data/details/traffic_details/nexdo.com) traffic rank

[25] Oddwiki (http://www.alexa.com/data/details/traffic_details/communitywiki.org) traffic rank

[26] OpenTeams (http://www.alexa.com/data/details/traffic_details/openteams.com) traffic rank

[27] Free for charitable nonprofits and read-only access

[28] Ourproject (http://www.alexa.com/data/details/traffic_details/ourproject.org) traffic rank

[29] PAUX (http://www.alexa.com/data/details/traffic_details/paux.com) traffic rank

[30] PBwiki (http://www.alexa.com/data/details/traffic_details/pbworks.com) traffic rank

[31] PicoWiki (http://www.alexa.com/data/details/traffic_details/picowiki.com) traffic rank

[32] ProjectForum (http://www.alexa.com/data/details/traffic_details/projectforum.com) traffic rank

[33] ProjectLocker (http://www.alexa.com/data/details/traffic_details/projectlocker.com) traffic rank

[34] Referata (http://www.alexa.com/data/details/traffic_details/referata.com) traffic rank

[35] Koren, Yaron (2009-01-24). " Custom license? (http://www.referata.com/wiki/Referata_talk:Features)".
     Referata. . Retrieved 2009-02-03.

[36] Russian wiki community (http://www.alexa.com/data/details/traffic_details/wiki-wiki.ru) traffic rank

[37] SeedWiki (http://www.alexa.com/data/details/traffic_details/seedwiki.com) traffic rank

[38] SnoutHold Cospire (http://www.alexa.com/data/details/traffic_details/cospire.com) traffic rank

[39] Socialtext (http://www.alexa.com/data/details/traffic_details/socialtext.net) traffic rank. Few wikis
     appear to be on the socialtext.net domain/ or most are not public wikis, so the Alexa rating doesn't seem very
     relevant.

[40] " SocialText Packages & Pricing (http://www.socialtext.com/products/pricing.php)". Socialtext.com. .
     Retrieved 2009-06-10.

[41] Swirrl (http://www.alexa.com/data/details/traffic_details/swirrl.com) traffic rank

[42] Swirrl Terms Of Service (http://www.swirrl.com/terms_of_service.html)

[43] Wetpaint (http://www.alexa.com/data/details/traffic_details/wetpaint.com) traffic rank

[44] Wik.is (http://www.alexa.com/data/details/traffic_details/wik.is) traffic rank

[45] Wikia (http://www.alexa.com/data/details/traffic_details/wikia.com) traffic rank

[46] Wikidot (http://www.alexa.com/data/details/traffic_details/wikidot.com) traffic rank

[47] Wikihost (http://www.alexa.com/data/details/traffic_details/wikihost.org) traffic rank

[48] Wiki-site (http://www.alexa.com/data/details/traffic_details/wiki-site.com) traffic rank

[49] Wikispaces (http://www.alexa.com/data/details/traffic_details/wikispaces.com) traffic rank

[50] Wiki Spot (http://www.alexa.com/data/details/traffic_details/wikispot.org) traffic rank

[51] Davis Wiki (http://www.alexa.com/data/details/traffic_details/daviswiki.org) traffic rank

[52] (For generally non-commercial projects. See Wiki Spot Community Guidelines)

[53] WikiZones.com (http://www.alexa.com/siteinfo/wikizones.com) traffic rank

[54] Wikkii (http://www.alexa.com/data/details/traffic_details/wikkii.com) traffic rank

[55] WikyBlog (http://www.alexa.com/data/details/traffic_details/wikyblog.com) traffic rank

[56] XWiki (http://www.alexa.com/data/details/traffic_details/xwiki.com) traffic rank

[57] YourWiki (http://www.alexa.com/data/details/traffic_details/yourwiki.net) traffic rank

[58] " ConstantSun: Image upload issues (http://constantsun.blogspot.com/2008/07/image-upload-issues.
     html)". Constantsun.blogspot.com. 2008-07-06. . Retrieved 2009-06-10.

[59] This is visible from the Control Panel (http://editthis.info/lumeniki/Control_Panel)

[60] Archiving Work Orders and Violation Reports, layered permissions, dynamic content, online forms, articles,
     blogs, slideshow, RSS/Atom, directory, classifieds, mail-in, mobile, newsletters.

[61] " Features (http://www.referata.com/wiki/Referata:Features)". Referata. 2008-11-25.. Retrieved
     2009-06-10.

[62] " viawiki.com (http://www.viawiki.com/levels.html)". viawiki.com. . Retrieved 2009-06-10.

[63] " wikia.com, Help:Semantic MediaWiki (http://help.wikia.com/wiki/Help:Semantic_MediaWiki)".
     wikia.com. . Retrieved 2009-07-22.

[64] http://pear.php.net/package/Text_Wiki/

[65] http://www.dmoz.org/Computers/Software/Groupware/Wiki/Wiki_farms/

[66] http://www.wikimatrix.org/

Wikitravel

	Wikitravel The Free Travel Guide
URL	http://wikitravel.org/
Type of site	→ Wiki
Available language(s)	18 languages
Owner	The copyright of the content is owned by the individual authors. The domain, server, and trademarks are owned by Internet Brands.
Created by	Evan Prodromou, Michele Ann Jenkins

Wikitravel is a Web-based project "to create a free, complete, up-to-date, and reliable worldwide travel guide."[1] Launched in July 2003 by Evan Prodromou and Michele Ann Jenkins, the Web site is based upon the → wiki model, using the Creative Commons Attribution ShareAlike license. In 2006, Internet Brands bought the trademark and servers and later introduced advertising to the website. Wikitravel received a Webby Award for Best Travel Website in 2007. That same year, Wikitravel's founders began **Wikitravel Press**, which publishes printed travel guides based on the Web site's content. The first print guides were released on February 1, 2008.

Description

Using a → wiki model, Wikitravel is built through collaboration of *Wikitravellers* from around the globe. Articles can cover any level of geographic specificity, from continents to districts of a city. These are logically connected in a hierarchy, by specifying that the location covered in one article "is in" the larger location described by another. The project also includes articles on travel-related topics, phrasebooks for travelers, and suggested itineraries. Wikitravel is a multilingual project available in 18 languages, with each language-specific project developed independently. While the project uses the MediaWiki software, which is also used by Wikipedia, Wikitravel is not a Wikimedia project; it was begun and is operated independently.

History

Wikitravel was started in July 2003 by Evan Prodromou and Michele Ann Jenkins, inspired in part by → Wikipedia.[2] Unlike Wikipedia, it uses the Creative Commons Attribution ShareAlike license rather than the GNU Free Documentation License. Among other things, this more easily allows individuals, tourism agencies, etc., to make free reprints of individual pages. Although both Wikipedia and Wikitravel are free-content resources, because of the incompatible licenses, content cannot be freely copied between them. Wikitravel's different objectives have also resulted in different policies and content guidelines. For example, Wikitravel eschews a neutral-point-of-view requirement, as it is written from the point of view of a traveler and, instead, encourages editors to "be fair."

On April 20, 2006, Wikitravel announced that it and → World66 — another open-content travel guide — had been acquired by Internet Brands, a publicly traded corporation.[3] The new owner hired Prodromou and Jenkins to continue managing Wikitravel as a consensus-based project. They explained that Internet Brands' long-term plan was for Wikitravel to continue to focus on collaborative, objective guides, while World66 would focus more on personal experiences and reviews. As a result, many authors of the German language community decided to fork the German Wikitravel, which was released on December 10, 2006, as Wikivoyage. The German language Wikitravel remains active. On April 1, 2008, Internet Brands added Google advertising to Wikitravel, with an opt-out procedure for registered users.

On May 1, 2007, Wikitravel received the Webby Award for Best Travel Website.[4]

On August 3, 2007, Prodromou, Jenkins, and long-time contributor Jani Patokallio started **Wikitravel Press**, a company that produces and sells print guidebooks based on material contributed to Wikitravel. The first Wikitravel Press guides, *Chicago* and *Singapore*, were officially launched on February 1, 2008.[5] Content in these guidebooks is available under the same Creative Commons Attribution ShareAlike license that Wikitravel material is licensed under.[6]

Milestones

- December 23, 2005 — 10,000 articles across all versions.
- June 11, 2006 — 10,000 articles on the English version.
- September 29, 2006 — 20,000 articles across all versions.
- May 1, 2007 — Wikitravel wins Webby Award for Best Travel Website.
- February 1, 2008 — publication of first printed Wikitravel Press guides.
- November 22, 2008 — 20,000 articles on the English version.
- August 21, 2009 — 50,000 articles across all versions.

External links

- Wikitravel [7] (*English version*)
- Wikitravel Press [8]
- Wikitravel Search Plugin For Firefox [9]

References

[1] " Wikitravel mainpage (http://wikitravel.org/en/Main_Page)". Wikitravel.org. . Retrieved 2008-07-03.

[2] WikiTravel Milestones (http://wikitravel.org/en/Wikitravel:Milestones)

[3] Internet Brands (20 April, 2006). " Internet Brands Acquires Wikitravel And World66 Online Travel Guides (http://www.corporate-ir.net/ireye/ir_site.zhtml?ticker=27587&script=410&layout=-6& item_id=845378)". Press release. .

[4] Webby Award (http://www.webbyawards.com/webbys/current.php#webby_entry_travel)

[5] " Wikitravel Press launches first printed Wikitravel guidebook (http://wikitravelpress.com/pr/20080201)". www.wikitravelpress.com. 2008-02-01. . Retrieved 2008-02-01.

[6] " Wikitravel:3 August 2007 (http://wikitravel.org/en/Wikitravel:3_August_2007)". www.wikitravel.org. 2007-08-03. . Retrieved 2008-01-30.

[7] http://wikitravel.org/en/Main_Page

[8] http://wikitravelpress.com/

[9] http://mycroft.mozdev.org/developer/devlist.html?email=winkywankywoo%40hotmail.com

World66

World66 was a Dutch company which embraced the open content idea and tried to transform it into a profitable business. It is now owned by El Segundo, California, based Internet Brands, Inc which acquired it in April 2006.

History

The site was founded in 1999 by Richard Osinga and Douwe Osinga as Osinga.com, but the name was changed to World66 in the same year and they were soon joined by Michael Manikowski. On November 29 2003, it expanded by absorbing the travel-related *CapitanCook* wiki. Internet Brands announced their acquisition of World66 on April 20, 2006. [1]

Technology

World66 uses → wiki-like software based on the Zope application server, which allows everyone to add or edit contents. The site claims more than 80,000 travel related articles covering about 10,000 destinations around the world and all of them are licensed under the Creative Commons Attribution-ShareAlike 1.0 Licence.

Issues

In 2004, World66 relicensed all content to an open license first a GNU FDL license and consequently to CC by-sa 1.0 - those who had contributed under GNU FDL license were informed of the change by e-mail and had the possibility to withdraw contributions.

See also

- → Wikitravel
- Travellerspoint
- WikiMapia

External links

- World66 [2]
- A BBC News article on collaborative travel guides [3]

References

[1] Internet Brands (April 20, 2006). " Internet Brands Acquires *Wikitravel* And *World66* Online Travel Guides (http://www.corporate-ir.net/ireye/ir_site.zhtml?ticker=27587&script=410&layout=-6& item_id=845378)". Press release. .
[2] http://www.world66.com/
[3] http://news.bbc.co.uk/2/hi/uk_news/magazine/3614517.stm

Susning.nu

Susning.nu was/is a Swedish language → wiki, started in October 2001 by Lars Aronsson (also the founder of Project Runeberg), and it ran for three years as an open wiki. In April 2004, Susning had over 60,000 articles on various topics, making it the largest Swedish wiki at the time. Aronsson's stated original aim for Susning was "to make it into whatever the users want it to be." As such, Susning was/is an encyclopedia, a dictionary, and a discussion forum about any concept of interest to its users. It was in direct competition with the Swedish Wikipedia and could perhaps be compared in scope to Everything2.

Skaffa dig en

Current logo of Susning.nu

On April 15, 2004, due to heavy vandalism by users who (amongst other things) included large quantities of pornography, all editing was disabled except for very few selected accounts. New account creation was also closed, effectively freezing the site. This state lasted for three years until about October 2007, when the site started to be opened during Sunday afternoons, and in about February 2008 this was expanded to include one hour every weekday. It is not clear whether this trend will continue or what Aronsson's current intentions are. It is likely that the problem of vandalism is greater for Susning.nu than for other wikis, since Susning.nu does not have any administrators who can block vandals 'in action'. The only one having administrative privileges is Lars Aronsson.

Unlike its main competitor the Swedish Wikipedia, Susning.nu places advertisements on practically all its articles. It also has no license agreement, so contributions remain copyrighted by their submitters (the right to modify is said to be implicit in the site's function). This, in turn, means that third parties, such as Wikipedia editors, cannot legally use Susning.nu materials contributed by others without permission. It also means that Susning.nu depends solely on Lars Aronsson's goodwill to continue. He has repeatedly stated that he sees the site as his own personal project, to do with whatever he wants to.

Susning uses a heavily-modified version of UseModWiki as its wiki engine. The domain name .nu, which belongs to the 260-km² island of Niue but is sold primarily to foreigners, was chosen because it means "now" in Swedish (and also in Danish and Dutch). *"Skaffa dig en Susning.nu"* is the slogan of Susning and translates to *"Get a clue.now"*. The standard top level domain for Sweden is .se.

See also

Other wiki encyclopedias:

- Enciclopedia Libre
- WikiZnanie (Russian)
- List of online encyclopedias

External links

- Susning.nu [1]
- Lars Aronsson: *Operation of a Large Scale, General Purpose Wiki Website. Experience from susning.nu's first nine months in service.* Presented on November 7, 2002, at the

ELPUB 2002 conference in Karlovy Vary [2], and printed in: João Álvaro Carvalho, Arved Hübler, Ana Alice Baptista (editors), Elpub 2002. Technology Interactions. Proceedings of the 6th International ICCC/IFIP Conference on Electronic Publishing held in Karlovy Vary, Czech Republic, 6-8 November, 2002, Verlag für Wissenschaft und Forschung Berlin, 2002, ISBN 3-89700-357-0, pages 27-37. Online copy [3].

References

[1] http://susning.nu/
[2] http://www.tu-chemnitz.de/elpub02/
[3] http://aronsson.se/wikipaper.html

WikiSym

WikiSym is a short hand for **International Symposium on Wikis and Open Collaboration**, or the *Wiki Symposium*, a conference dedicated to → wiki research and practice. Its proceedings are published in the ACM Digital Library.

2008 WikiSym logo

WikiSym 2009 (Orlando, FL (U.S.A.))

WikiSym 2009 will be held in Orlando, FL, on October 25-27, 2009.

WikiSym 2008 (Porto, Portugal)

WikiSym 2008 was held in Porto, Portugal, in 8-10 September, 2008, at the Faculty of Engineering [1] of the University of Porto and supported ("in-cooperation agreement") by the ACM.[2] [3] Keynotes were given by George Landow, Professor of Art and English at Brown University[4] and Stewart Nickolas, IBM Emerging Technologies while Dan Ingalls, Sun Microsystems Laboratories gave an invited talk. The Conference Chair was Ademar Aguiar and Program Chair was Mark Bernstein.

WikiSym 2007 (Montreal, Canada)

WikiSym 2007 was co-located with OOPSLA 2007, an ACM conference, in Montreal, Quebec, Canada on October 21-23, 2007.[5] Invited speakers were Jonathan Grudin and Ward Cunningham. Speakers Peter Turchi as well as Jim Purbrick and Mark Lentczner were shared with OOPSLA. Conference chair was Alain Désilets and program chair was Robert Biddle.[6]

WikiSym 2006 (Odense, Denmark)

WikiSym 2006 was co-located with ACM Hypertext 2006 from August 21-23, 2006 in Odense, Denmark.[7] Invited speakers included Angela Beesley ("How and Why Wikipedia Works"), Doug Engelbart and Eugene Eric Kim ("The Augmented Wiki"), Mark Bernstein ("Intimate Information: organic hypertext structure and incremental formalization for everyone's everyday tasks"), and Ward Cunningham ("Design Principles of Wiki: How can so little do so much?"). Conference chair was Dirk Riehle and program chair was James Noble.[8]

WikiSym 2005 (San Diego, CA, U.S.A.)

WikiSym 2005 was co-located with ACM OOPSLA 2005, held in San Diego, California, USA, October 14– 16, 2005.[9] Speakers included Ward Cunningham and Jimmy Wales. Sponsors of the event included Google. Conference chair was Dirk Riehle.[10]

See also

- → Wikimania
- RecentChangesCamp

External links

- Main WikiSym [11] website

References

[1] http://www.fe.up.pt
[2] 2008 WikiSym website (http://www.wikisym.org/ws2008)
[3] "Utilização de wikis reduz a troca de emails." Sept. 9, 2008. *Sol.* (http://sol.sapo.pt/PaginaInicial/ Tecnologia/Interior.aspx?content_id=108411). Accessed Feb. 7, 2009. **(Portuguese)**
[4] "Especialistas mundiais de wikis reúnem-se entre segunda e quarta-feira no Porto" Sept. 7, 2008. cienciahoje.pt (http://www.cienciahoje.pt/index.php?oid=?7768&op=all). Accessed Feb. 7, 2009. **(Portuguese)**
[5] WikiSym 2007 website (http://www.wikisym.org/ws2007)
[6] Désilets, Alain; Biddle, Robert, eds. (2007), *Proceedings of the 2007 International Symposium on Wikis* (http:// portal.acm.org/toc.cfm?id=1296951&coll=ACM&dl=ACM&type=proceeding&idx=SERIES11299& part=series&WantType=Proceedings&title=ISW), ACM Press,
[7] WikiSym 2006 website (http://www.wikisym.org/ws2006)
[8] Riehle, Dirk; Noble, James, eds. (2006), *Proceedings of the 2006 International Symposium on Wikis* (http:// portal.acm.org/toc.cfm?id=1149453&coll=ACM&dl=ACM&type=proceeding&idx=SERIES11299& part=series&WantType=Proceedings&title=ISW), ACM Press,
[9] WikiSym 2005 website (http://www.wikisym.org/ws2005)
[10] Riehle, Dirk, ed. (2005), *Proceedings of the 2005 International Symposium on Wikis* (http://portal.acm.org/ toc.cfm?id=1104973&coll=ACM&dl=ACM&type=proceeding&idx=SERIES11299&part=series& WantType=Proceedings&title=ISW), ACM Press,
[11] http://www.wikisym.org

Wikimania

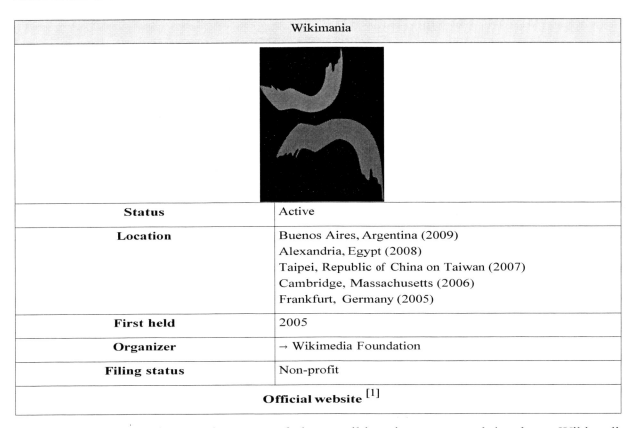

Wikimania	
Status	Active
Location	Buenos Aires, Argentina (2009) Alexandria, Egypt (2008) Taipei, Republic of China on Taiwan (2007) Cambridge, Massachusetts (2006) Frankfurt, Germany (2005)
First held	2005
Organizer	→ Wikimedia Foundation
Filing status	Non-profit
Official website [1]	

Wikimania is a conference for users of the → wiki projects operated by the → Wikimedia Foundation. The first conference was held in Frankfurt, Germany, August 4– 8, 2005; the second ran August 4– 6, 2006, in Cambridge, Massachusetts, USA; the third conference was held August 3– 8, 2007, in Taipei, Taiwan; and the fourth conference was held in Alexandria,
Egypt from July 17-19, 2008. Topics of presentations and discussions include Wikimedia Foundation projects, other wikis, open source software, and free content.

Overview

Wikimania conferences

Conference	Date	Place	Continent	Attendance
Wikimania 2005 [2]	5 August – 7 August 2005	Frankfurt, Germany	Europe	380[3]
Wikimania 2006 [4]	4 August – 6 August 2006	Cambridge, Massachusetts, US	North America	400[5]
Wikimania 2007 [6]	3 August – 5 August 2007	Taipei, Republic of China on Taiwan	Asia	440
Wikimania 2008 [7]	17 July – 19 July 2008	Alexandria, Egypt	Africa	625
Wikimania 2009 [1]	26 August – 28 August 2009	Buenos Aires, Argentina	South America	
Wikimania 2010 [8]	9 July – 11 July 2010	Gdańsk, Poland	Europe	

Wikimania 2005

The first Wikimania conference was held in the *Haus der Jugend* at Frankfurt, Germany, August 4 to August 8 2005.

The week of the conference included four "Hacking Days", from August 1– 4, when some 25 developers gathered to work on code and discuss the technical aspects of MediaWiki and of running the Wikimedia projects. The main days of the conference, despite its billing as being "August 4– 8", were Friday to Sunday of that week, August 5 – 7. Presentation sessions were scheduled all day during those three days.

Global Voices Panel at the 2005 conference. Shown are Hossein Derakhshan, Ting Chen, Isam Bayazidi, and Milton Ainehuranga.

Keynote speakers included Jimmy Wales, Ross Mayfield, Ward Cunningham and Richard Stallman (who spoke on *"Copyright and community in the age of computer networks"*). The majority of sessions and conversations were in English, although a few were in German.

Sponsors of the event included Answers.com, SocialText, Sun Microsystems, DocCheck [9], and Logos Group.

Wikimania 2006

Wikimania 2006 took place from August 6 to August 8 2006, at Harvard Law School's Berkman Center for Internet & Society in Cambridge, Massachusetts in the United States. It had about 400[5] -500[10] attendees.

Speakers included Jimmy Wales, Lawrence Lessig, Brewster Kahle, Yochai Benkler, Mitch Kapor, Ward Cunningham, and David Weinberger. Dan Gillmor held a citizen journalism unconference the day after.

Attendees break for lunch.

Wales' plenary speech was covered by the Associated Press, and printed in numerous worldwide newspapers. He chronicled how the Foundation evolved from him "sitting in his pajamas" to the maturing corporate structure that it is now; the frequent push for quality over quantity; Wikipedia will be included on computers distributed through One Laptop per Child; both Wikiversity and the creation of an advisory board were approved by the Foundation board; and that Wiki-WYG is in development thanks to private investment by Wikia, Inc. and Socialtext.[11]

Answers.com was the Wikimania 2006 Patron sponsor, while Amazon.com, the Berkman Center for Internet & Society at Harvard Law School, Nokia, WikiHow were Benefactors-level sponsors, Wetpaint, Ask.com, Yahoo!, and Socialtext were Friends-level sponsors, and IBM, FAQ Farm, Elevation Partners, One Laptop per Child, and the Sunlight

Foundation were Supporter-level sponsors of the conference.[12]

Three other teams submitted hosting bids, for the cities of London, Milan, Boston, and Toronto; only Toronto and Boston were passed to the second round of consideration by Wikimania organizers. Toronto would have hosted the event in the University of Toronto's Bahen Centre.

Wikimania 2007

As announced on September 25, 2006, Wikimania 2007 [13] was held in Taipei, Republic of China on Taiwan from August 3, 2007 to August 5, 2007. It was the first to hold a volunteer training course.[14]

Three other teams submitted hosting bids, for the cities of London, Alexandria, and Turin. Official bids from Hong Kong, Singapore, Istanbul, and Orlando failed to make the shortlist. Bids for Geneva, Chicago, and Las Vegas were never made official.[15]

The press conference for the Chunghwa Telecom sponsoring Wikimania 2007 in Taipei

On August 3, 2007, *New York Times* reporter Noam Cohen reported: "The conference has attracted about 440 attendees, a little more than half from Taiwan, who want to immerse themselves for three days in the ideas and issues that come up making an entirely volunteer written encyclopedia. The workshops cover practical topics like how to collaborate peacefully; what importance to give 'expertise' in a project that is celebrated for allowing anyone to contribute, including anonymous editors."[16]

Wikimania 2008

Wikimania 2008 was held in Alexandria, Egypt from July 17 to July 19, 2008. The venue was the Bibliotheca Alexandrina. Three cities were in the running at the end, the other two being Atlanta and Cape Town. Karlsruhe, London and Toronto submitted official bids, but later withdrew. There was a controversy about the conference because of Egypt's alleged censorship and imprisoning of bloggers.[17] [18]

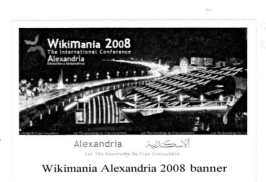

Wikimania Alexandria 2008 banner

Wikimania 2009

Wikimania 2009 will be held in Buenos Aires, Argentina, on August 26 – 28, 2009. Final selection
was made between Buenos Aires and Toronto. Brisbane and Karlsruhe submitted official bids, but later withdrew from consideration.

Wikimania Buenos Aires 2009 banner

Wikimania 2010

Wikimania 2010 will be held in the Polish Baltic Philharmonic in Gdańsk, Poland. Bids for Amsterdam and Oxford lost by a small margin.

2010 Gdańsk Wikimania banner

External links

- Taipei chosen to host Wikimania 2007
- Day 1 report of Wikimania 2006
- Interview: Wikinewsie Kim Bruning discusses Wikimania
- Wikimedia Foundation's first Wikimania convention held in Germany

Wikimania 2005

- Wikimania 2005 proceedings [19]
- "Worldwide Wikimania" [20] Sean Dodson, The Guardian, August 11, 2005
- "Rewriting the rule books" [21] Alan Connor, the BBC, August 15, 2005

Wikimania 2006

- Official site
- "The Many Voices of Wikipedia, Heard in One Place" [22] Robert Levine, The New York Times, August 7, 2006
- "Anybody can edit: A weekend of Wikimania" [23] Ian Sands and Jess McConnell, The Boston Phoenix, August 11, 2006
- "The Neutrality of this Article is Disputed" [24] Katherine Mangu-Ward, Reason, August 15, 2006

Wikimania 2007

- Official site
- The China Post - "Wikipedia founder rewards volunteers" Monday, August 6, 2007 - By Dimitri Bruyas [25]

Wikimania 2008

- Official site
- Videos of Wikimania sessions on Kaltura's devwiki [26]

Wikimania 2009

- Official site

Wikimania 2010

- Gdańsk presentation on meta [27]

References

[1] http://wikimania2009.wikimedia.org

[2] http://wikimania2005.wikimedia.org

[3] Main Page - Wikimania (http://wikimania2005.wikimedia.org/wiki/Main_Page)

[4] http://wikimania2006.wikimedia.org

[5] The Many Voices of Wikipedia, Heard in One Place (http://www.nytimes.com/2006/08/07/technology/07wiki.html?ex=1312603200&en=c7f5a3bc5ad54239&ei=5088&partner=rssnyt&emc=rss)

[6] http://wikimania2007.wikimedia.org

[7] http://wikimania2008.wikimedia.org

[8] http://www.wikimania2010.pl/wiki/Strona_g%C5%82%C3%B3wna

[9] http://www.doccheck.com

[10] Reason Magazine - The Neutrality of this Article is Disputed (http://www.reason.com/news/show/36969.html)

[11] MP3 of Jimmy Wales' plenary speech at Wikimania 2006 (http://www.supload.com/listen?s=SI0OG2vN04i)

[12] Wikimania 2006: Sponsors (http://wikimania2006.wikimedia.org/wiki/Sponsors)

[13] http://wikimania2007.wikimedia.org/wiki/Main_Page

[14] http://wikimania2007.wikimedia.org/wiki/Volunteer_training/20061209

[15] http://meta.wikimedia.org/wiki/Talk:Wikimania_2007/Bid_list

[16] New York Times (http://bits.blogs.nytimes.com/2007/08/03/in-taipei-wikipedians-talk-of-fundraising-and-wikiwars/) article *In Taipei, Wikipedians Talk Wiki Fatigue, Wikiwars and Wiki Bucks* report by Noam Cohen and edited by Saul Hansell published August 3, 2007

[17] Is there a boycott of Wikimania 2008? | Technology | Los Angeles Times (http://latimesblogs.latimes.com/technology/2008/07/boycott-wikiman.html)

[18] In Egypt, Wikipedia is more than hobby - International Herald Tribune (http://www.iht.com/articles/2008/07/21/business/link21.php)

[19] http://meta.wikimedia.org/wiki/Wikimania05

[20] http://www.guardian.co.uk/online/story/0,,1546162,00.html

[21] http://news.bbc.co.uk/1/hi/magazine/4152860.stm

[22] http://www.nytimes.com/2006/08/07/technology/07wiki.html?ex=1312603200&en=c7f5a3bc5ad54239&ei=5088&partner=rssnyt&emc=rss

[23] http://www.thephoenix.com/article_ektid19620.aspx

[24] http://www.reason.com/news/show/36969.html

[25] http://www.chinapost.com.tw/taiwan/2007/08/06/117187/Wikipedia-founder.htm

[26] http://www.kaltura.com/devwiki/index.php/Wikimania_Sessions

[27] http://meta.wikimedia.org/wiki/Wikimania_2010/Bids/Gda%C5%84sk

Wikimedia Foundation

Logo of the Wikimedia Foundation

Type	501(c)(3) charitable organization
Founded	St. Petersburg, Florida, US June 20 2003
Headquarters	San Francisco, California United States
Staff	Michael Snow, Chair of the Board Jimmy Wales, Chairman Emeritus[1] Sue Gardner, Executive Director
Area served	Worldwide
Focus	Free, open content, → wiki-based internet projects
Method	→ Wikipedia, Wiktionary, Wikiquote, Wikibooks (including Wikijunior), Wikisource, Wikimedia Commons, Wikispecies, Wikinews, Wikiversity, Wikimedia Incubator and MetaWiki
Revenue	$5,032,981 (2007-2008)[2]
Volunteers	350,000 (2005)[3]
Employees	23 (as of November 2008)[4]
Website	wikimediafoundation.org [5]

The **Wikimedia Foundation, Inc.** is a non-profit charitable organization headquartered in San Francisco, California, United States, and organized under the laws of the state of Florida, where it was initially based. It operates several online collaborative → wiki projects including → Wikipedia, Wiktionary, Wikiquote, Wikibooks (including Wikijunior), Wikisource, Wikimedia Commons, Wikispecies, Wikinews, Wikiversity, Wikimedia Incubator and Meta-Wiki[6]. Its flagship project, the English-language Wikipedia, ranks among the top ten most-visited websites worldwide.[7]

The creation of the foundation was officially announced on June 20, 2003 by → Wikipedia co-founder Jimmy Wales,[8] who had been operating Wikipedia under the aegis of his company Bomis.[9]

Goals

The Wikimedia Foundation falls under section 501(c)(3) of the US Internal Revenue Code as a public charity. Its National Taxonomy of Exempt Entities (NTEE) code is B60 (Adult, Continuing Education).[10] [11] The foundation's by-laws declare a statement of purpose of collecting and developing educational content and to disseminate it effectively and globally.[12]

The Wikimedia Foundation's stated goal is to develop and maintain open content, → wiki-based projects and to provide the full contents of those projects to the public free of charge.[13] This is possible thanks to its Terms of Use (updated and approved on June 2009, to adopt CC-BY-SA license).

In addition to the multilingual general encyclopedia → *Wikipedia*, the foundation manages a multi-language dictionary and thesaurus named *Wiktionary*, an encyclopedia of quotations named *Wikiquote*, a repository of source texts in any language named *Wikisource*, and a collection of e-book texts for students (such as textbooks and annotated public domain books) named *Wikibooks*. *Wikijunior* is a subproject of Wikibooks that specializes in books for children.

Operations

The continued technical and economic growth of each of the Wikimedia projects is dependent mostly on donations but the Wikimedia Foundation also increases its revenue by alternative means of funding such as grants, sponsorship, services (*datafeed*) and brand merchandising. In March 2008 the foundation announced its largest donation to date: a three-year, $3 million grant from the Alfred P. Sloan Foundation.[14]

History and growth

The Wikimedia Foundation was created from Wikipedia and Nupedia on June 20, 2003.[15] It applied to the United States Patent and Trademark Office to trademark *Wikipedia* on September 17, 2004. The mark was granted registration status on January 10, 2006. Trademark protection was accorded by Japan on December 16, 2004, and in the European Union on January 20, 2005. Technically a service mark, the scope of the mark is for: "Provision of information in the field of general encyclopedic knowledge via the Internet." There are plans to license the use of the Wikipedia trademark for some products, such as books or DVDs.[16]

Jimmy Wales, the Founder of the Wikimedia Foundation, in December 2008

The name "Wikimedia" was coined by Sheldon Rampton in a post to the English Wikipedia's mailing list in March 2003.[17]

With the foundation's announcement, Wales also transferred ownership of all Wikipedia, Wiktionary and Nupedia domain names to Wikimedia along with the copyrights for all materials related to these projects that were created by Bomis employees or Wales himself. The computer equipment used to run all the Wikimedia projects was also donated by Wales to the foundation, which also acquired the domain names "wikimedia.org" and "wikimediafoundation.org".

In April 2005, the US Internal Revenue Service approved (by letter) the foundation as an educational foundation in the category "Adult, Continuing Education", meaning all contributions to the Wikimedia Foundation are tax deductible for U.S. federal income tax purposes.

On December 11, 2006, the Wikimedia Foundation board noted that the corporation could not become the membership organization initially planned but never implemented due to an inability to meet the registration requirements of Florida Statute. Accordingly, the bylaws were amended to remove all reference to membership rights and activities. The decision to change the bylaws was passed by the board unanimously.

On September 25, 2007, the Wikimedia Foundation board gave notice that the operations would be moving to the San Francisco Bay Area. Major considerations cited for choosing San Francisco were proximity to like-minded organizations and potential partners as well as cheaper and more convenient international travel than is available from St. Petersburg.[18] [19] [20]

Board of Trustees

- In January 2004, Jimmy Wales appointed his business partners Tim Shell and Michael Davis to the board of the Wikimedia Foundation. In June 2004, an election was held for two user representative board members. Following one month of campaigning and two weeks of online voting, Angela Beesley and Florence Nibart-Devouard were elected to join the board. In late 2004, Wales and Beesley launched a startup company, Wikia, affiliated with neither Wikimedia nor Bomis, except for their presence as principals/trustees. In July 2005, Beesley and Nibart-Devouard were re-elected to the board.

- On July 1, 2006, Beesley resigned from the board effective upon election of her successor, expressing concern about "certain events and tendencies that have arisen within the organization since the start of this year," but stating her intent to continue to participate in the Wikimedia projects, and in the formation of an Australian chapter. A special election was held in September to finish Beesley's term, ending with the mid-2007 election. The election was won by Erik Möller.

- In October 2006, Nibart-Devouard replaced Wales as chair of the Foundation. On December 8, 2006, the board expanded to seven people with the appointments of Kat Walsh and Oscar van Dillen. Effective December 15, 2006, Jan-Bart de Vreede was appointed to replace Shell.

- In the June 2007 election, Möller and Walsh were reelected; van Dillen, who ran for re-election, was narrowly edged by Frieda Brioschi.

- Davis left the board in November 2007. Nibart-Devouard's elected term expires in June 2008. The appointed terms for Wales and de Vreede expired in December 2008. Brioschi's and Walsh's elected terms expired in June 2009.

- In December 2007, Möller resigned from the Board of Trustees, and was hired as the foundation's deputy director by the executive director.

- In February 2008, Florence Devouard announced the addition of two new board members: Michael Snow, an American lawyer and chair of the Communication Committee; and Domas Mituzas, a Lithuanian computer software engineer, MySQL employee, and longtime member of the core tech team.[21]
- In April 2008, the board announced a restructuring of its membership, increasing the number of board positions to 10 overall, as follows:
  - Three community-elected seats
  - Two seats to be selected by the chapters
  - One board-appointed 'community founder' seat, to be occupied by Jimmy Wales
  - Four board-appointed 'specific expertise' seats[22]
- In the June 2008 board election, Ting Chen was elected for a one-year term, then Frieda Brioschi resigned to be elected at the board of Wikimedia Italia.
- In August 2009 board election, Ting Chen (reelected), Kat Walsh and Samuel Klein are elected. Their positions will be effective until July 2011

Volunteer committees and positions

In 2004, the foundation appointed Tim Starling as developer liaison to help improve the MediaWiki software, Daniel Mayer as chief financial officer (finance, budgeting and coordination of fund drives), and Erik Möller as content partnership coordinator.

In May 2005, the foundation announced the appointment of seven people to official positions:[24]

In April 2009, Wikimedia Foundation conducted → Wikipedia usability study questioning users about the editing mechanism[23]

- Brion Vibber as chief technical officer (Vibber was also an employee of the Foundation, with other duties)
- Domas Mituzas as hardware officer
- Jens Frank as developer liaison
- Möller as chief research officer
- Danny Wool as grants coordinator
- Elisabeth Bauer as press officer
- Jean-Baptiste Soufron as lead legal coordinator

Möller resigned in August 2005, due to differences with the board, and was replaced by James Forrester. In February 2007, Forrester resigned, and the board appointed Gregory Maxwell to the position, renamed "chief research coordinator".[25]

In January 2006, the foundation created several committees, including the Communication Committee, in an attempt to further organize activities essentially handled by volunteers at that time.[26] Starling resigned that month to spend more time on his PhD program.

Employees

The functions of the Wikimedia Foundation were, for the first few years, executed almost entirely by volunteers. In 2005, the foundation had only two employees, Danny Wool, a coordinator, and Brion Vibber, a software manager. Though the number of employees has grown, the foundation's staff is still very small, and the bulk of foundation work continues to be done by volunteers.

The current staff are listed on the Foundation website, here.

As of October 4, 2006, the Wikimedia Foundation had five paid employees:[28] two programmers, an administrative assistant, a coordinator handling

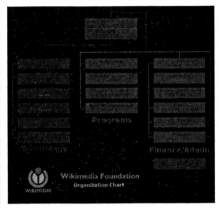

Organization chart as of January 2008[27]

fundraising and grants, and an interim executive director,[29] Brad Patrick, previously the foundation's general counsel. Patrick ceased his activity as interim director in January 2007, and then resigned from his position as legal counsel, effective April 1, 2007. He was replaced by Mike Godwin as general counsel and legal coordinator in July 2007.[30] Three further technical contractors were also appointed in December 2006: part-time hardware manager Kyle Anderson in Tampa, full-time MediaWiki software developer Tim Starling, and part-time networking coordinator Mark Bergsma.

In January 2007, Carolyn Doran was named chief operating officer and Sandy Ordonez came on board as head of communications.[31] Doran had begun working as a part-time bookkeeper in 2006 after being sent by a temporary agency. Doran later left the foundation in July 2007, and Sue Gardner was hired as consultant and special advisor (later CEO). Some months after Doran's departure, it was determined[32] that she was a convicted felon, with a DUI arrest during her tenure at the foundation and a substantial criminal history, including shooting her boyfriend and complicity in credit card forgery.[33] Her departure from the organization was cited as one of the reasons the foundation took about seven months to release its fiscal 2007 financial audit.[34]

Danny Wool, officially the grant coordinator but also largely involved in fundraising and business development, resigned in March 2007. In February 2007, the foundation added a new position, chapters coordinator, and hired Delphine Ménard,[35] who had been occupying the position as a volunteer since August 2005. Cary Bass was hired in March 2007 in the position of volunteer coordinator. In May 2007, Vishal Patel was hired to assist in business development.[36] Oleta McHenry was brought in as accountant in May, 2007, through a temporary placement agency and made the official fulltime accountant in August, 2007. In January 2008, the foundation appointed three new staff: Veronique Kessler as the new chief financial and operating officer, Kul Wadhwa to replace Vishal Patel as head of business development, and Jay Walsh as head of communications.

In June 2008, the foundation announced two staff additions in fundraising: Rebecca Handler as major gifts officer and Rand Montoya as head of community giving.[37] Soon afterward, Sara Crouse was hired as head of partnerships and foundation relations.[38] In fall 2008, the foundation hired three software developers: Tomasz Finc, Ariel Glenn, and Trevor Parscal.[39]

Current Board of Trustees

These are the current members of the Board:[40]

- Michael Snow, chair
- Jimmy Wales, chairman emeritus
- Jan-Bart de Vreede, vice-chair
- Arne Klempert, chapter selected seat
- Domas Mituzas, executive secretary
- Stuart West, treasurer
- Kat Walsh
- Ting Chen

Advisory Board

The Advisory Board is an international network of experts who have agreed to give the foundation meaningful help on a regular basis in many different areas, including law, organizational development, technology, policy, and outreach.[41] The current members are:

- Angela Beesley Leinonen
- Ward Cunningham MacKinnon
- Melissa Hagemann Mackintosh
- Mitch Kapor
- Neeru Khosla
- Trevor Neilson
- Florence Nibart-Devouard
- Achal Prabhala
- Clay Shirky
- Ethan Zuckerman

- Teemu
- Rebecca
- Wayne
- Benjamin Mako Hill
- Roger McNamee

Wikimedia projects

The launch dates shown below are when official domains were established for the projects and/or beta versions were launched; preliminary test versions at other domains are not considered.

The Wikimedia projects logo family

Name	URL	Launching date	Description
→ Wikipedia	www.wikipedia.org [210]	2001-01-15	Encyclopedia containing more than 10 million articles in 264 languages.
Meta-Wiki	meta.wikimedia.org [42]	2001-11-09	Wiki devoted to the coordination of the Wikimedia projects.
Wiktionary	www.wiktionary.org [43]	2002-12-12	Dictionary cataloging meanings, synonyms, etymologies and translations.
Wikibooks	www.wikibooks.org [44]	2003-07-10	Collection of free educational textbooks and learning materials.
Wikiquote	www.wikiquote.org [45]	2003-07-10	Collection of quotations structured in numerous ways.
Wikisource	www.wikisource.org [46]	2003-11-24	Project to provide and translate free source documents, such as public domain texts.
Wikimedia Commons	commons.wikimedia.org [47]	2004-09-07	Repository of images, sounds, videos and general media, containing over 4,400,000 files.
Wikimedia Incubator	incubator.wikimedia.org [48]	2006-06-02	Used to test possible new languages for existing projects.
Wikispecies	species.wikimedia.org [49]	2004-09-13	Directory of species data on animalia, plantae, fungi, bacteria, archaea, protista and all other forms of life.
Wikinews	www.wikinews.org [50]	2004-12-03	News source containing original reporting by citizen journalists from many countries.
Wikiversity	www.wikiversity.org [51]	2006-08-15	Educational and research materials and activities.

Finances

The Wikimedia Foundation relies on public contributions and grants to fund its mission of providing free knowledge to every person in the world.[52] It is exempt from federal income tax[52] [53] and from state income tax.[52] [54] It is not a private foundation, and contributions to it qualify as tax-deductible charitable contributions.[52]

At the beginning of 2006, the foundation's net assets were $270,000. During the year, the organization received support and revenue totaling $1,510,000, with concurrent expenses of $790,000. Net assets increased by $720,000 to a total of over one million dollars.[52] In 2007, the foundation continued to expand, ending the year with net assets of $1,700,000.[55] Both income and expenses nearly doubled in 2007.[55]

In August 2009, the Omidyar Network issued a potential $2 million in "grant" funding to Wikimedia.[56] At the same time, an Omidyar partner, Matt Halprin, was nominated to the Wikimedia Foundation Board of Trustees. The Omidyar Network also invested part of $4 million into Wikia, Inc.,[57] which was co-founded by Wikimedia Foundation chairman emeritus, Jimmy Wales.

Local chapters

Wikimedia projects have an international scope. To continue this success on an organizational level, Wikimedia is building an international network of associated organizations.

Local chapters are self-dependent organizations that share the goals of the Wikimedia Foundation and support them within a

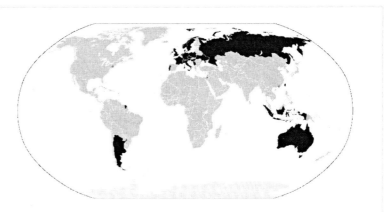

World map showing countries that have local chapters in blue.

specified geographical region. They support the foundation, the Wikimedia community and Wikimedia projects in different ways — by collecting donations, organizing local events and projects and spreading the word of Wikimedia, free content and Wiki culture. They also provide the community and potential partners with a point of contact capable of fulfilling specific local needs.

Local chapters are self-dependent associations with no legal control of nor responsibility for the websites of the Wikimedia Foundation and vice versa.

Country	Title	URL	Since
Argentina	Wikimedia Argentina	www.wikimedia.org.ar [58]	September 1, 2007
Australia	Wikimedia Australia	www.wikimedia.org.au [59]	March 1, 2008
Austria	Wikimedia Österreich	www.wikimedia.at [60]	February 26, 2008
Czech Republic	Wikimedia Česká republika	www.wikimedia.cz [61]	March 6, 2008
Denmark	Wikimedia Danmark		July 3, 2009
France	Wikimédia France	www.wikimedia.fr [62]	October 23, 2004
Germany	Wikimedia Deutschland	www.wikimedia.de [63]	June 13, 2004
Hong Kong	香港維基媒體協會	www.wikimedia.hk [64]	March 1, 2008
Hungary	Wikimédia Magyarország	wiki.media.hu [65]	September 27, 2008
Indonesia	Wikimedia Indonesia	wikimedia.or.id [66]	October 7, 2008
Israel	Wikimedia Israel	il.wikimedia.org [67]	June 26, 2007
Italy	Wikimedia Italia	www.wikimedia.it [68]	June 17, 2005
Netherlands	Wikimedia Nederland	nl.wikimedia.org [69]	March 27, 2006
Norway	Wikimedia Norge		June 23, 2007
Poland	Wikimedia Polska	pl.wikimedia.org [70]	November 18, 2005

Portugal	Wikimedia Portugal		July 3, 2009
Russia	Викимедиа РУ	wikimedia.ru [71] (not yet working)	May 24, 2008
Serbia	Wikimedia Србије	rs.wikimedia.org [72]	December 3, 2005
Sweden	Wikimedia Sverige	se.wikimedia.org [73]	December 11, 2007
Switzerland	Wikimedia CH	www.wikimedia.ch [74]	May 14, 2006
Republic of China	中華民國維基媒體協會	www.wikimedia.tw [75]	July 4, 2007
Ukraine	Вікімедіа Україна	www.wikimedia.org.ua [76]	July 3, 2009
United Kingdom	Wikimedia UK	uk.wikimedia.org [77]	January 12, 2009
New York City	Wikimedia New York City		January 12, 2009

Wikimania

Wikimedia organizes each year Wikimania, a conference for users of the Wikimedia Foundation projects. It was first organized in Frankfurt (Germany), 2005.

External links

- Wikimedia Foundation website [5]
- Wikimedia blog [78]
- Wikimedia technical blog [79]
- Wikimedia Foundation annual report [80]
- Wikimedia Foundation bylaws [81]PDF (259 KiB)
- Wikimedia on freenode [82]
- Financial statements 2004-2005-2006 [83]PDF (90.2 KiB)
- Public Record for Wikimedia Foundation Inc. [84] from Florida Department of State web site
- Sheldon Rampton's WikiEN-l post [85]

References

[1] Cbrown1023. " Board of Trustees (http://wikimediafoundation.org/w/index.php?title=Board_of_Trustees& oldid=24547)". Wikimedia Foundation. Archived from the original (http://wikimediafoundation.org/wiki/ Board_of_Trustees) on 2008-01-15. . Retrieved 2008-01-19.

[2] " Finance report (http://upload.wikimedia.org/wikipedia/foundation/4/4c/Wikimedia_20072008_fs.pdf)". Wikimedia Foundation. . Retrieved 2009-07-05.

[3] **(French)** Open for business (2007), Jaap Bloem & Menno van Doorn (trad. Audrey Vuillermier), éd. VINT, 2007 (ISBN 978-90-75414-20-2), p. 93. No official number available since 2006 (http://stats.wikimedia.org/ WikimediaProjectsGrowth.png)

[4] " Wikimedia Foundation's "Staff" page (http://wikimediafoundation.org/wiki/Current_staff)". Wikimedia Foundation. . Retrieved 2008-11-29.

[5] http://wikimediafoundation.org/wiki/Home

[6] http://en.wikipedia.org/w/index.php?title=m%3AMain+Page

[7] " Top 500 (http://www.alexa.com/site/ds/top_sites?ts_mode=global&lang=none)". Alexa. . Retrieved 2007-12-04.

[8] Bergstein, Brian (2007-03-25). " Sanger says he co-started Wikipedia (http://abcnews.go.com/Technology/ wireStory?id=2980046)". *ABC News* (Associated Press). . Retrieved 2007-07-31. "The nascent Web encyclopedia Citizendium springs from Larry Sanger, a philosophy Ph.D. who counts himself as a co-founder of

Wikipedia, the site he now hopes to usurp. The claim doesn't seem particularly controversial — Sanger has long been cited as a co-founder. Yet the other founder, Jimmy Wales, isn't happy about it."

[9] Wales, Jimmy (2003-06-20). " Wikipedia English mailing list message (http://lists.wikimedia.org/pipermail/ wikipedia-l/2003-June/010743.html)". .

[10] " NTEE Classification System (http://www.guidestar.org/npo/ntee.jsp)". . Retrieved 2008-01-28.

[11] " NCCS definition for Adult Education (http://nccs2.urban.org/ntee-cc/b.htm#b60)". . Retrieved 2008-01-28.

[12] Jd. " Wikimedia Foundation bylaws (http://wikimediafoundation.org/w/index. php?title=Wikimedia_Foundation_bylaws&oldid=20641#ARTICLE_II_-_STATEMENT_OF_PURPOSE)". Wikimedia Foundation. Archived from the original (http://wikimediafoundation.org/wiki/ Wikimedia_Foundation_bylaws#ARTICLE_II_-_STATEMENT_OF_PURPOSE) on 2007-04-20. . Retrieved 2008-01-28.

[13] Devouard, Florence. " Mission statement (http://wikimediafoundation.org/w/index. php?title=Mission_statement&oldid=21859)". Wikimedia Foundation. Archived from the original (http:// wikimediafoundation.org/wiki/Mission_statement) on 2007-09-01. . Retrieved 2008-01-28.

[14] " Sloan Foundation to Give Wikipedia $3M (http://ap.google.com/article/ ALeqM5i8x-wlh7nMm12x_kVQ6MZxrYWK9QD8VKMV1G0)". Associated Press. .

[15] Jimmy Wales: " Announcing Wikimedia Foundation (http://lists.wikimedia.org/pipermail/wikipedia-l/ 2003-June/010743.html)", June 20, 2003, <Wikipedia-l@wikipedia.org>

[16] Nair, Vipin (December 5, 2005). " Growing on volunteer power (http://www.thehindubusinessline.com/ew/ 2005/12/05/stories/2005120500070100.htm)". Business Line. . Retrieved 2008-12-26.

[17] Rampton, Sheldon (2003-03-16). " Wikipedia English mailing list message (http://mail.wikipedia.org/ pipermail/wikien-l/2003-March/001887.html)". .

[18] Carlos Moncada (2007-09-25). " Wikimedia Foundation Moving To Another Bay Area (http://www2.tbo.com/ content/2007/sep/25/wikimedia-foundation-moving-another-bay-area/?news-breaking)". *The Tampa Tribune*. .

[19] Richard Mullins (2007-09-26). " Online Encyclopedia To Leave St. Petersburg For San Francisco (http:// www.tbo.com/news/money/MGBNF5F517F.html)". *The Tampa Tribune*. .

[20] Kim, Ryan (2007-10-10). " Wikipedia team plans move to San Francisco (http://www.sfgate.com/cgi-bin/ article.cgi?f=/c/a/2007/10/10/BU69SNMQ2.DTL&tsp=1)". *San Francisco Chronicle*. .

[21] Devouard, Florence (2008-02-13). " [Foundation-l] [Announcement] Welcome to our two new board members (http://lists.wikimedia.org/pipermail/foundation-l/2008-February/038528.html)". . Retrieved 2008-02-13.

[22] Walsh, Jay. " Board of Trustees Restructure Announcement (http://wikimediafoundation.org/w/index. php?title=Board_of_Trustees/Restructure_Announcement&oldid=26599)". Wikimedia Foundation. Archived from the original (http://wikimediafoundation.org/wiki/Board_of_Trustees/Restructure_Announcement) on 2008-04-27. . Retrieved 2008-04-26.

[23] http://usability.wikimedia.org/wiki/UX_and_Usability_Study

[24] Snow, Michael (2005-05-30). " Wikimedia names seven to official positions (http://en.wikipedia.org/wiki/ Wikipedia:Wikipedia_Signpost/2005-05-30/Foundation_official_positions)". *The Wikipedia Signpost*. . Retrieved 2008-03-10.

[25] Möller, Erik. " Resolution:Chief Research Coordinator (http://wikimediafoundation.org/w/index. php?title=Resolution:Chief_Research_Coordinator&oldid=19693)". Wikimedia Foundation. Archived from the original (http://wikimediafoundation.org/wiki/Resolution:Chief_Research_Coordinator) on 2007-03-01. . Retrieved 2007-03-01.

[26] Devouard, Florence. " Resolutions (http://wikimediafoundation.org/w/index.php?title=Resolutions& oldid=24632)". Wikimedia Foundation. Archived from the original (http://wikimediafoundation.org/wiki/ Resolutions) on 2008-01-21. . Retrieved 2008-02-04.

[27] January 2008 Wikimedia Organization employee descriptions (http://lists.wikimedia.org/pipermail/ foundation-l/2008-January/037383.html)

[28] Jimmy Wales. (internet video). *Charlie Rose (46:22)* (http://video.google.com/ videoplay?docid=5184822358876183858). [TV-Series]. Google Video: Charlie Rose. . Retrieved 2006-12-08.

[29] Korg. " Wikimedia Foundation Announces Interim Executive Director (http://wikimediafoundation.org/w/ index.php?title=Press_releases/Wikimedia_Foundation_Announces_Interim_Executive_Director& oldid=13996)". Wikimedia Foundation. Archived from the original (http://wikimediafoundation.org/wiki/ Press_releases/Wikimedia_Foundation_Announces_Interim_Executive_Director) on 2006-06-12. . Retrieved 2006-06-12.

[30] Mailing list post (http://lists.wikimedia.org/pipermail/foundation-l/2007-July/031128.html) by the Chair of the Wikimedia Foundation's Board of Trustees announcing the appointment.

[31] Danny. " Current staff (http://wikimediafoundation.org/w/index.php?title=Current_staff&oldid=19370)". Wikimedia Foundation. Archived from the original (http://wikimediafoundation.org/wiki/Current_staff) on

2007-02-01. . Retrieved 2007-02-01.

[32] Metz, Cade (2007-12-13). " Wikipedia COO was convicted felon (http://www.theregister.co.uk/2007/12/13/wikimedia_coo_convicted_felon/)". . Retrieved 2007-12-27.

[33] Bergstein, Brian (2007-12-21). " Felon Became COO of Wikipedia Foundation (http://ap.google.com/article/ALeqM5hcWLu3fg-aDeJNfWTY6hlbz93oCwD8TM0HVG0)". . Retrieved 2007-12-27.

[34] Ral315 (2007-11-19). " *Signpost* interview: Florence Devouard (http://en.wikipedia.org/wiki/Wikipedia:Wikipedia_Signpost/2007-11-19/Anthere_interview)". *The Wikipedia Signpost*. . Retrieved 2008-02-19.

[35] " Resolution:Chapters coordinator (http://wikimediafoundation.org/wiki/Resolution:Chapters_coordinator_-_Delphine_MÃ©nard)". .

[36] Bass, Cary. " Current staff (http://wikimediafoundation.org/w/index.php?title=Current_staff&oldid=21206)". Wikimedia Foundation. Archived from the original (http://wikimediafoundation.org/wiki/Current_staff) on 2007-05-18. . Retrieved 2007-05-18.

[37] Kessler, Veronique (2008-06-26). " Wikimedia Foundation announces new staff appointments (http://blog.wikimedia.org/2008/06/26/wikimedia-foundation-announces-new-staff-appointments/)". *Wikimedia Blog*. Wikimedia Foundation. . Retrieved 2008-06-28.

[38] Kessler, Veronique (2008-07-12). " Welcome Sara Crouse to the WMF staff (http://blog.wikimedia.org/2008/07/12/welcome-sara-crouse-to-the-wmf-staff/)". *Wikimedia Blog*. Wikimedia Foundation. . Retrieved 2008-07-17.

[39] " Staff (http://wikimediafoundation.org/wiki/Staff)". Wikimedia Foundation. . Retrieved 2008-11-29.

[40] Walsh, Jay. " Board of Trustees (http://wikimediafoundation.org/wiki/Board_of_Trustees)". Wikimedia Foundation. . Retrieved 2008-04-27.

[41] Garsided. " Advisory Board (http://wikimediafoundation.org/w/index.php?title=Advisory_Board&oldid=25007)". Wikimedia Foundation. Archived from the original (http://wikimediafoundation.org/wiki/Advisory_Board) on 2008-02-01. . Retrieved 2008-02-12.

[42] http://meta.wikimedia.org/

[43] http://www.wiktionary.org/

[44] http://www.wikibooks.org/

[45] http://www.wikiquote.org/

[46] http://wikisource.org/wiki/Main_Page

[47] http://commons.wikimedia.org/wiki/Main_Page

[48] http://incubator.wikimedia.org/wiki/Main_Page

[49] http://species.wikimedia.org/wiki/Main_Page

[50] http://www.wikinews.org/

[51] http://www.wikiversity.org/

[52] " Wikimedia Foundation, Inc. - Financial Statements — June 30, 2006, 2005, and 2004 (http://upload.wikimedia.org/wikipedia/foundation/2/28/Wikimedia_2006_fs.pdf)" (PDF). Wikimedia Foundation. 2006-12-06. . Retrieved 2006-12-06.

[53] See also Section 501(c)(3) of the Internal Revenue Code of the Florida Statutes

[54] See also Chapter 220.13 of the Florida Statutes

[55] Finance report 2007

[56] Press release (http://news.prnewswire.com/DisplayReleaseContent.aspx?ACCT=104&STORY=/www/story/08-25-2009/0005082868&EDATE=), *Omidyar Network Commits $2 Million Grant to Wikimedia Foundation*, August 25, 2009.

[57] CNET News (http://news.cnet.com/8301-10784_3-6054663-7.html), Margaret Kane, March 28, 2006.

[58] http://www.wikimedia.org.ar/

[59] http://www.wikimedia.org.au

[60] http://www.wikimedia.at

[61] http://www.wikimedia.cz

[62] http://www.wikimedia.fr/

[63] http://www.wikimedia.de/

[64] http://www.wikimedia.hk/

[65] http://wiki.media.hu/

[66] http://wikimedia.or.id

[67] http://il.wikimedia.org/

[68] http://www.wikimedia.it/

[69] http://nl.wikimedia.org/

[70] http://pl.wikimedia.org/

[71] http://wikimedia.ru/

[72] http://rs.wikimedia.org/
[73] http://se.wikimedia.org/wiki/Huvudsida
[74] http://www.wikimedia.ch/
[75] http://www.wikimedia.tw/
[76] http://www.wikimeda.org.ua
[77] http://uk.wikimedia.org/
[78] http://blog.wikimedia.org/
[79] http://techblog.wikimedia.org/
[80] http://wikimediafoundation.org/wiki/Annual_Report
[81] http://www.wikimediafoundation.org/bylaws.pdf
[82] irc://irc.freenode.net/wikimedia
[83] http://upload.wikimedia.org/wikipedia/foundation/2/28/Wikimedia_2006_fs.pdf
[84] http://www.sunbiz.org/scripts/cordet.exe?action=DETFIL&inq_doc_number=N03000005323&
    inq_came_from=NAMFWD&cor_web_names_seq_number=0000&names_name_ind=N&
    names_cor_number=&names_name_seq=&names_name_ind=&
    names_comp_name=WIKIMEDIAFOUNDATION&names_filing_type=
[85] http://mail.wikipedia.org/pipermail/wikien-l/2003-March/001887.html

Comparison of wiki software

The following tables compare general and technical information for a number of wiki software packages.

General Information

WARNING: Table could not be rendered - ouputting plain text.
Potential causes of the problem are: (a) table contains a cell with content that does not fit on a single page (b) nested tables (c) table is too wide

Creator First public release date Latest stable release Stable release date Predecessor Cost (USD) Software licenseLicenses here are a summary, and are not taken to be complete statements of the licenses. Some packages may use libraries under different licenses. Open source Encoding Multilingual Programming language Data managementData backendArtificialMemory ArtificialMemory Semantic Wiki April 1, 2003October 1, 2007 N/A Enterprise Subscriptions start at +$500/monthProprietary softwareProprietary No ??ASP.NET/C Sharp (programming language)C#Microsoft SQL ServerAxosoft OnTime Axosoft October 1, 2007December 5, 2007 N/A Free for 1 User, $395 and up for teams Proprietary softwareProprietary No ? Yes ASP.NET/C Sharp (programming language)C#Microsoft SQL ServerBitweaver Bitweaver.org April 4, 2004 2.6.1 May 14, 2009 N/A Free LGPL Yes ? Yes PHPMySQL PostgreSQL Oracle FirebirdBrainKeeper BrainKeeper, Inc. April 19, 2006January 15, 2007 N/A Subscriptions start at $5/monthProprietary softwareProprietary No ? Supports Multilingual Content J2EE/Java (programming language)JavaRDBMS BusinessWiki Divante, Inc.January 5, 2007MediaWikiSubscriptions start at $150/monthGPL Yes UTF-8 Yes PHP, C Sharp (programming language)C# on Mono (software)MONOMySQLCentral Desktop Central Desktop Inc. October 1, 2005 Winter Release '07 November 12, 2007 N/A Free Ver

Available, Paid plans start at $25/monthProprietary softwareProprietary No ??PHPPostgreSQLClearspaceJive SoftwareJanuary 7, 2007 2.5.7 February 9, 2009 N/A For internal collaboration and communities of practice: free for up to 5 users, additional users $59/user/yearProprietary softwareProprietary No ISO8859-1, UTF-8, ... Yes J2EE/Java (programming language)JavaSQL/LDAP including: MySQL, Oracle databaseOracle, PostgreSQL, IBM DB2 and Microsoft SQL ServerComindwork Comindwork February 5, 2007February 1, 2009 N/A Free for 1 project, $29 and up for moreProprietary softwareProprietary No UTF-8 Yes ASP.NET/C Sharp (programming language)C#Microsoft SQL ServerCodeBeamer (software)codeBeamerIntland Software2002 5.3.1 May 2009 N/A Proprietary softwareProprietary No UTF-8 No Java (programming language)JavaMySQL, Oracle DatabaseOracle, Apache Derby or PostgresAtlassian ConfluenceConfluenceAtlassian Software SystemsMay 12, 2004 3.0.0 June 2, 2009 N/A Free (open source project or community or personal), $1200–8000 commercial, $600–4000 academicCommercial, Academic, Community, Personal, Open Source Project No ISO8859-1, UTF-8, ... Yes Java (programming language)Java, Java EERelational databaseRDB (PostgreSQL, MySQL, Oracle databaseOracle, DB2, MS SQL Server)Corendal Wiki Thierry Danard May 14, 2005February 12, 2007 N/A Free GNU General Public LicenseGPL Yes ??Java (programming language)JavaMySQL or Oracle databaseOraclecoWiki Daniel T. Gorski; Paul Hanchett March 2002 0.3.4 February 24, 2005 N/A Free GNU General Public LicenseGPL Yes ??PHP5MySQLMindTouch DekiMindTouch & community July 25, 2006 8.08.2 December 6, 2008MediaWikiFree & open-source edition, paid enterprise edition, and free and paid hosted versions offered.GNU General Public LicenseGPL/Lesser GNU General Public LicenseLGPL, Apache License Yes UTF-8 Yes PHP, C Sharp (programming language)C# on Windows or Mono (software)MonoMySQLDidiWiki Matthew Allum ? 0.5 September 30, 2004 N/A Free GNU General Public LicenseGPL Yes ??C (programming language)CFile systemDokuWiki Andreas Gohr July 2004February 14, 2009February 14, 2009 Free GNU General Public LicenseGPL v2 Yes UTF-8 Yes PHPFile systemEditMe EditMe, LLC August 1, 2002 2007.06.25 June 25, 2007 N/A From $5/mo Proprietary No ??Java (programming language)Java (Hosted)MySQLFlexWiki David Ornstein ? 2.0 February 2, 2008 N/A Free Common Public LicenseCPL Yes ??ASP.NET, C Sharp (programming language)C#File system, Microsoft SQL ServerFoswiki Foswiki Community December 26, 2008 1.0.6 June 21, 2009TWiki Free GNU General Public LicenseGPL Yes ISO8859-1, UTF-8 Yes PerlFlat-file, Revision Control SystemRCS; no SQL-based storage Foswiki mailing list - Database store (somewhat)Gitit (software)Gitit John MacFarlane November 8, 2008 0.5.3 February 1, 2009 [-] Free GNU General Public LicenseGPL Yes UTF-8 Yes Haskell (programming language)HaskellGit (software)Git, Revision Control SystemRCSGroupSwim CollaborationTN20September 23, 2007 5.0 September 23, 2007 N/A For internal collaboration: priced on a per user/month basisProprietary softwareProprietary No ? ? Java (programming language)JavaMySQLHOAwiki CMS/groupware Troxler Inc. June 1, 2008 2.2 December 31, 2008 N/A Subscriptions start at $28/monthProprietary softwareProprietary No UTF-8 Yes PHPMYSQLInstiki David Heinemeier Hansson ? 0.13.0 March 17, 2008 N/A Free Ruby LicenseInstiki - Ruby License Instiki is distributed under the same terms as Ruby itself, per the Ruby license. Yes ??Ruby programming languageRubyRuby on Rails#ModelActive RecordIpbWikiGlobalSoftFebruary 25, 2006 1.7.1 September 25, 2007 N/A Free for the basic version, 30$/year for full version Proprietary No ??PHPMySql, Microsoft SQL Server or Oracle DatabaseOracleJAMWiki Various June 30, 2006 0.7.0 February 28, 2009MediaWiki Free GNU Lesser General Public

LicenseLGPL Yes UTF-8 Yes Java (programming language)Java Most JDBCJDBC compliant databases, or HSQLfile system using HSQLJotSpot JotSpot October 2004 2.0 July 24, 2006 N/A From $100/mo Proprietary No ??Java (programming language)JavaFile system, XMLJSPWiki Janne Jalkanen July 6, 2001 2.8.2 March 31, 2009 N/A Free Apache Public License 2.0 Yes UTF-8 Yes Java (programming language)JavaFlat-file, Revision Control SystemRCS, Subversion (software)SVNKanopia Kanopia, Inc. August 1, 2007 0.1 August 1, 2007 N/A Free GNU General Public LicenseGPL v2 Yes ??PHPMySQL, PostgreSQLKerika Kerika, Inc. May 1, 2005 1.1 August 1, 2007 N/A $9.95/month/user; free for anyone with ".edu" email address Proprietary No ??Java (programming language)JavaObject-oriented databaseMediaWikiWikimedia FoundationJanuary 25, 2002 1.15.1 July 13, 2009 N/A Free GNU General Public LicenseGPL v2 Yes UTF-8 Yes PHPMySQL, PostgreSQL, SQLiteMidgard (software)Midgard WikiHenri BergiusSeptember 29, 2004 1.8.3 April 25, 2007 N/A Free GNU Lesser General Public LicenseLGPL Yes ??PHPMySQL and Revision Control SystemRCSMoinMoin Jurgen Hermann; Thomas Waldmann; ... July 28, 2000 1.7.2 September 9, 2008 PikiPiki Free GNU General Public LicenseGPL Yes UTF-8 Yes Python (programming language)PythonFlat-fileMojoMojo Marcus Ramberg & community August 29, 2007 0.999032 August 2, 2009 N/A Free Perl Yes UTF-8 Yes PerlPostgreSQL, SQLite, MySQL, others Near-Time Near-Time, Inc. November 20, 2005 2007.28.0 June 27, 2007 N/A Starts at $24.99 per month for unlimited spaces and unlimited usersProprietary No ??Ruby on RailsmySQLOddMuseWiki Alex Schroeder UseModWiki 0.9 Free GNU General Public LicenseGPL Yes ??PerlFlat-fileOpenWiki ? 0.78 sp1 March 19, 2002 N/A Free ????Active Server PagesASP, VBScriptMS Access and Microsoft SQL ServerOpenLink Wiki ? Free GNU General Public LicenseGPL and Commercial License ?????PAUX From €300/mo Free and Commercial License?????PBworks David Weekly May 30, 2005TipiWikiFree & Paid options available Proprietary No UTF-8?PHPMogileFS, Squid cacheSquid, MySQL, Pound (networking)Pound, lighttpdPicoWikiPaul KlippMay 20, 2008June 22, 2008May 20, 2008 Free Proprietary No UTF-8 No PHPMySQLPersonal_PPC_WikiPersonal PPC Wiki Tony Steward November 2008 1.6.4 February 2009 N/A Free GNU General Public LicenseGPL Yes ??Basic4ppcFile SystemPerspective (software)Perspective Alan Slater March 2004 0.922 February 6, 2007 N/A Free GNU General Public LicenseGPL Yes ??ASP.NET, C Sharp (programming language)C#, XSL TransformationsXSLTMicrosoft Indexing Service, XMLPhpWiki Steve Wainstead, ... December 1999 1.3.14 July 1, 2007WikiWikiWeb Free GNU General Public LicenseGPL Yes ISO8859-1, UTF-8 Yes PHPBerkeley DB, Flat-file, MySQL, PostgreSQL, Microsoft SQL Server, Oracle 8, Firebird Pier_(software)Pier Lukas Renggli ? 1.0.17 September 23, 2008SmallWiki Free MIT LicenceMIT Yes ??Smalltalk, Squeak Image-based, and pluggable PmWiki Patrick Michaud February 6, 2002 2.2.0 January 18, 2009 N/A Free GNU General Public LicenseGPL Yes ISO8859-1, UTF-8 Yes PHPFlat-file. MySQL, SQLite (plug-ins) Portili TeamWikihttp://portili.comJune 17, 2009 1.00 June 17, 2009 N/A Enterprise edition: $339. Free version for personal use. Proprietary softwareProprietary No UTF-8 No PHPMySQLQwikiWikiFebruary 1, 2008 N/A Free BSD License Yes ISO8859-1, UTF-8 ? PHPFlat-fileSamePageeTouch SystemsJanuary 2007 March 2009 March 1, 2009 N/A For internal collaboration and knowledge management: SaaS & hosted pricingProprietary softwareProprietary No ? Yes J2EE/Java (programming language)JavaSQL/LDAPScrewTurn Wiki ScrewTurn Software September 3, 2006 2.0.36 January 10, 2009 N/A Free GPL Yes ? Yes ASP.NET, C Sharp (programming language)C#MySql, Microsoft SQL Server or flat-fileSmallWiki Lukas Renggli, ... ???? Free MIT LicenceMIT Yes ??Squeak?Socialtext Socialtext 2003 3.0.2.1 October 2008 3.0.2.1

Pricing varies. Available deployment options include: free open-source and VMware image downloads, hosted services and dedicated appliances.Open-source and commercial licensing options? No ?PerlPostgreSQLSpringnoteOpenmaru; NCsoftMarch 2007 Beta October 2007 N/A Free Proprietary No ISO8859-1, UTF-8, Shift JIS, EUC-KR Yes Ruby on RailsMySQLSwikiMark Guzdial; Jochen Rick October 1999 1.5 December 6, 2005 N/A Free GNU General Public LicenseGPL Yes ??SqueakFile systemSycamore (software)Sycamore Philip Neustrom May 2006 1.0 May 17, 2006MoinMoin Free GNU General Public LicenseGPL Yes ??Python (programming language)PythonPostgreSQLThoughtFarmer ThoughtFarmer May 2006 3.5.1 June 3, 2009 N/A $109/user Proprietary No UTF-8 Yes ASP.NET, C Sharp (programming language)C#Microsoft SQL ServerTiddlyWiki Jeremy Ruston September 2004 2.4.1 August 4, 2008 N/A Free BSD licensesBSD Yes ??JavaScript Single file, MySQL (mod) TigerWiki Chabel.org July 2005 2.19 November 2, 2006roWiki Free GNU General Public LicenseGPL Yes ??PHPFile systemTikiWiki CMS/Groupware Luis Argerich (200+ devs nowadays) October 9, 2002 3.1 June 27, 2009 N/A Free GNU Lesser General Public LicenseLGPL Yes UTF-8 Yes PHPMySQL, PostgreSQL or Oracle databaseOracle via ADOdbTraction TeamPage Traction Software December 1, 1999 4.1 December 24, 2008 N/A Enterprise wiki, blog, discussion, live blogging, tagging, document management for internal / external collaboration and communities: free for up to 5 users, pricing starts at $3750 / year for 25 usersProprietary softwareProprietary No UTF-8, ... Supports multi-lingual content(and supports i18n) Java SE/Java (programming language)Java Flat File and File System / WebDAV for Attachments TWiki Peter Thoeny October 1998 4.2.2 August 11, 2008JosWikiFree download at twiki.org; twiki.net offers Certified TWiki Virtual Appliance with/without support, and paid hosting solutionsGNU General Public LicenseGPL Yes ISO8859-1, UTF-8 Yes PerlFlat-file, Revision Control SystemRCS, pluggable storage backend UseModWiki Clifford Adams January 22, 2000 1.0 September 12, 2003AtisWiki Free GNU General Public LicenseGPL Yes ??PerlFlat-fileWackoWiki Roman Ivanov March 2003 R4.3.rc September 12, 2008WakkaWiki Free BSD licenseBSD Yes ? Yes PHPMySQLWiclear David Jobet June 25, 2004 0.10 March 26, 2006 N/A Free GNU General Public LicenseGPL Yes ??PHPMySQLWiki ServerApple Computer comes with OS X Server Proprietary softwareProprietary No WikiCrowd Stas Davydov June 4, 2009 0.0.7 July 20, 2009 N/A Free LGPL Yes UTF-8 Yes PHP, XSL, JavaScriptXMLWikispaces Tangient LLC March 18, 2005May 15, 2009Free & Paid options available Proprietary No UTF-8 Yes PHPMySQL, MogileFSWikiwig Steve Goldman (Formerly Starcrouz) July 20, 2004 R5.01 May 28, 2008 Wikiwig 4.x Free GNU General Public LicenseGPL Yes ? Yes PHPMySQLWikkaWiki Wikka Development Team May 16, 2004 1.1.6.7 June 15, 2009WakkaWiki Free GNU General Public LicenseGPL Yes ISO8859-1 No PHPMySQL wiki, WikiWikiWebWard Cunningham 1995 ? ? Apple HyperCard see QuickWiki ? ? ? Perl ? WikkiTikkiTavi Tavi ? 0.26 ? N/A Free GNU General Public LicenseGPL Yes ??PHPMySQLWikyBlog Josh Schmidt September 2005 1.7.1.1 March 3, 2009 N/A Free GNU General Public LicenseGPL Yes UTF-8 Yes PHPMySQLXWiki Ludovic Dubost February 2004 1.8.3 May 9, 2009 Twiki Free GNU Library General Public LicenseLGPL Yes UTF-8 Yes Java (programming language)JavaPostgreSQL, MySQL, Oracle, Apache Derby, HSQLDB ZWiki Simon Michael November 5, 1999 0.61.0 October 28, 2008 N/A Free GNU General Public LicenseGPL Yes UTF-8 Yes Python (programming language)PythonZope Object DatabaseZODB - Zope Object Database Creator First public release date Latest stable release Stable release date Predecessor Cost (USD) Software license Open source Encoding Multilingual Programming language Data managementData backend

Target audience

Wiki software	Public	Private	Corporate/Enterprise	Education	Intranet	Personal
ArtificialMemory	No	No	Yes	Yes	Yes	Yes
Axosoft OnTime	No	Yes	Yes	Yes	Yes	
Bitweaver	Yes	Yes	Yes	Yes	Yes	Yes
BrainKeeper	Yes	Yes	Yes	Yes	?	
BusinessWiki	Yes	Yes	Yes	Yes	Yes	Yes
Central Desktop	Yes	Yes	Yes	Yes	No	
Clearspace	Yes	Yes	Yes	Yes	Yes	No
codeBeamer	Yes	Yes	Yes	Yes	Yes	Yes
Comindwork	Yes	Yes	Yes	Yes	Yes	
Confluence	Yes	Yes	Yes	Yes	Yes	Yes
Corendal Wiki			Yes			
coWiki	Yes	Yes	Yes			
MindTouch Deki	Yes	Yes	Yes	Yes	Yes	
DidiWiki						Yes
DokuWiki	Yes	Yes	Yes	Yes	Yes	Yes
EditMe	Yes	Yes	Yes	Yes	Yes	
FlexWiki	Yes	Yes	Yes			
Foswiki	Yes	Yes	Yes	Yes	Yes	Yes
Gitit	Yes	Yes	Yes	Yes	Yes	Yes
GroupSwim Collaboration	Yes	Yes	Yes	Yes	Yes	
HOawiki CMS/groupware	Yes	Yes	Yes	Yes	Yes	Yes
Instiki	Yes	Yes				Yes
IpbWiki	Yes	Yes	Yes			
JAMWiki	Yes	Yes	Yes	Yes	Yes	
JotSpot	Yes	Yes	Yes			
JSPWiki	Yes	Yes	Yes	Yes	Yes	
Kerika	Yes	Yes	Yes	Yes		
MediaWiki	Yes	No[28]	Yes			
Midgard Wiki	Yes	Yes	Yes			
MoinMoin	Yes	Yes	Yes	Yes	Yes	Yes

Wiki software	Public	Private	Corporate/Enterprise	Education	Intranet	Personal
MojoMojo	Yes	Yes	Yes	Yes	Yes	Yes
Near-Time	Yes	Yes	Yes	Yes	Yes	
OddMuseWiki	Yes	Yes	Yes	Yes	Yes	
OpenWiki	Yes	Yes	Yes			
PBworks	Yes	Yes	Yes	Yes	Yes	
Personal_PPC_Wiki						Yes
Perspective						
PhpWiki	Yes	Yes	Yes	Yes	Yes	
PmWiki	Yes	Yes				
Portili TeamWiki	Yes	Yes	Yes	Yes	Yes	Yes
SamePage	Yes	Yes	Yes	Yes	No	
ScrewTurn Wiki	Yes	Yes	Yes	Yes	Yes	
Socialtext	Yes	Yes	Yes	Yes	Yes	
Springnote	Yes	Yes	Yes	Yes	Yes	
Swiki	Yes	Yes		Yes		
Sycamore	Yes	Yes				
ThoughtFarmer			Yes		Yes	
TiddlyWiki		Yes				Yes
TigerWiki	Yes	Yes	Yes	Yes	Yes	
TikiWiki CMS/Groupware	Yes	Yes	Yes	Yes	Yes	Yes
Traction TeamPage	Yes	Yes	Yes	Yes	Yes	
TWiki	Yes	Yes	Yes	Yes	Yes	
UseModWiki	Yes	Yes	Yes	Yes	Yes	
WackoWiki	Yes	Yes	Yes	Yes	Yes	
Wiclear	Yes	Yes				
WikiCrowd	Yes	Yes	Yes	Yes	Yes	Yes
Wikispaces	Yes	Yes	Yes	Yes	Yes	Yes
Wikiwig	Yes	Yes	Yes	Yes	Yes	
WikkaWiki	Yes	Yes	Yes	Yes	Yes	Yes
WikkiTikkiTavi	Yes					
WikyBlog	Yes	Yes	Yes	Yes	Yes	Yes
XWiki	Yes	Yes	Yes	Yes	Yes	Yes
ZWiki	Yes	Yes	Yes	Yes	Yes	

Features 1

	File uploading / attachments	Spam prevention	Page access control[29]	Inline HTML[30]	User-customizable interface[31]	Document renaming	
ArtificialMe	Yes	No	Yes	Yes	Yes	Yes	
Axosoft OnTime	Yes	No	Yes	Yes	Yes	Yes	
Bitweaver	Yes	Yes, CAPTCHA for registration and anonymous edits or comments.	Yes	Yes	Yes, themes, modules, layout	Yes	
BrainKeeper	Yes	Yes, CAPTCHA	No	Yes	Yes[32]	Yes	
BusinessWi	Yes	Yes, CAPTCHA	Yes	Yes	Yes, templates and themes, html and css	Yes, links are updated	
Central Desktop	Yes	Yes, CAPTCHA	No	Yes	Yes, templates and themes, html and css	No	
Clearspace	Yes	optional	Yes, extensive permissions API	Yes	Yes	No, scheduled for 3.0	
Comindwo	Yes	No	Yes	Yes	Yes, templates and themes	Yes	
codeBeam	Yes	No	Yes	optional	Partial - JSP pages + CSS	Yes, links don't break	
Confluence	Yes	Yes, CAPTCHA	Yes	optional	Yes, templates and themes + CSS	Yes, links are updated	
Corendal Wiki	Yes	No	Yes	Yes	Partial - Velocity templates + CSS	Yes	
coWiki	No	No	Yes, due to UNIX-style permissions	No	Partial - hand-edited templates, document "Print version"	Yes, all pages are seamlessly updated	
MindTouch Deki	Yes	Yes	Yes	optional	Yes	Yes	

	File uploading / attachments	Spam prevention	Page access control[29]	Inline HTML[30]	User-customizable interface[31]	Document renaming	
DidiWiki	No	No	No	escaped	Partial - style-sheets	rename the document file	
DokuWiki	Yes	Yes, blacklist	Yes, optional	Yes, optional	Yes, templates, CSS, PHP; heavily documented PHP API [33]	Yes, plugin	
EditMe	Yes	No, blacklist	Yes, optional	Yes	Partial - CSS, XSLT, user editable navigation	Yes	
FlexWiki	Yes	Yes, blacklist, CAPTCHA, nofollow	Yes	Yes, plugin	Partial - CSS, templates, WikiTalk	Yes, old page becomes a redirect	
Foswiki	Yes	Yes[34]	Yes	Yes	templates, skins, user CSS	Yes, fixing backlinks	
Gitit	Yes	Yes: reCaptcha, blacklist, etc.	Yes	Yes	templates, user CSS	Yes	
GroupSwim Collaboration	Yes	Yes, blacklist, CAPTCHA	Yes	Yes	Partial - preset skins	Yes	
HOAwiki	Yes	Yes, CAPTCHA for registration & anonymous edits or comments, banning, encrypted email addresses	Yes	Yes	Yes - themes, User CSS, templates, modules	Yes	
Instiki	Yes	No	No	Yes	Partial - CSS	No	
	File uploading / attachments	Spam prevention	Page access control[29]	Inline HTML[30]	User-customizable interface[31]	Document renaming	
IpbWiki	Yes	Yes	Yes	Yes	Partial - many features are user-customizable, templates	Yes, old page becomes a redirect	
JAMWiki	Yes	Yes, content by regexp	Yes	Yes, optional	Yes - templates and editable CSS stylesheet topic	Yes, old page becomes a redirect	
JotSpot	Yes	No	Yes	Yes, optional	Partial - CSS	Yes	

JSPWiki	Yes	Yes, content by regexp, CAPTCHA, Akismet, bot detection	Yes	Yes, optional	Partial - templates	Yes
Kerika	Yes	Yes, ACL for each project	Yes	No	Partial - customizable toolbar	Yes, full document management
MediaWiki	Yes	Yes, URL blacklist, word blacklist, IP blocking, captchas (as used on wikinews)[35]	Yes	Yes	Partial - many features are user-customizable, templates	Yes, old page becomes a redirect
Midgard Wiki	Yes	No	Yes	Yes	Partial templates, CSS	No
MoinMoin	Yes	Yes, BadContent filtering via Regular Expressions, Textchas	Yes, very flexible ACLs, wiki-editable groups	Yes - safe	Yes - Themes, templates, CSS, XSLT, user editable navigation	Yes, old page can be a redirect
MojoMojo	Yes	Yes, CAPTCHA	Yes, Cascading ACL control allowing stewardship of topics	Yes - safe	Yes - Themes, CSS	Yes, current: page redirect, soon: Node moving
Near-Time	Yes	Yes	Yes	Yes	Yes, templates, html, custom navigation portal, custom data fields, CSS	Yes
OddMuseW	Yes	Yes	Yes	Yes, plugin	CSS	Yes
OpenWiki	Yes	Yes	Yes	No		
OpenLink Wiki	Yes	Yes	Yes	Yes	templates, skins, user CSS, XSLT	Yes
PAUX	Yes	Yes	Yes	Yes	templates, skins, user CSS	Yes
PBworks	Yes	Yes - passwords, SSO-capable integration, ACLs, IP whitelisting/blacklisting	Yes	Yes, and plugins	Partial - CSS	No

	File uploading / attachments	Spam prevention	Page access control[29]	Inline HTML[30]	User-customizable interface[31]	Document renaming	
Personal_PPC_	No	No	No	Yes	Partial - style-sheets	rename the document file	
Perspective	Yes		Yes (per collection)	parameterized Raw Includes, in-page XSLT	XSLT, CSS	Yes, with aliases	
PhpWiki	Yes	Yes, CPAN Blog::SpamAssassin	Yes	plugin	themes; un-documented	Yes	
PmWiki	Yes	Yes[36]	Yes	Yes, module	Yes, themes, per page/per group CSS, ...	Yes, module	
Portili TeamWiki	Yes	Yes, only authorized users can edit pages. Anonymous comments (if enabled) are disguised from spam robots.	Yes, includes user/group management functions	Yes, Safe	Yes, CSS	Yes	
SamePage	Yes	Yes	Yes	Yes	Yes	Yes	
Socialtext	Yes	Yes	Yes	Yes	Yes	Yes	
	File uploading / attachments	**Spam prevention**	**Page access control[29]**	**Inline HTML[30]**	**User-customizable interface[31]**	**Document renaming**	
Springnote	Yes	Yes	Yes	Yes	Background color customization	Yes	
Swiki	Yes	Yes, block IP Addresses, words, UserIDs	Yes	Yes	For AniAniWebs, CSS	Yes, updating all backlinks	
Sycamore	Yes	Yes, block IP Addresses, UserIDs, hidden email addresses, CAPTCHA	Yes	No	user CSS, themes	Yes, old page redirects	
ThoughtFar	Yes	N/A	Yes	Yes	Yes	Yes	
TiddlyWiki	No	No	No	Yes, plugin	Yes, themes, user CSS, modules	Yes	

TigerWiki	No	No, to be coded	Yes, password protection	No	Partial - style-sheets, template	No	
TikiWiki CMS/Groupware	Yes	Yes, CAPTCHA for registration and anonymous edits or comments, encrypted email addresses. [37]	Yes	Yes	themes, user CSS, modules	Yes	
Traction TeamPage	Yes, with WebDAV versioning	Yes, CAPTCHA for registration, block lists	Yes	Yes Safe	Yes, workspace templates, color templates, and developer tools	Yes, links are updated automatically and name history maintained	
TWiki	Yes	Yes[38]	Yes	Yes	templates, skins, user CSS	Yes, fixing backlinks	
UseModWi	Yes	Yes, IP blacklist	Yes?	Yes?	CSS	Yes, admins only	
WackoWiki	Yes	Yes, referrer blacklist	Yes	Yes - configurable/safe	themes, style-sheets	Yes	
Wiclear	Yes	Yes, blacklist captcha	Yes, available for plugin too	Yes	themes, style-sheets	Yes	
WikiCrowd	No	No	Yes	No	No	No	
Wikispaces	Yes	Yes, CAPTCHA	Yes	Yes	Yes, themes, HTML, CSS	Yes	
Wikiwig	Yes	Yes,Captcha	Yes	Yes	Partial	Yes	
WikkaWiki	Yes	Yes, referrer blacklist (module), HTTP REQUEST analysis (module)	Yes	Yes - configurable/safe	style-sheets	No	
WikkiTikkiT	Yes	Yes, Captcha	No	Yes - configurable/safe	style-sheets	No	

WikyBlog	Yes	Yes, Captcha, ACL	Yes	Yes	Yes - html, CSS	Yes	
XWiki	Yes	{{yes, Captcha, ACL}}	Yes	Yes	style-sheets, templates, themes	Yes	
ZWiki	Yes	Yes	Yes	Yes	style-sheets, templates, skins	Yes	
	File uploading / attachments	Spam prevention	Page access control[29]	Inline HTML[30]	User-customizable interface[31]	Document renaming	

Features 2

	WYSIWYG editing	Web feeds	Extensibility	Cross-wiki support	Other features
ArtificialMemory	Yes	Yes, RSS	No	No	[39]
Axosoft OnTime	Yes	No	Yes	No	[40]
BrainKeeper	Yes	Yes, RSS			[41]
Bitweaver	Yes, with FCKeditor or via Quicktag [42] insertion	Yes	Yes	Yes, through PEAR plugins	[43]
BusinessWiki	Yes	Yes, RSS, Newsletter	Plug-ins, Mediawiki extensions, Google Gadgets, Google Apps		[44]
Central Desktop	Yes	Yes, RSS			[45]
Clearspace	Yes	Yes	Yes, both functionality and theme via plugins	No	
Comindwork	Yes	Yes, RSS	No	No	[46]
codeBeamer	Yes with TinyMCE or Microsoft Word	No	Yes, Java Plug-ins		[47]
Confluence	Yes	Yes, RSS	Java Plug-ins, User Macros in Apache Velocity		[48]
Corendal Wiki	Yes	No	patch mechanism		[49]
coWiki	?	Yes, RSS[50]	plugins via an OOP interface		[51]

	WYSIWYG editing	Web feeds	Extensibility	Cross-wiki support	Other features
MindTouch Deki	Yes	Yes, RSS, XML, JSON	API, Service Oriented Architecture		[52]
DidiWiki	No	No			[53]
DokuWiki	Yes Quickbuttons [54]	Yes, RSS/Atom[55]	Yes, Plugin API	Yes	[56]
EditMe	Yes	Yes, RSS	javascript		[57]
FlexWiki	No	Yes, RSS	ASP, WikiTalk, .Net Reflection plugins		Forms, Scripting, Integrated Weblog and Threaded Message Forum
Foswiki	Yes, pre-installed plugin	Yes, RSS/Atom, with search string	400+ extensions; Plugin API for developers; Topic markup/scripting for users to create wiki applications	Yes, user selectable wiki syntax with EditSyntaxPlugin	[58]
Gitit	Markdown	No		No	[59]
UseModWiki	Nc?	Yes	extensions		
GroupSwim Collaboration	Yes	Yes, RSS, Daily Digests	Plug-ins, Google Gadgets and docs, Zoho Docs	Yes	[60]
HOAwiki CMS/groupware	Yes, with FCKeditor	Yes, RSS/Atom/RDF	Hundreds of features, plugins, modules & mods	Yes	[61]
Instiki	No	Yes, RSS	fairly trivial with minimal Ruby knowledge	Yes, can use different administrator-set) markup languages.	[62]
	WYSIWYG editing	**Web feeds**	**Extensibility**	**Cross-wiki support**	**Other features**
IpbWiki	No	Yes, RSS/Atom	actions, handlers		[63]
JAMWiki	Partial, optional editing buttons	Yes, RSS			Plugin wiki syntax parser (default is Mediawiki syntax)
JotSpot	Yes	Yes, RSS, per page	plugins, server-side Javascript		[64]

JSPWiki	Partial, alpha	Yes, RSS, per page	plugins, filters, providers		Weblog integration
Kerika	Yes, full graphical Wiki features	No	not yet		[65]
MediaWiki	No	Yes, RSS/Atom	actions, handlers		[66]
Midgard Wiki	No	Yes, RSS, all changes	PHP component architecture		CMS integration
MoinMoin	Yes, v1.5+	Yes, RSS, last changes	different plugin types	Yes, selectable parsers	[67]
MojoMojo	Yes, With live preview	Yes, RSS	Yes, plugins and custom additions types	Yes, Multiple markup parsers available	[68]
Near-Time	Yes	Yes, RSS in/out	API		[69]
OddMuseWiki	Yes, plugin	Yes	plugins		[70]
OpenWiki	No				
OpenLink Wiki	Yes	Yes, RSS/Atom/RDF	plugins, Virtuoso hosted PHP integration	Yes, publish wiki in other formats (Docbook and HTML)	[71]
PAUX	Yes	Yes, RSS/Atom/RDF	actions		[72]
PBworks	Yes	Yes, RSS/Atom	API, AuthAPI, plugins, wikilets		[73]
P_ersonal_PPC_Wi	No	No			[74] [75]
Perspective	Yes, IE, Mozilla & Firefox	Yes, RSS (last day's changes)	HTML Includes, XSLT includes that can take external URL contents, .Net action classes		[76]
PhpWiki		Yes RSS/Atom/RDF: global, per page or per user	plugins		support all databases
PmWiki	No	Yes	very, 100+ plugins	WikiCreole (option) [77]	[78]
Portili TeamWiki	Yes	No	Yes, This wiki will integrate seamlessly with Portili blog & other Portili web-apps (to be launched soon).	No	Exceptionally easy to use with easy user/group management.
SamePage	Yes	Yes, RSS feeds,	plugins		

	WYSIWYG editing	Web feeds	Extensibility	Cross-wiki support	Other features
Socialtext	Yes	Yes, RSS feeds, Google/Technorati search results	using REST/SOAP APIs		[79]
Springnote	Yes	Yes, RSS feeds, Google search results	API, plugins, mashups, widgets	No	[80]
Swiki	No		Some		[81]
Sycamore	No	Yes, RSS each page, bookmarks RSS			[82]
ThoughtFarmer	Yes	Yes	Plugins, API used by ThoughtFarmer Professional Services		[83]
TiddlyWiki	No	Yes, RSS	plugins		
TigerWiki	No	Yes, RSS with plugin	Code modification		[84]
TikiWiki CMS/Groupware	Yes, with FCKeditor or via Quicktag [85] insertion	Yes, RSS/Atom/RDF	Hundreds of features, plugins, modules & mods	No	[86]
Traction TeamPage	Yes	Yes, Dynamic RSS inbound / outbound	Plug-in architecture for widgets, forms, interface and function modifications		[87]
TWiki	Yes, pre-installed plugin	Yes, RSS/Atom, with search string	400+ extensions; Plugin API for developers; TWiki markup/scripting for users to create wiki applications	Yes, user selectable wiki syntax with EditSyntaxPlugin	[88]
UseModWiki	No?	Yes	extensions		
WackoWiki	Yes, WikiEdit [89]	Yes, RSS	actions, handlers		[90]
Wiclear	No	Yes, RSS/Atom	plugins		[91]
Wikispaces	Yes	Yes, RSS/Atom	API, widgets, single sign-on (SSO)		[92]
Wikiwig	Yes, Xinha	No	Some		

WikkaWiki	Yes, WikiEdit [89]	Yes, Single page/Comments/Global	actions, handlers		[93]
WikkiTikkiTavi	No		bunch of custom stuff in php		
WikyBlog	No	Yes	Plugins, Plugin API		
XWiki	Yes, using TinyMCE	Yes, RSS	plugins, macros, scripts, applications		[94]
ZWiki	Yes, using Epoz	Yes, RSS/Atom	all Zope plugins, LaTeX, and more		[95]
	WYSIWYG editing	**Web feeds**	**Extensibility**	**Cross-wiki support**	**Other features**

Installation

	Platform	**Ease of installation[96]**	**Web-server required**	**Other software required**	**Installable to USB stick**
ArtificialMemory	SaaS - hosted	Hosted - no installation or setup required	None	None	
Axosoft OnTime	SaaS (hosted) or Installed on MS Platform	Hosted requires no installation or Installed has easy-to-use Wizard	IIS	MS SQL Express or Full MS SQL Server	
Bitweaver	Linux, Unix, MSW & others	Easy	Any Web-server with PHP	PHP	
BrainKeeper	NA - hosted	Hosted - no installation or setup required	None	None	
BusinessWiki	Linux, Unix, MSW & others OR hosted (no set required)	Moderately simple	Apache or IIS with PHP 5.0+	MySQL, PHP5	
Central Desktop	NA - hosted	Hosted - no set required	None	None	

Clearspace	Java 1.5 + one of: Windows Server 2003 SP2, Linux (2.6 Kernel), Solaris 10	Easy, configuration wizard or hosted	Tomcat, WebLogic, WebSphere	MS SQL, Postgres, MySQL or Oracle	
Comindwork	SaaS (hosted) or Installed on MS Platform	Hosted - no installation or setup required	IIS	MS SQL Express or Full MS SQL Server	
codeBeamer	Any OS that supports Java 1.5 and servlet 2.4	Easy	Tomcat included, or use your own servlet container.	Java 1.5	
Confluence	Any OS that supports Java 1.4 and servlet 2.4	Easy, Configuration Wizard	Tomcat included, or use your own servlet container.	Java 1.4	
Corendal Wiki	Any OS that supports Java 1.4 and servlet 2.4	Moderately simple	Tomcat, Oracle Application Server	Java, MySQL or Oracle, Tomcat or Oracle Application Server	
coWiki	Linux, Unix, MSW & others		Apache with PHP	MySQL, PHP	
MindTouch Deki	Linux, Unix, MSW & others	Hosted [97], Moderately simple, Appliance [98]	Apache, IIS6, IIS7, IIS8	Mono, MySQl, PHP	
DidiWiki	Linux, Unix, MSW & others	simple	None (built-in)	none	
DokuWiki	Linux, Unix, MSW & others	Moderately simple	Should work on any web server with PHP	PHP	Yes

EditMe	hosted	None Required	None Required	None	
FlexWiki	Linux, Unix, MSW & others	Moderately simple	IIS/Apache	ASP.Net/Mono	
Foswiki	Linux, Unix, MSW & others	Native install: Easy on *nix, moderately difficult on MS-Windows.	Any Web-server with cgi support. Web-server included in VMware appliance downloads.	Perl, RCS	
GroupSwim Collaboration	SaaS - hosted	Hosted - no installation required	None	None	N/A
HOAwiki CMS/Groupware	SaaS - hosted	Hosted - no installation or setup required	None	None	N/A
Instiki	Linux, Unix, MSW & others	Trivial	None (built-in)	Ruby	
	Platform	**Ease of installation**[96]	**Web-server required**	**Other software required**	
IpbWiki	Linux, Macs, Unix, MSW & others	Moderately simple	Apache or IIS with PHP 4+	MySQL, PHP	
JAMWiki	Any OS that supports Java 1.4 and servlet 2.4	Simple, WAR file and one page web-based form	Any servlet 2.4-compliant application server	Java 1.4	
JotSpot	Linux, Unix, MSW & others	Easy, VMware virtual appliance	None (built-in)	VMware Player	
JSPWiki	Any OS that supports Java 1.5 and servlet 2.4	Moderately simple	any servlet 2.4-compliant web server	Java 1.5	

Kerika	Any OS that supports Java 1.5	Very easy (under 2 minutes)	None	Java 1.5	
MediaWiki	Linux, Unix, MSW & others	Moderately simple	Apache or IIS with PHP 5.0+	MySQL, PHP5	
Midgard Wiki	Linux, Unix & others	Easy, requires root	Apache with PHP	MySQL, PHP	
MoinMoin	Linux, Macs, Unix, MSW & others	Easy for Desktop version	None for Desktop version	Python	
MojoMojo	Linux, Macs, Unix, MSW, others	Easy - 4-step process	None - builtin server suitable for desktop or production use	SQL database (MySQL, PostgreSQL, Sqlite)	
Near-Time	NA - hosted	Hosted: no set-up or installation required	None	None	
OddMuseWiki	Linux, Unix, MSW & others	Easy	Any web server with cgi support	Perl	
OpenWiki	MSW & others	Easy	IIS	ASP	
OpenLink Wiki	Linux, Unix, MSW & others	Easy	OpenLink Virtuoso	OpenLink Virtuoso	
PAUX	Any OS that supports Java 1.5	Easy	None (built-in)	Java	
PBwiki	SaaS - hosted	Hosted - no installation or setup required	None	None	
Personal_PPC_Wiki	Windows XP, Windows Mobile 5	simple	None (built-in)	none	Yes
Perspective	MSW & others	Moderately simple	IIS	.NET Runtime 1.1	
PhpWiki	Linux, Unix, MSW & others	Moderately simple	Any Web-server with PHP	PHP	

	Platform	Ease of installation[96]	Web-server required	Other software required	
PmWiki	Linux, Unix, MSW & others	Very Easy	Any Web-server with PHP, can run without a web server.	PHP	Yes
Portili TeamWiki	Linux, Unix, MSW & others	Moderately simple	Apache or IIS with PHP 5.0+	MySQL, PHP5	
Socialtext	NA - hosted	hosted service without installation as an option; appliance option available with managed service for remote upgrades and administration	no, all required components included	no, all required components included	
	Platform	**Ease of installation[96]**	**Web-server required**	**Other software required**	
Springnote	NA - hosted	Hosted - no installation or setup required	None	None	
Swiki	Linux, Unix, MSW & others	Very Easy: Just drag the image file over the executable or (non-GUI) just use the image file as an executable parameter	None--installs own server. Can coexist with IIS and Apache by running on alternate port	None	
Sycamore	Linux, Unix & others	Easy	Apache	Python (with Image Library), MySQL/PostgreSQL, Xapian	
ThoughtFarmer	MSW & others	Managed installation -- Easy	MS-Windows Server 2003 or 2008	MS SQL Server 2005 or 2008	
TiddlyWiki	MSW & others	Easy	None	None	Yes
TigerWiki	Linux, Unix & others	Easy	Any Web-server with PHP	PHP	
TikiWiki CMS/Groupware	Linux, Unix, MSW & others	Moderately simple via install script. Telnet/ssh is useful but not necessary.	Any Web-server with PHP	PHP	Yes
Traction TeamPage	Any OS capable of running Java 2 Virtual Machine	Easy, Installation Wizard installs all components	None (Built-In)	None	

	Platform	Ease of installation[96]	Web-server required	Other software required	Installable to USB stick
TWiki	Linux, Unix, MSW & others	Native install: Easy on *nix, moderately difficult on MS-Windows.	Any Web-server with cgi support. Web-server included in VMware appliance [99] and TWiki for MS-Windows Personal [100].	Perl, RCS	
UseModWiki	Linux, Unix, MSW & others	Easy	Any web server with cgi support	Perl	
WackoWiki	Linux, Unix, MSW & others	Quick and easy, multilingual installer	Apache v1.3.x (v2 recommended), IIS	MySQL, PHP	
Wiclear	Linux, Unix & others	Easy, in 4 steps, update wizard	Apache with PHP. IIS untested	MySQL, PHP	
Wikispaces	SaaS - hosted	Hosted - no installation or setup required	None	None	
Wikiwig	Linux, Unix, MSW & others	Easy	Any with PHP	MySQL, PHP	
WikkaWiki	Linux, Unix, MSW & others	Easy installation/upgrade, through web-wizard	Any Web-server with PHP	MySQL/PHP	
WikkiTikkiTavi	Linux, Unix & others	Moderate	Any Web-server with PHP	MySQL/PHP	
WikyBlog	Linux, Unix, MSW & others	Moderately simple	Apache or IIS with PHP 4.1+	MySQL 4.0+	
XWiki	Java Platform	Simple package for MS-Windows Available, Simple JAR autoinstaller for any platform	Any J2EE webserver	Java	
ZWiki	Linux, Unix, MSW & others	Moderate (easy if Zope is already installed)	Zope	Python (included with most Zope installs)	

See also

- → Comparison of wiki farms
- List of wiki software
- → List of wikis
- Wiki software

External links

- What Is Wiki [101] - general Wiki info.
- Wiki Matrix [66] - Comparison of wikis and features selected by the user.

References

[1] Licenses here are a summary, and are not taken to be complete statements of the licenses. Some packages may use libraries under different licenses.

[2] Enterprise Subscriptions start at +$500/month

[3] Subscriptions start at $5/month

[4] Subscriptions start at $150/month

[5] Free Ver Available, Paid plans start at $25/month

[6] For internal collaboration and communities of practice: free for up to 5 users, additional users $59/user/year

[7] including: MySQL, Oracle, PostgreSQL, IBM DB2 and Microsoft SQL Server

[8] Free for 1 project, $29 and up for more

[9] Free (open source project or community or personal), $1200– 8000 commercial, $600– 4000 academic

[10] Commercial, Academic, Community, Personal, Open Source Project

[11] (PostgreSQL, MySQL, Oracle, DB2, MS SQL Server)

[12] Free & open-source edition, paid enterprise edition, and free and paid hosted versions offered.

[13] Foswiki mailing list - Database store (somewhat) (http://n2.nabble.com/ Database-store-(somewhat)-td3443836.html#a3443836)

[14] For internal collaboration: priced on a per user/month basis

[15] Subscriptions start at $28/month

[16] Instiki - Ruby License Instiki is distributed under the same terms as Ruby itself, per the Ruby license (http:// ruby.mirror.easynet.be/en/LICENSE.txt).

[17] Free for the basic version, 30$/year for full version

[18] $9.95/month/user; free for anyone with ".edu" email address

[19] Starts at $24.99 per month for unlimited spaces and unlimited users

[20] Free and Commercial License

[21] Free & Paid options available

[22] For internal collaboration and knowledge management: SaaS & hosted pricing

[23] Pricing varies. Available deployment options include: free open-source and VMware image downloads, hosted services and dedicated appliances.

[24] Open-source and commercial licensing options

[25] Enterprise wiki, blog, discussion, live blogging, tagging, document management for internal / external collaboration and communities: free for up to 5 users, pricing starts at $3750/ year for 25 users

[26] Free download at twiki.org; twiki.net offers Certified TWiki Virtual Appliance with/without support, and paid hosting solutions

[27] Free & Paid options available

[28] http://www.mediawiki.org/wiki/Manual:Preventing_access#Simple_private_wiki

[29] Page Access Control: Some wiki engines allow (optional) read/write access restriction to users or user groups on a per-page basis (e.g. through Access control lists).

[30] Inline HTML *Safe* means that several features of HTML are restricted. This is better than *Full*, for security reasons. Users with complete access to HTML could, for example, create spoof forms to trick users.

[31] User-customizable interface: Many items have administrator hand-editable templates. Even items which use hard-coded templates could still be modified if the source is available.

[32] templates, html, custom navigation portal, custom data fields

[33] http://dev.splitbrain.org/reference/dokuwiki/nav.html?inc/template.php.html

[34] IP blacklist, content by regexp, excessive activities, scripted registration prevention (plugin), hidden e-mail addresses

[35] URL anding are available using a MediaWiki extension. (http://mail.wikipedia.org/pipermail/wikitech-l/2005-December/033270.html)

[36] word/URL block (addon, auto-upd. database), URL-approval (option), encrypt e-mails (addon), nofollow, Captcha (addon)

[37] Documentation about Spam Protection for TikiWiki. (http://doc.tikiwiki.org/Spam+Protection)

[38] IP blacklist, content by regexp, excessive activities, scripted registration prevention (plugin), hidden e-mail addresses

[39] Ajax UI; Semantic Wiki; natural language/text import of entities, attributes, and relations; inlclusions (articles in articles); innovative features aimed at cutting edge knowledge workers

[40] Windows and Web UI; Powerful Search; Project Hierarchy; Auto TOC Creation; Latest Edits Page; Powerful security; Integrated project management tools

[41] Enterprise-level Search, Interactive Dashboard, Tagging, Content Workflow, Custom Data Fields, Simple but Comprehensive Administration

[42] http://www.bitweaver.org/wiki/QuicktagsPackage

[43] ACLs, calendar, email notification, maps, multisites, forum, blogs, articles, filegalleries

[44] Enterprise level security, Lotus Notes & Sharepoint integrations, Enterprise admin interface, Idea Management Plugin, TimeTracker plugin, Open Plug-in API, Tagging, E-Mail Notifications, Fully supported

[45] Block architecture, Calendars, Discussions, Database feature, Tasks and Milestones Blocks available

[46] Ajax UI; Semantic Wiki; inlclusions (articles in articles); Tagging, Email-notifications, Enterprise security

[47] Enterprise level security, Integration with Issue Tracker / Document Manager / Continuous Integration, Open API, Tagging, E-Mail Notifications, Commercial support

[48] Enterprise level security, Simple admin interface, Open Plug-in API, Tagging, E-Mail Notifications, Fully supported

[49] For Corporate environments. Articles hierarchy. Integrated with Active Directory users and groups, NTLM authentication, Workflow, Revisions, Subscriptions, WYSIWYG editor, Access Control (Read and Write)

[50] http://www.cowiki.org/184.html

[51] Data saved hierarchic (web trees) and in XML, per-page threaded comments, comfortable installation wizard

[52] Highly usable, stores in XML, SOA, API, enterprise arch and business focused, fully supported by MindTouch company website (http://www.mindtouch.com)

[53] extremely fast and requires very little RAM, built-in web server

[54] http://wiki.splitbrain.org/wiki:quickbuttons

[55] http://wiki.splitbrain.org/wiki:syndication

[56] Section Editing, XHTML-Compliant, nice tables, side-by-side diff, namespaces, Interwiki

[57] Multi-level access controls, hosted solution, side-by-side diff, Email notifications

[58] Revision control, ACLs for topics, tagging, blogging, calendaring, charting, global search & replace, email notification, form handling and reporting, platform to build wiki applications, graphing, slideshow presentations, 13 translations, plotting, multistyle diffs, advanced searching, spreadsheet calculations, WYSIWYG supports TML, available as a VMware appliance

[59] Version control with [Git|Git_(software)] or now [darcs|Darcs], slideshow presentations, LaTeX math, readers can output pages in RTF, ODT, LaTeX,

[60] Multi-level access controls, hosted solution, side-by-side version comparison, Email notifications

[61] Calendaring, charting, directory, newsletters, email notification, form handling and reporting, slideshow presentations, spreadsheet calculations and GRAPHS, mobile, GIS (MapServer), 3d Browsing, Workflows, accounting package, invoicing, ecommerce

[62] Trivial to set up on any platform that supports Ruby. Supports inline HTML, Textile, Markdown, and RDoc.

[63] Integration with Invision Power Board, bbcode support

[64] Support for server-side Javascript, VMware virtual appliance

[65] Graphical wiki with hybrid peer-to-peer networking, can send project updates by email to non-users, can create private networks

[66] Per-article discussion page, watchlist, searching, email notification (built in, but currently disabled on Wikipedia)

[67] Enterprise level security, authentication, and authorization, Email notification, additional desktop edition, XML-RPC content synchronization, searching in attachments (v1.6+).

[68] Hierarchical node structure and cascading permissions system allows for stewardship of topics. Version control and ability to do 3-way merge on conflict.

[69] Enterprise level security, Simple admin interface, Categorizing and Tagging, Analytics, Premium Business Engine, Fully supported

[70] very easily extensible, themeable, easy setup of wiki farms

[71] Based on WebDAV can be maintained by any WebDAV user agent, LDAP Integration, OpenLink Data Space Integration, Wiki Cluster and Tag support, WYSIWIG Editor, Revisions, Access Control List

[72] Individualized publication of dynamic content, which contains reusable semantic content objects. They are able to represent knowledge in its full complexity, and they make knowledge available as filterable content for Websites, semantic Wiki, detailed-evaluated eLearning and individualized print media.

[73] SideBars; Discussions; email notifications w/diffs; SSO integration capability; Statistics; PDF output; HTML slideshows; integrated modules for calendars, spreadsheets, audio chat, and more; fully UTF-8 compliant; Tagging.

[74] extremely fast and requires very little RAM, built-in web server

[75] Open-source and commercial licensing options

[76] Searching over MS Office documents, can search files in folders outside of the Wiki (including MS Office files), Active Directory integration, User authorisation based on AD Group membership, Private Content

[77] The PmWiki markup rules are easily modifiable and replaceable by plug-ins, should a need for another wikimarkup family be demonstrated.

[78] Highly sophisticated support for customization. Practically cameleon-like

[79] accessible through REST/SOAP APIs

[80] API that provides usage of all service features, Opensource WYSIWYG editor - Xquared, importing of various file formats (doc, odt, txt, html), multi-file uploading, clean UI, group wiki, XML-RPC, tags, revision control, full text search, e-mail notification, various templates, video insertion features

[81] Installs own webserver (Commanche) and can co-exist with IIS or Apache. AniAniWeb function provides owner control of granular access and creates access groups. Users tracked by email address.

[82] Javascript based quick edit, web based configuration, searching, built-in map function

[83] Structured wiki, granular access controls, faceted browsing, revision control, full text search, email notification, photo albums

[84] All minimal features that a wiki needs

[85] http://doc.tikiwiki.org/Quicktags

[86] ACLs, calendaring, charting, email notification, form handling and reporting, slideshow presentations, spreadsheet calculations and GRAPHS, mobile, GIS (MapServer), JGraphPad for drawings inside wikipages, 3d Browsing, Workspaces, Workflows, OpenOffice WYSIWYG editing of Tikiwiki content, Multitiki installations

[87] Enterprise level security, Multiple workspaces on same TeamPage server, Faceted permissioned search crossing workspaces using content or tag navigation, Page and Comment Moderation, Social tagging, Threaded discussion, Paragraph or page level comments, Document versioning and management via WebDAV, Page Name history to support complex refactoring, Mobile Interface, E-Mail Notifications and Newsletter, IM Notification, Simple web based admin, Authenticate using LDAP or Active Directory (including LDAP queries for group definition, NTLM support for single signon, Optional FAST module provided permission aware drill-down content navigation as well as wiki + attached document search, Java SDK (no charge for Java source and documentation), extensible SDL (Skin Definition Language), Fully supported

[88] Revision control, ACLs for topics, tagging, blogging, calendaring, charting, global search & replace, email notification, form handling and reporting, platform to build wiki applications, graphing, slideshow presentations, 13 translations, plotting, multistyle diffs, advanced searching, spreadsheet calculations, WYSIWYG supports TML, available as a VMware appliance

[89] http://wackowiki.org/Dev/Projects/WikiEdit

[90] WYSIWYG-like editor, ACLs, subpages, comments, files, email notification, cloning of pages, installation wizard...

[91] hierarchical pages, linked translations, multilingual, ACLs, section editing, XHTML compliant, side-by-side diff, email notifications, admin panel, moderator/admin/user

[92] Discussion pages, tagging, email notification, full-text search, user dashboard, localization

[93] FreeMind support, ACLs, cloning of pages, advanced syntax highlighting using GeSHi, *on-the-fly* downloading of codeblocks

[94] Platform to build wiki applications, Forms and Scripting, Multilingual, Database storage, Fulltext search, GraphViz, SVG, Freemind, Lucene, Charting, photo albums, presentations, blogging, calendar, e-mail plugin, virtual wikis, simple table computations, sortable tables, section editing, portlet integration, integrated statistics, XML-RPC API, Tags, PDF/RTF export

[95] hierarchical pages, revision control, fulltext search, email notification, issue tracker, LaTeX integration

[96] " Ease of installation" is expressed relative to other server software packages, and not to desktop applications.

[97] http://wik.is

[98] http://www.mindtouch.com

[99] http://twiki.org/cgi-bin/view/Codev/TWikiVMDebianStable
[100] http://twiki.org/cgi-bin/view/Codev/TWikiForWindowsPersonal
[101] http://www.wiki.org/wiki.cgi?

Content management system

A **content management system (CMS)** such as a document management system (DMS) is a computer application used to manage work flow needed to collaboratively create, edit, review, index, search, publish and archive various kinds of digital media and electronic text.[1]

CMSs are frequently used for storing, controlling, versioning, and publishing industry-specific documentation such as news articles, operators' manuals, technical manuals, sales guides, and marketing brochures. The content managed may include computer files, image media, audio files, video files, electronic documents, and Web content. These concepts represent integrated and interdependent layers. There are various nomenclatures known in this area: Web Content Management, Digital Asset Management, Digital Records Management, Electronic Content Management and so on. The bottom line for these systems is managing content and publishing, with a workflow if required.

Types of CMS

There are six main categories of CMS, with their respective domains of use:

- Enterprise CMS (ECMS)
- Web CMS (WCMS)
- Document management system (DMS)
- Mobile CMS
- Component CMS
- Media content management system
- Also a company CMS Software Limited of Upminster Essex

Enterprise content management systems

An enterprise content management (*ECM*) system is concerned with content, documents, details and records related to the organizational processes of an enterprise. The purpose is to manage the organization's unstructured information content, with all its diversity of format and location.

Web content management systems

A '*web content management*' (WCM) system is a CMS designed to simplify the publication of Web content to Web sites, in particular allowing content creators to submit content without requiring technical knowledge of HTML or the uploading of files.

See also

- Content management
- Digital asset management
- Document management system
- Enterprise content management
- Flash CMS
- List of content management systems
- Semantic wiki

References

[1] " What is a Content Management System, or CMS? (http://www.contentmanager.eu.com/history.htm)". .
    Retrieved 2008-05-18.

List of wikis

This page contains a **list of notable websites that use a → wiki model**.

Name	Focus	Notes	Articles	License
→ Wikipedia	Encyclopedic	Umbrella, multilingual MediaWiki project	12000000+	CC-BY-SA
English Wikipedia	Encyclopedic	Public access, most prominent English wiki	3000000+[1]	CC-BY-SA
Citizendium	Encyclopedic	Requires real names; guided by expert input while allowing edits from the general public	10800+[2]	CC-by-sa 3.0
Scholarpedia	Encyclopedic	Written exclusively by professionals focusing on their field of expertise; subject to peer review	1619 [3]	Copyrighted
Knol	Encyclopedic	A wiki-like technology from Google	100000+[4]	CC-by 3.0
Wikibooks	General—textbooks	A wikimedia project	115200+[5]	GFDL + other
NotePub	General purpose	An online notepad that allows for both public and private content.		
Wikiversity	General—Self-directed learning	Supports free learning communities, projects, materials, and learners; a wikimedia project		GFDL + other
wikiHow	General instruction	A how-to manual	56651+[6]	CC-by-nc-sa 2.5
WikiAnswers	General knowledge	Compiles answers to questions posed	3625500+ Answers [7]	Copyrighted
Everything2	Personal essays	A wiki-like project for essays	273900+[8]	Copyrighted

MeatballWiki	Communities—Online communities		4900+ [9]	Copyrighted
Wikitruth	Social—Criticism of → Wikipedia		200+ [10]	GFDL
Conservapedia	Encyclopedia	Information and articles are written from a Conservative Christian viewpoint aimed at correcting the perceived liberal bias of Wikipedia	30600+ [11]	Copyrighted (free use)
Encyclopedia Dramatica	Satire of Internet memes	A satirical wiki	7400+[12]	Fair use
Uncyclopedia	Satire—Parody	A satirical encyclopedia dedicated to parody	134000+ [13]	CC-by-nc-sa 2.0
Wikiquote	Reference—Quotations	A quote repository, a wikimedia project	90200+[14]	GFDL
Wikisource	Reference—Primary sources	Dedicated to use on → Wikipedia; a wikimedia project	586400+[15]	GFDL
Wikimedia Commons	Misc—Electronic media	A repository of free electronic media; a wikimedia project		CC-SA and other
Biographicon	Misc—Biographies of people	A directory of personal profiles		GFDL
MyWikiBiz	Misc—Business directory	Allows people and enterprises to write about themselves		
International Music Score Library Project	Music	A wiki library of public domain musical scores	14800+[16]	GFDL
LyricWiki	Music—Lyrics	A listing of lyrics by album	722000+[17]	CC-BY-SA
Whole Wheat Radio	Music—Indie music	An online community radio station featuring independent music		
→ Memory Alpha	Fiction—*Star Trek*	Contains canon-only material	29900+[18]	CC-NC 2.5
Wookieepedia	Fiction—*Star Wars*	Science fiction encyclopedia	65000+	GFDL
A Million Penguins	Fiction—collaboratively-written novel		491[19]	Copyrighted
Galaxiki	Fictional galaxy	Dedicated to the creation of a fictional galaxy		
Lostpedia	Fiction—*Lost*			
→ WikiWikiWeb	Computer programming, specifically design patterns	World's oldest wiki (began circa 1995)	33886[20]	GPL
Javapedia	Computers—Java	An online encyclopedia for developing Java		

SWiK	Computers—Open source software			
GeoNames	Places	A geographical database that links specific names with unique features		
City wiki	Places	An umbrella term for a variety of wikis dedicated to cities or other geographic regions		
The Student Room	Place—UK University and student life	Offers UK university guides, revision notes, examples of university personal statements and information on student life and university courses		
DavisWiki	Place—Davis, California	A city wiki dedicated solely to Davis; at one point the largest city wiki	13000+[21]	CC-by 3.0
Galbijim Wiki	Place—South Korea	Written by, and for an audience of South Korean expatriates		
WikiPilipinas	Place—The Philippines	A combined non-academic encyclopedia, web portal, directory and almanac for Philippine-based knowledge		
Travellerspoint	Places—Travel	A social networking site dedicated to sharing stories and recommendations about travel	2400+[22]	CC-SA 3.0
OpenStreetMap	Places—Maps	Uses GPS, aerial photography and other free sources of images to create a map of the world		CC-SA 2.0
WikiMapia	Places—On-line map	Combines Google Maps with a wiki system; currently supports 35 languages		
→ Wikitravel	Places—Travel	A travel guide using wikimedia's software, but otherwise unconnected to the Wikimedia Foundation. 20 supported languages	48000+[23]	CC-SA 1.0
→ World66	Places—Travel	A formerly Dutch company now owned by Internet Brands	46100+[24]	CC-SA 1.0
Baidu Baike	Encyclopedic/Chinese	A Chinese encyclopedia	1519920[25]	Copyrighted

WikiZnanie	Encyclopedic/Russian	A Russian language encyclopedia released under the FreeBSD Documentation License		
Enciclopedia Libre Universal en Español	Encyclopedic/Spanish	A Spanish language fork of Wikipedia		GFDL
Vikidia	Encyclopedic/Spanish and French	A Spanish and French language encyclopedia for children ages 8– 13		GFDL
→ Susning.nu	Encyclopedic/Swedish	A Swedish language encyclopedia, which competes with Swedish Wikipedia	63400+[26]	Copyrighted
Wikinews	General—News	Collaborative news service, a wikimedia project		GFDL and other
GCPEDIA	Government	Internal Government of Canada Wiki		
ZineWiki	Social—Independent media	A zine encyclopedia		
WikiCandidate	Fictional presidential campaign	A virtual campaign for a fictional U.S. presidential candidate. A project of Cornell University.		
Congresspedia	Government—United States Congress	A separately branded sub-section of SourceWatch		GFDL
Diplopedia	Government—Diplomacy	Encyclopedia of the U.S. Department of State collecting items related to international relations and diplomacy		
Jurispedia	Government—Law	A multi-lingual academic encyclopedia, including Arabic, Chinese, English, French, German and Spanish		CC-NC
SourceWatch	Social—Propaganda	Formerly Disinfopedia, discusses propaganda and includes organizations that seek to influence public opinion		GFDL
Wikileaks	Social—Whistleblowers	Allows people to leak documents anonymously		-
Intellipedia	Government—Intelligence	Three non-accessible wikis running on networks that link the U.S. intelligence community		
WikiTimeScale	General—Human history	An interactive timeline of history		GFDL

OpenWetWare	Science—Biology	Promotes sharing and dissemination of knowledge related to biological research		CC-SA
Wikispecies	Science—Biology	A directory of species; wikimedia project		GFDL...
BOWiki	Science—Gene function	An ontology curation framework and gene function editor		GFDL
SNPedia	Science—Biology	A database of research and information about single-nucleotide polymorphisms	3000+[27]	CC-by-nc-sa 3.0
Psychology wiki	Science—Psychology	Promotes sharing and dissemination of knowledge related to psychological research		
Sensei's Library	Misc—Go (game)		18200+	OPL
PlanetMath	Misc—Mathematics	Free wiki-style mathematical encyclopedia		GFDL
ATWiki	Misc—Assistive technology	Also addresses disabilities related to assistive technology		
ShopWiki	Misc—Products	A shopping wiki and product comparison search engine featuring buying guides and shopping resources		
RitchieWiki	Reference—Construction Equipment	An equipment wiki geared for the construction industry. Includes equipment specifications. Also available in French and Spanish.		
Foodista.com	Reference—Food and Cooking	A Creative Commons structured wiki about foods, recipes, and other culinary information.		CC-BY
Appropedia	English	Appropriate technology and sustainable development.		
Ekopedia	Multilingual—Encyclopedic	Environmental sustainability.		CC-SA 3.0
Heroes Wiki	Fiction—*Heroes*			CC-NC-ND
Medpedia	Encyclopedic Medical/health	Requires real names; guided by medical expert input while allowing edits from the general public		GFDL
WiserEarth	Social and Environmental Responsibility			

Catawiki	Catalogues	Dutch language only	200000+	
Collegewikis	Information exchange among college students			
Uninotes.org				
AboutUs.org	Internet directory	originally with MediaWiki software, but now largely with Ruby on Rails	14,000,000+	GFDL and CC-BY-SA
SKYbrary	Aviation safety information			

See also

- → Comparison of wiki farms
- → History of wikis
- List of online encyclopedias
- List of wiki software
- Nupedia, a defunct, expert-based precursor to wikipedia
- UseModWiki
- Wiki farm
- Wiki software

External links

- Open content encyclopedias [28] at the Open Directory Project
- meta:Interwiki map
- meta:List of largest wikis
- Wiki1001.com [29] – a directory of all wikis
- WikiIndex.org [30] – a wiki of wiki and new wikis [31]
- wikindex.com [32]—wikis ranked by size, popularity, usage
- A complete list of Wikia community sites [33]

References

[1] http://en.wikipedia.org/wiki/Special:Statistics
[2] Citizendium - Category:CZ Live (http://en.citizendium.org/wiki/Category:CZ_Live) lists the number of clusters. Citizendium also contains subpages: see Citizendium - Special:Statistics (http://en.citizendium.org/wiki/Special:Statistics) for details.
[3] http://www.scholarpedia.org/article/Special:Statistics
[4] http://googleblog.blogspot.com/2009/01/100000th-knol-published.html
[5] http://meta.wikimedia.org/wiki/List_of_Wikibooks
[6] http://www.wikihow.com/Special:Statistics
[7] http://wiki.answers.com/
[8] http://www.surveytome.com/e2/Stats/General.aspx
[9] http://www.usemod.com/cgi-bin/mb.pl?action=index
[10] http://www.wikitruth.info/index.php?title=Special:Statistics
[11] http://www.conservapedia.com/Special:Statistics
[12] http://www.encyclopediad*amatica.com/Special:Statistics
[13] http://uncyclopedia.info/wiki/Main_Page
[14] http://meta.wikimedia.org/wiki/Wikiquote#List_of_Wikiquotes
[15] http://meta.wikimedia.org/wiki/Wikisource/List
[16] http://imslp.org/wiki/Special:Statistics
[17] http://lyricwiki.org/Special:Statistics?action=raw
[18] http://memory-alpha.org/en/index.php/Special:Statistics

[19] http://www.amillionpenguins.com/wiki/index.php/Special:Statistics

[20] http://meta.wikimedia.org/w/index.php?title=List_of_largest_wikis

[21] http://meta.wikimedia.org/w/index.php?title=List_of_largest_wikis&oldid=1415712

[22] http://www.travellerspoint.com/wiki_stats.cfm

[23] http://wikitravel.org/shared/Multilingual_statistics

[24] http://meta.wikimedia.org/w/index.php?title=List_of_largest_wikis

[25] http://meta.wikimedia.org/w/index.php?title=List_of_largest_wikis

[26] http://meta.wikimedia.org/w/index.php?title=List_of_largest_wikis

[27] http://www.snpedia.com/index.php/Special:Statistics

[28] http://www.dmoz.org//Computers/Open_Source/Open_Content/Encyclopedias//

[29] http://wiki1001.com

[30] http://wikiindex.org

[31] http://wikiindex.org/WikiProject:Wikis_to_Add

[32] http://wikindex.com

[33] http://www.wikia.com/wiki/Wikia

Mass collaboration

Mass collaboration is a form of collective action that occurs when large numbers of people work independently on a single project, often modular in its nature. Such projects typically take place on the internet using social software and computer-supported collaboration tools such as → wiki technologies, which provide a potentially infinite hypertextual substrate within which the collaboration may be situated.

A key aspect which distinguishes mass collaboration from other forms of large-scale collaboration, is that the collaborative process is mediated by the content being created - as opposed to being mediated by direct social interaction as in other forms of collaboration.

Factors

Modularity

Modularity enables a mass of experiments to proceed in parallel, with different teams working on the same modules, each proposing different solutions. Modularity allows different "blocks" to be easily assembled, facilitating decentralised innovation that all fits together.[1]

Differences

Cooperation

Mass collaboration differs from mass cooperation in that the creative acts taking place requires the joint development of shared understandings. Conversely, group members involved in a cooperation needn't engage in a joint negotiation of understanding, they may simply execute instructions willingly.

Another important distinction is the borders around which a mass cooperation can be defined. Due to the extremely general characteristics and lack of need for fine grain negotiation and consensus when cooperating, the entire internet, a city and even the global economy may be regarded as a mass cooperation. Thus a mass collaboration is more refined and complex in its process and production on the level of collective engagement.

Online forum

Although an online discussion is certainly collaborative, mass collaboration differs from a large forum, email list, bulletin board, chat session or group discussion in that the discussion's structure of separate, individual posts generated through turn-taking communication means the textual content does not take the form of a single, coherent body. Of course the conceptual domain of the overall discussion exists as a single unified body, however the textual contributors can be linked back to the understandings and interpretations of a single author. Though the author's understandings and interpretations are most certainly a negotiation of the understandings of all who read and contribute to the discussion, the fact that there was only one author of a given entry reduces the entry's collaborative complexity to the discursive/interpretive as opposed to constructive/' negotiative' levels[2] [3] [4]

Coauthoring

From the perspective of individual sites of work within a mass collaboration, the activity may appear to be identical to that of coauthoring. In fact, it is, with the exception being the implicit and explicit relationships formed by the interdependence that many sites within a mass collaboration share through hypertext and coauthorship with differing sets of collaborators. This interdependence of collaborative sites coauthored by a large number of people is what gives a mass collaboration one of its most distinguishing features - a coherent collaboration emerging from the interrelated collection of its parts.

Changes

Business

In the book Wikinomics - how mass collaboration changes everything [5], Don Tapscott and Anthony D Williams list four powerful new ideas that the new art and science of wikinomics is based on:

- being open
- peering
- sharing
- acting globally

The concept of mass collaboration has led to a number of efforts to harness and commercialize shared tasks. Collectively known as crowdsourcing, these ventures typically involve on an online system of accounts for coordinating buyers and sellers of labor. Amazon's Mechanical Turk system follows this model, by enabling employers to distribute minute tasks to thousands of registered workers.

Government

The power of Mass-collaboration is evidenced by the scope and accuracy of the Wikipedia project. On his website Mass-Collaboration.net [6], Kevin St.Onge discusses the opportunities that mass collaboration presents to the world in achieving a global democracy. He argues that governments as we know them will be dissolved and replaced by the collaborative efforts of the entire world population.

The role of discussion

In traditional collaborative scenarios discussion plays a key role in the negotiation of jointly developed, shared understandings (the essence of collaboration), acting as a point of mediation between the individual collaborators and the outcome which may or may not eventuate from the discussions. Mass collaboration reverses this relationship with the work being done providing the point of mediation between collaborators, with associated discussions being an optional component. It is of course debatable that discussion is optimal, as most (if not all) mass collaborations have discussions associated with the content being developed. However it is possible to contribute (to → Wikipedia for instance) without discussing the content you are contributing to. (Smaller scale collaborations might be conducted without discussions especially in a non-verbal mode of work - imagine two painters contributing to the same canvas - but the situation becomes increasingly problematic as more members are included.)

For an example of a discussion accompanying mass collaboration, see the [Israel talk page]. In addition to such points of discussion, fora, IRC (chat) and email lists often support and augment this negotiation.

Non-textual mass collaboration

Although the only widely successful examples of mass collaboration thus far evaluated exist in the textual medium, there is no immediate reason why this form of collective action couldn't work in other creative media. It could be argued that some projects within the open source software movement provide examples of mass collaboration outside of the traditional written language (see below), however, the code collaboratively created still exists as a language utilizing a textual medium. Music is also a possible site for mass collaboration, for instance on live performance recordings where audience members' voices have become part of the standard version of a song. Most "anonymous" folk songs and "traditional" tunes are also arguably sites of long term mass collaboration.

Further reading and listening

- A. Désilets, L. Gonzalez, S. Paquet, M. Stojanovic (2006). "Translation the Wiki Way [7]". *Proceedings of the WIKISym*: 19. doi:10.1145/1149453.1149464 [8]. http://iit-iti. nrc-cnrc.gc.ca/iit-publications-iti/docs/NRC-48736.pdf.
- A. Désilets (2007). "Translation Wikified: How will Massive Online Collaboration Impact the World of Translation?". *Proceedings of Translating and the Computer*.
- Leadbeater, Charles (2008). *We-Think – Mass innovation not mass production*. Profile Books. ISBN 9781861978929.
- Laurie Taylor (Presenter), Charles Leadbeater (Guest). (2008-03-05). *Thinking Allowed* [9]. [Radio]. London, UK: BBC Radio 4. Event occurs at start. http://www.bbc.co.uk/ radio4/factual/thinkingallowed/thinkingallowed_20080305.shtml. Retrieved 2008-03-12.

References

[1] http://www.linux.com/archive/feature/130024?theme=print

> The sudden and unexpected importance of the Wikipedia, a free online encyclopedia created by tens of thousands of volunteers and coordinated in a deeply decentralized fashion, represents a radical new modality of content creation by *massively distributed collaboration*. This talk will discuss the unique principles and values which have enabled the Wikipedia community to succeed and will examine the intriguing prospects for application of these methods to a broad spectrum of intellectual endeavors

[3] Cover story: Google's Next Big Dream, Imagine what you could do with the world's mightiest computer (http://www.businessweek.com/magazine/content/07_52/b4064048925836.htm?chan=magazine+channel_top+stories), BusinessWeek, 2007-12-24.

"democracy comes into being after the poor have conquered their opponents, slaughtering some and banishing some, while to the remainder they give an equal share of freedom and power; and this is the form of government in which the magistrates are commonly elected by lot...

"the forgiving spirit of democracy, and the 'don't care' about trifles, and the disregard which she shows of all the fine principles which we solemnly laid down at the foundation of the city... how grandly does she trample all these fine notions of ours under her feet, never giving a thought to the pursuits which make a statesman, and promoting to honour any one who professes to be the people's friend...

"in what manner does tyranny arise? — that it has a democratic origin is evident..."

(http://classics.mit.edu/Plato/republic.9.viii.htmlhttp://classics.mit.edu/Plato/republic.9.viii.html)

And see generally Eric Havelock, *The Liberal Temper in Greek Politics* (London: Jonathan Cape, 1957), (New Haven: Yale University Press, 1964).

[5] http://wikinomics.com/
[6] http://www.mass-collaboration.net
[7] http://iit-iti.nrc-cnrc.gc.ca/iit-publications-iti/docs/NRC-48736.pdf
[8] http://dx.doi.org/10.1145%2F1149453.1149464
[9] http://www.bbc.co.uk/radio4/factual/thinkingallowed/thinkingallowed_20080305.shtml

Universal edit button

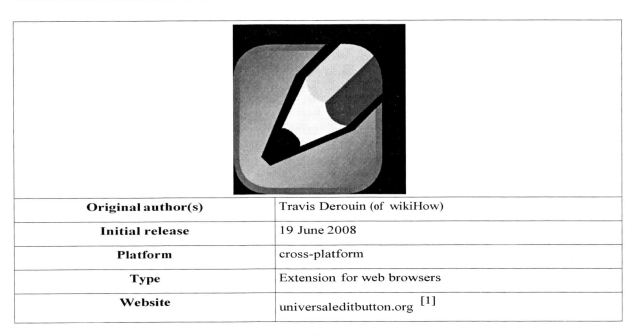

Original author(s)	Travis Derouin (of wikiHow)
Initial release	19 June 2008
Platform	cross-platform
Type	Extension for web browsers
Website	universaleditbutton.org [1]

The **Universal Edit Button** is a green pencil icon in the address bar of a web browser that indicates whether a web page (most often a → wiki) is editable. It is similar to the orange "broadcast" RSS icon (" ") that indicates that there is a web feed available. Clicking the icon opens the edit window. It was invented by a collaborative team of wiki enthusiasts, including Ward Cunningham, Jack Herrick, and many others. The concept was first conceived during the 2007 RecentChangesCamp in Montréal. After coding by Travis Derouin, Brion Vibber and other programmers, the button was officially launched on June 19 2008.[2]

Description

The Universal Editing Button (UEB) allows a web surfer to quickly recognize when a site — such as a → wiki — may be edited. According to the UEB's creators, "it is a convenience to web surfers who are already inclined to contribute, and an invitation to those who have yet to discover the thrill of building a common resource. As this kind of public editing becomes more commonplace, the button may become regarded as a badge of honor. It serves as an incentive to encourage companies and site developers to add publicly-editable components to their sites, in order to have the UEB displayed for their sites."

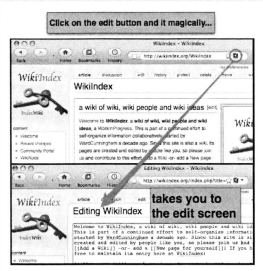

A screenshot from WikiIndex.org showing the Universal Edit Button in action.

Tim Berners-Lee's initial vision for the web was a read-write medium.[3] Yet as the web matured, very few web sites offered users the ability to write or edit. The web became primarily a "read only" medium. Everyone web surfed but few got to enjoy web editing.

Over the years, → wiki practitioners and other edit-friendly folks spread the idea that the web should be editable by anyone at any time. The success of → Wikipedia, and the increasing utility of wikis like wikiHow, AboutUs.org, wikiTravel and Wikia demonstrates that open editing creates usable information resources. "Read only" sites are increasingly adding the ability for anyone to participate. Wikis appear in enterprise software products and in consumer offerings. As the Internet becomes more editable by the day, web users are becoming more adept and creative in the tools that allow information to be shared.[4]

History

Conversations on this idea started at RoCoCo[5] (a RecentChangesCamp) in Montreal in 2007, and discussions continued on the AboutUs wiki.[6] At the Palo Alto RCC in 2008, a handful of people explored the idea, got excited about the ability to have the button automatically detected by browsers, and helped spread the idea. The current icon was selected after a lengthy discussion involving multiple suggestions, but is not necessarily intended as a permanent choice.

Websites

Websites supporting the Universal Edit Button include WikiHow, AboutUs.org, Wikimedia (including → Wikipedia, Wiktionary, Wikimedia Commons and all other Wikimedia projects)[7], MediaWiki software, DokuWiki[8], MoinMoin, Oddmuse, PhpWiki, Socialtext[9], TWiki[10], the Creative Commons wiki[11], Foodista, Wikia, PBwiki[12], WikkaWiki[13], → Memory Alpha, Wired's How-To blog,[14] and WordPress (as a Plug-in)[15].

External links

- The Universal Edit Button homepage [1]
- A podcast on the Universal Edit Button [16] by Ward Cunningham (inventor of the wiki), Mark Dilley (AboutUs.org), and Peter Kaminski (Socialtext).
- Universal Edit Button at Mozilla Addons [17]
- The Epiphany extension [18]

References

[1] http://universaleditbutton.org/Universal_Edit_Button

[2] Cleaver, Martin (2008-06-19). " The Universal Edit button launches today (http://www.wikisym.org/?p=37)". WikiSym. . Retrieved 2009-03-17.

[3] Tim Berners-Lee (2005-12-12). " So I have a blog (http://dig.csail.mit.edu/breadcrumbs/node/38)". Decentralized Information Group (DIG). . Retrieved 2009-03-17.

[4] " About the Universal Edit Button (http://universaleditbutton.org/About)". Universaleditbutton.org. . Retrieved 2009-03-17.

[5] " RoCoCo (http://rocococamp.info)". Rocococamp.info. 2008-04-30. . Retrieved 2009-03-17.

[6] Discussions on the AboutUs wiki (http://www.aboutus.org/UniversalWikiEditButton) — AboutUs.org

[7] " Wikimedia announcement (http://blog.wikimedia.org/2008/06/19/firefox-3-and-the-wiki-edit-button/)". Blog.wikimedia.org. . Retrieved 2009-03-17.

[8] Gohr, Andreas (2008-06-20). " plugin:ueb (http://www.dokuwiki.org/plugin:ueb)". DokuWiki. . Retrieved 2009-06-11.

[9] Niall Kennedy June 28, 2008 11:21 PM (2008-06-28). " Socialtext announcement (http://www.socialtext.com/blog/2008/06/a-universal-edit-button-for-th.html)". Socialtext.com. . Retrieved 2009-03-17.

[10] " TWiki announcement (http://twiki.org/cgi-bin/view/Blog/2008-06-20-universal-wiki-edit-button-for-twiki)". Twiki.org. . Retrieved 2009-03-17.

[11] " Creative Commons announcement (http://creativecommons.org/weblog/entry/8387)". Creativecommons.org. 2008-06-22. . Retrieved 2009-03-17.

[12] " PBwiki announcement (http://blog.pbwiki.com/2008/06/20/the-universal-edit-button/)". Blog.pbwiki.com. . Retrieved 2009-03-17.

[13] " WikkaWiki announcement (http://docs.wikkawiki.org/WhatsNew1166)". Docs.wikkawiki.org. . Retrieved 2009-03-17.

[14] Wikis Rally Around Universal Edit Button (http://www.webmonkey.com/blog/Wikis_Rally_Around_Universal_Edit_Button) — Webmonkey

[15] " WordPress plugin (http://universaleditbutton.org/WordPress_plugin)". Universaleditbutton.org. . Retrieved 2009-03-17.

[16] http://siliconflorist.com/2008/06/27/universal-edit-button-ward-cunningham-mark-dilley-and-peter-kaminski/

[17] https://addons.mozilla.org/en-US/firefox/addon/7804

[18] http://johannes.sipsolutions.net/Projects/epiphany-extensions

Article Sources and Contributors

Wiki *Source*: http://en.wikipedia.org/w/index.php?oldid=308350490 *Contributors*: -OOPSIE-, 02pollajo, 05jasm01, 0lexa0, 0pera, 10nitro, 119, 16@r, 17Drew, 2004-12-29T22:45Z, 21655, 2bar, 3Jane, 62.82.226.xxx, 99DBSIMLR, A Man In Black, AAA765, ABShipper, ACupOfCoffee, AGrobler, AK7, AaronRoe, Ablewisuk, Abstract Idiot, Abune, Acadamenorth, Academic Challenger, Accurizer, Acidburn24m, Acooley, Adam Bishop, Adam1213, Adashiel, Aeconley, Aenar, Aeusoes1, Agathoclea, AgentPeppermint, Ahoerstemeier, Ahy1, Aim Here, AirBa, Aitias, Ajmint, Aksi great, Akuyume, Alanlastufka, Aldie, Aldrich Hanssen, Aled2912, Alerante, Alex S, AlexRampaul, Alexa411, Alexf, Alhutch, Alias Flood, Alibaasit, Alikaalex, Allenc28, AllisonDavis, AllyGator, Alphax, Altenmann, Alterego, Amberrock, Amcaja, American Eagle, Amren, Ancheta Wis, Andre Engels, Andreas Toth, Andrew c, Andrewpmk, Andrewski, Andris, Android79, Andyabides, Andycjp, Andypandy.UK, Angela, Angr, Anig168, Anoriega, Anote-Cred 001, Ant.silver, Antandrus, Anthony, AntiOnline, Antonielly, Aoi, Apatterno, Apoltix, Aranel, Arcadie, Archimedo, Arcturus, Arcy, Arhold, Ariaconditzione, Arm, Armin756, Art LaPella, Artisol2345, Artw, Arvindn, Ashinberry, Ashro, Astronouth7303, Atkint, Avedomni, Avernet, Avillia, Awien, AxelBoldt, Axeman89, BD2412, Babajobu, Badanbarman, BadgerOfDarkness, Baldmonkey, Banes, BanyanTree, Bardeep1, Barneyboo, Bart133, Bartosz, Bayerischermann, Bbatsell, Bcorr, Bdesham, Bdude, Beano, Beefly, Beeglebug, Bellatrix411, Benandorsqueaks, Berek, Berria, Betelgeuse, Bevo, Beyondthislife, Bfrank9, Bhadani, Bibliomaniac15, Big boss si, Bigbluefish, Bigjim1475, Bigtop, Bigwyrm, Bitbit, Blackjack48, Blacknova, Blanchardb, Blankfaze, Blavkisblack, Blu Aardvark, Blue520, Bluemask, Bmearns, Bmicomp, Bob51, Bobbis, Bobblewik, Bobet, Bobo192, Bogdangiusca, Bomac, Bongwarrior, Bookofjude, Boonbs, Boothy443, Borislav, Bornhj, BozMo, Bozoid, Bradley1976, BrainyBabe, Branddobbe, Bratsche, Breakpoint, BrenDJ, Brian Kendig, Brian0918, Brianjd, Brighterorange, Brockert, BrokenSegue, Brokenfrog, Brusselsshrek, Bryan Derksen, Brynnbop, Btw, Btwied, Bucketsofg, Buickid, BurnDownBabylon, Buron444, Butros, Buzztootight, Bwithh, C.Fred, C3o, CAPS LOCK, CHANDER, CJGB, CP-sakha, Cactus.man, Caesura, Cailpearce, Caim, CambridgeBayWeather, Cammo1818, Can't sleep, clown will eat me, Canadian-Bacon, CanadianCaesar, Canderson7, CanisRufus, CaptainVindaloo, Carbon-16, Carnal Abhorrence, Catfoo, Cazcazcaz, Cbrown1023, Cconnett, Cdc, Centrx, Cerevox, Cganske, Chanting Fox, CharlesC, Charlie MacKenzie, Chatfecter, Chcknwnm, Chealer, ChildofMidnight, Chinasanyo, Chinneeb, Chocolateboy, Cholmes75, Chris 73, Chris G, Chris Roy, Chris is me, ChrisG, Chrisforster, Chrismoore123, Christian List, Christinewales, Christopher Parham, Chrstnrckr08, Chuck Marean, Chud50, Cinnamon Apple, CinnamonApril, Citizen Premier, Cjfsyntropy, Ckg, Claygate, ClockworkSoul, CloudNine, Clowning, Clubjuggle, CmdrRickHunter, Codex Sinaiticus, ColinMcMillen, Colinjl, Collins.mc, Color probe, Computerjoe, Connect2shashi, Connelly, ConnorJack, Conrad.Irwin, Constanz, Conti, Conversion script, CopperMurdoch, Coredesat, Cormaggio, Cosoce, Cowpriest2, CrazyLegsKC, CrazyTiger, Cronullasoutherland, CryptoDerk, Cthia, CthulhuRlyeh, Curps, Cva india, Cyan, CyberSkull, Cybercobra, Cyp, Cyrius, D1ma5ad, DEmerson3, DJ Clayworth, DVD R W, Daekharel, Daf, Dagav, Damian Yerrick, Damicatz, Dan100, DanKeshet, DanMS, Daniel MacKay, Daniel Olsen, Daniel5127, DanielCD, DanielVonEhren, Dansiman, Dantheman531, DarkHorizon, Darrel Stadlen, Darrenhusted, Dave6, David Andel, David Johnson, David Latapie, DavidCary, DavidH, DavidLevinson, Dawn Bard, Dbenbenn, Dbtfz, Dcandeto, Deadcorpse, Deanos, Decumanus, Delirium, Delldot, Delta Tango, Demmy, Dennis Valeev, DerHexer, Derktar, Desen, Detruncate, Dharris, Diberri, Dierssen, Digitalme, Digression from a tangent, Dimo414, Dina, Dirk Riehle, DisturbedFan, DjNockles, Djmackenzie, Djr xi, Dlewis3, Dmn, Dmoss, Dmr2, Doc glasgow, Doctorevil64, Docu, Dogbone, Dollydimple, Donama, Donthem, Dori, Doug W, Dparsons62, Dposse, DrBob, Draeco, DragonflySixtyseven, Dreaded Walrus, DreamGuy, Drini, Dsavalia, Dsleaton, Dub4u, Duksandfish, Durin, DvnInspiration, Dweekly, Dwheeler, DylanLake, Dysbiote, Dysepsion, Dysprosia, E David Moyer, EAi, EEPROM Eagle, ESkog, Eal, Earle Martin, EatsWontons, EddEdmondson, Edgar181, Edward, Edwy, Eeee, Efe, Effeietsanders, Egil, Egmonster, Eidako, Eivind, El C, ElTyrant, Electrojimmy, Eliasbizannes, ElinorD, Elkman, Ellsass, Eloquence, Emiellaiendiay, Emmelie, Emurph, Emurphy42, Encephalon, Endcruelty, Endroit, EngineerScotty, Ensa, Epbr123, Epochbb, Epolk, Eric outdoors, Ericl234, Ericpi, Eriter, Errabee, Essjay, Estel, EvanProdromou, Evercat, Everyking, Evie em, Evil Monkey, Evil saltine, EvocativeIntrigue, Ezhiki, F Notebook, FCYTravis, FOTEMEH, FR Soliloquy, FT2, Fahadsadah, Fahim, Fang Aili, Fawcett5, Fdp, Feinoha, Felixdakat, FellowWikipedian, Fennec, Fergking, Ferkelparade, Ff1959, Firefoxman, Fish and karate, Fishal, Fistfull of me, Flatulant, Flauros, Flcelloguy, Flizack, Flockmeal, Florian Cauvin, Floschneck, Flying Hamster, Fnfd, FogDevil, ForDorothy, ForJustice74, Fornost, Francs2000, Frank1101, FrankCostanza, Frankk74, Franklinhigh123, Frazzydee, Freakofnurture, Frecklefoot, Fred Bauder, Fredrick day, Fredrik, FreplySpang, FrummerThanThou, Frymaster, Fulou, Furrykef, Fuzheado, Fvw, GChriss, GHe, GJeffery, GSGSGSG, Gabbe, Gadfium, Gaius Cornelius, Galactor213, Galoubet, Gamaliel, Garlicbreadboi, Gary King, Geeks2go, Gemtpm, General Eisenhower, Geni, Geoffrey, George Kontopoulos, Georgebolton14, Geraki, Geschichte, Ghyll, Giantgrawp, Gilgamesh, Gilliam, Gimboid13, Gioto, Glacier Wolf, Gladeator204, Glen, Gnangarra, Gnewf, Golbez, Goodboy7557, Goosehonk1, Goplat, Gothkidd1, Gotyear, Gracenotes, GraemeL, Grand krishna deva rayas, Grandgrawper, Gravity, Grawp, GreatWhiteNortherner, Greeneto, Greenrd, Gregfitzy, GregorB, Grin, Grunt, Grye, Gscshoyru, Gsf, Gsheld, Guaka, Guanaco, Guillermo181, Gunmetal Angel, Gurch, Gurchzilla, Gutworth, Guy M, Gwernol, Hadal, HaeB, Hammer of the year, Handface, Harryjayan, Haukurth, Hawaiian717, Hayabusa future, Haza-w, Hcheney, Hdt83, Heimstern, Hej30251, Helikophis, Helixblue, Hello32020, Hemanshu, Hemanth 020784, Henriquevicente, Henry Flower, Henrygb, Hephaestos, Hetar, Hikari Tajiri, Histrion, Hojimachong, Homefill, Honta, Hooverbag, Horsten, Hottsie2, Hsvenforcer, Huangdi, Hugh7, Husond, Huwr, Hyad, IGod, ILovePlankton, IMSoP, IRP, Iambbscom, Icairns, Icq628, Id the MildlyConfused, Idohschool, Idont Havaname, Iediteverything, If62668, Ihope127, IkBenDeMan, Ilyanep, Indivisible, Infire, Infrogmation, Inkypaws, Insanephantom, Inter, Interesdom, Intgr, Intiendes, Iridescent, Irishguy, Isetmyfriendsonfire, Itntennis, Ivenms, Ixfd64, Izehar, J Crow, JCarriker, JFPerry, JFreeman, JIP, JImbo Wales, JLaTondre, JONJONAUG, JWSchmidt, JYolkowski, Jacek Kendysz, JackLumber, Jacobko, Jacoplane, Jahiegel, Jaimedv, Jamesmarkhetterley, Jaxl, Jay, Jcw69, Jdforrester, Jdk0ac, JeLuF, Jedwl, Jeffrey.Kleykamp, JeffyJeffyMan2004, Jello moses, Jeltz, Jemmy Button, JeremyA, Jezmck, Jiang, Jimbo D. Wales, Jimmy4, Jimp, Jinkleberries, Jivetio, Jmabel, Jmfranks03, Jnc, Jni, JoanneB, Joe Sewell, Joeblakesley, Joestrand, Johanvs, John Abbe, John Fader, John Vandenberg, John254, JohnMcDonnell, JohnOwens, JohnWittle, Johnleemk, Johnmarkh, Johnsolo, Jon1999, Jon2000, JonGarfunkel, Jonnabuz, Jonny92, Jonsafari, Joorgan, JoseGonzalez66, Josh Grosse, Joshbuddy, Jossi, Joyous!, Jpbowen, Jpgordon, Jrdioko, Jrgetsin, Jrockley, Jtkiefer, Ju66l3r, JulesH, Julesd, Jumbo Snails, Jusjih, JustAnotherJoe, JustinHagstrom, Justinsomnia, Jwissick, JzG, KAtremer, KConWiki, KED, KF, KNHaw, KYPark, Kakurady, KamuiShirou, Kantos, Karada, Karimarie, KaseyGirl, Kate, Katie-cassidy, Kauymatty7, Kazrak, Kazvorpal, Kbdank71, Kedithe tramp, Keegan, Keilaron, KellyMartin, Kenwarren, Kerowyn, Kessaris, Kessler, Kevinkor2, Kewp, Keyzi, Khalid, Khalid hassani, Khivi, Kidstand, Kimchi.sg, Kine, KingsOfHearts, Kingturtle, Kirc1184, KissL, Kissall, Kjoonlee, Klalalala, Knowledge Seeker, KnowledgeOfSelf, Kochas, Kon-Tiki001, Konman72, Konstable, Korath, Korg, Korny O'Near, Kosebamse, Kotjze, Koweja, Kowey, Koyaanis Qatsi, Kozuch, Kpjas, KrakatoaKatie, Krellis, Ksnortum, KumoriKen, Kungfuadam, KurtRaschke, Kuru, Kurykh, Kwamikagami, Kwekubo, Kyle Barbour, Kylemew, L.sogabe, LOL, Lachatdelarue, Langec, Laparapa, Larry_Sanger, Larryincinci, Lars Washington, Lda523287, Le savoir et le savoir-faire, Leandrod, Lectonar, Lee Daniel Crocker, Leebo, Leif, Leithp, Leo Trollstoy, LeoDV, Leopold Stotch, Lethaniol, Lexi Marie, Li-sung, Liftarn, Light current, Lightdarkness, Lights, Likemeplz, Limetom, Linuxbeak, Lionyroxursox, Listre, LittleDan, LizardWizard, Localbatman, Location x3, Locoseprix, Lomn, Longhair, Lord Voldemort, Lornova, Loudsox, Lucasbfr, Luckyjill, Lumos3, Luna Santin, Lunchboxhero, Lupin, Lupo, Luuke21, Lysdexia, M Blissett, M0RHI, MC MasterChef, MER-C, MFH, MHD, MRSC, Ma8thew, Mac, MacGyverMagic, Macaddct1984, Mackeriv, Magnaexim, Magnus Manske, Mahnol, Maitch, Majorly, Malcolm Farmer, Malo, Man vyi, Mange01, Manscher, Marcmaguire, MarkGallagher, MarkWiseman, Markhu, Markw here, Mars200125, Marsvin, MartinHarper, Martinp23, Martsax, Marysunshine, Marzedu, Master82, Matchups, Matteh, Mattfatrat, Matthew 8965, Matthew0028, Matthieupinard, MattisManzel, Mattisse, Mauri1980, Mav, Max Schwarz, MaxInsanity, Maxamegalon2000, Maximillion Pegasus, Maximus Rex, Mbarbier, Mburkeb, Mccready, Mcmillin24, Mdchachi, Meelar, Meeples, Mefroats, Megalodon99, Melaen, Melsaran, Memamo2, Mendel, Merovingian, Merphant, Mesosade, Messatsu, Methedemon, Methnor, Mets501, Mg76734, Mga, Mggeep, Mhazard9, Mibrad, Micaarzur, Michael Hardy, Michael Snow, MichaelJE2, MichaelMcGuffin, Micov, Mightyxander, MiiInc, Mike Christie, Mike Rosoft, Mike6271, MikeX, Mikellewis, Mikelove1, Milo257, Mimithebrain, MindlessIQ, Mindmatrix, Mindspillage, Minghong, Mintguy, Mirv, Misza13, Mitaphane, Mnemeson, Mo0, Moa3333, Modestyle, Modular, Moink, Molerat, Monuko, Moonrat506, Moormand, Moosebumps, Moretz, Moriori, Mormegil, Morwen, Mosdefinitely, Mostly magic, Mp, Mr Adequate, Mr. Lefty, Mr. Strong Bad, Mr. Wiki, Mr.Z-man, MrGBug, Mrajkovic, Mrholybrain, Mrmaniac2, Msikma, Muffyn, Muness, Muriel Gottrop, Mushroom, Musical Linguist, MuthuKutty, Muthukumartsm, Mxn, Mydogategodshat, Mysekurity, Mysidia, Mário, N-Man, N00b314159, NIRVANA2764, NSK, NSLE, NSR, Nach0king, Nadavspi, Nae'blis, Nakon, NawlinWiki, Ndentzel, Nealmcb, Neiche, NeilN, Nelly1234, Nentuaby, Neo-Jay, Neomasterjon78, Netizen, Netmouse, Neutrality, Newton2, Nex699, NicholasTurnbull, Nick Watts, Nick125, Nick683, NickBush24, NickelShoe, Nickptar, Nieghtdog, NigelR, Nikola Smolenski, Nilfanion, Nique1287, Nishkid64, Nitya Dharma, Nixnews1, Nlu, No Guru, Noahcs, Noelledge, Nohat, Noobrune, Noodlenozzle, Norm, Not a dog, Notheruser, Novacatz, Nsh, Nsigniacorp, NuclearWarfare, Nufy8, Numbo3, Nunquam Dormio, Nurg, Nut er, Nwagg1234, OGoncho, Octane, Oddboy10, Ohmygod, Okiefromokla, Omicronpersei8, Omm3, Onorem, Oobopshark, OrbitOne, Orenm2, Oskard, Osman Amanat, Ottre, Outoftuneviolin, Outriggr, Owen, OwenX, Owiebut, Ozzyslovechild, P3net, PDH, PFHLai, PQN, Pablomartinez, PaePae, Pahari Sahib, Pakaran, Paleorthid, Palica, Peripitus, Persian Poet Gal, Peruvianllama, Peter, Petri Krohn, Pevarnj, Pgecaj, Pgk, Phil Boswell, Philipemarlow, Phoenix X, Phyzome, Pickers1988, Pie4all88, Pies are blue guy, Piguy, Pilotguy, PinchasC, Pintman, Piotrus, Pious7, Pipedreamergrey, Pizza1512, Pjacobi, Plbogen, Plobnob, Plop, Pluke, Poccil, Ponder, Poopman100, Popsracer, Porqin, Postmodern Beatnik, Praveshphp, PrimeCupEevee, Prodego, Professorbikeybike, Proteus, Psb777, Pschemp, PseudoNym, PseudoSudo, Pstudier, Psy guy, Psych0, PsychicMaster, Puchku, Purcelce, Pwiscombe, Pyrospirit, Pyroven, QBorg, Qmwne235,

QuackGuru, Quackor, Quentint, Quercusrobur, Qwertzy2, Qxz,R'n'B, R9tgokunks, RHaworth, RN, RTC, RW, RaCha'ar, Ral315, Ram-Man, Ramin Nakisa, Ran, Random Rowen, Random832, Ranveig, Rapha, Rasimkilic, Raul654, Raven4x4x, Rawlife, Rbonvall, Rdsmith4, RebekahThorn, Red lace, RedWordSmith, Redeyed Treefrog, Redvers, Reedy, Reginmund, ReiniUrban, Remember the dot, RexNL, Rfc1394, Rfl, Rhobite, Rholton, Rich Farmbrough, Richard W.M. Jones, RickK, Ricky81682, Rieg, Rikatee, Rippawallet, RippleEffect, Rjstanford, Rjwilmsi, Rlee0001, Rmhermen, Rna33857, Robchurch, Robertissimo, Robertvan1, Robin cash flo, Robin63, Robofish, RockMFR, Roland2, Ron Barker, Rookkey, Rooseter5, Root4(one), Ropers, Rory096, Rossmay, Rotem Dan, RoyBoy, Royalguard11, Rs2, Rsgranne, Rsm99833, Rumpelstiltskin223, Runch, Runefrost, Ruyn, RxS, Ryan Roos, RyanCross, Ryanaxp, Rye93, Ryulong, SGBailey, SMcCandlish, SPUI, ST47, SWAdair, Sade, Sai1981, Salix alba, SallyForth123, Sam Francis, Sam Hocevar, Sam Korn, Sam Vimes, Sam63912, Samaritan, Samir, Samsara, Sandahl, Sandipsonu, Sango123, Sangrito, Sannse, Sarcasticninja, Sasper, Sayden, Sbmehta, Sceptre, SchfiftyThree, Schizmatic, SchuminWeb, Schzmo, Scientizzle, Scifiintel, Scohoust, Scorpion451, ScotchMB, Scott Seals, Scriberius, ScudLee, SeanMack, SebastianBreier, Secretlondon, Seedat, Seidenstud, Semper331fi, Sephiroth storm, Serlin, Sesquiannual, Sesshomaru, Seth Ilys, Seventeen four, Sgkay, Sh33dyIV, Shabnam.garg, Shacharg, Shaizakopf, Shakeer, Shanel, Shanes, Shantavira, Shatner, ShaunES, Sheepo39, Shell Kinney, Shii, Shimgray, Shinuzi, Shizane, Shlomi Hillel, Shoaler, Shocking Blue, Sietse Snel, Silsor, Silver hr, Simeon H, SimonP, SineWave, Sing66, Sir Lewk, Sir Nicholas de Mimsy-Porpington, Siroxo, Sj, Sjakkalle, Sjorford, Skizzik, SkyWalker, Sleepy42, Slmader, SlowkingMan, Sm8900, Small business, SmartGuy, Snoutholder, Snoyes, Soccerolive7, Solidrage, Solitude, SomeStranger, SonicAD, SonicTailsKnuckles, Soosed, Sopranosmob781, Sorpigal, Sourapples, Spalding, Spangineer, SparsityProblem, Spartan000, Speaker219, Spebi, Specialnet, SpeedyGonsales, Spellcast, Spencaz, Sperril, Splash, Spliffy, Spookfish, Springnuts, Squash, Srikeit, Srl, Srleffler, Stalchild, Starx, Stavaface, Stbodie, Steel, SteffenPoulsen, Steinsky, Stephen, Stephen Gilbert, Stephenb, Stereotek, Steven Walling, Stevertigo, Stevietheman, Stillnotelf, Stormie, Stormreaever, Stormwriter, Strehler, StuartDouglas, Stupidstupidstupid, Sum0, SuperDude115, Superman826, SusanLesch, Suso, Susurrus, Susvolans, Sverdrup, Swzine, THE KING, TJDay, TMK, TNLNYC, TPK, Tachyon01, Tagishsimon, TakuyaMurata, Talrias, Tamiera, Tangotango, Tapir Terrific, Tariqabjotu, Tarquin, Taw, Tawker, Taxman, Tbyrne, Tdonne, TenPoundHammer, Teratornis, Terence, Terjepetersen, TestPilot, TexasAndroid, Texastwister, Texture, Thalter, ThanosMadTitan23, ThatAdamGuy, Thatdog, The Anome, The Cunctator, The Land, The wub, TheBoyNextDoor, TheJC, TheKMan, TheLimbicOne, TheMidnighters, TheRoyalNavy, Theopapada, Theresa knott, Thewayforward, Thinboy00, This user has left wikipedia, ThomasPaine1776, Thorpe, ThurnerRupert, Tide rolls, Tierlieb, TigerShark, Tikko1, Tim Starling, Tim-lees, Tim1988, Tim1988 2, Timhowardriley, Timneu22, Timrem, Timwi, Tinlv7, Titoxd, Tjnewell, Tlogmer, Tmopkisn, Tobias Bergemann, Tobias Escher, Tobin Richard, Tom-, Tomalak geretkal, TomasBat, Tomfulton, Tommot22, Tony1, Tonyseeker, TorqueSmackey, Toughpigs, Tpbradbury, Trampled, Trav.company, Travelbird, TreasuryTag, Tree Biting Conspiracy, Tregoweth, Trevor MacInnis, TreyHarris, Trilobite, Triona, Tristan Schmelcher, Ttwaring, Twinxor, UH Collegian, Ucanlookitup, Ugen64, Ugur Basak, Ukexpat, Ukpcdaz, Ulrich.fuchs, Ultratomio, Umapathy, Ummit, Uncle G, Unfree, UninvitedCompany, UrsaFoot, Usarmymilitary, Utcursch, VampWillow, Vedexent, Verdatum, Versus22, Vgracecar, Vicenarian, VickiBrown, Vilerage, Voice of All, Vondort, Vonsnip, Vykk, W3stfa11, WadeSimMiser, Waggers, Wainwra, Waisbrot, Wakka, Walabee, Wangandthegang, Wangi, Wavej4, Wavelength, Wayward, Webmaster 2.0, Wegates, Wereon, West Brom 4ever, Weyes, Whocouldibe2, Whomp, Whosyourjudas, Wik, Wiki Wikardo, Wiki alf, WikiTerra, WikiToaster, Wikimancer, Wikipedia Admin, Wikipedia is Communism, Wikipediarules2221, Wikipeditor, Wiktionary4Prez!, WildTurkey, Will Beback, WillMak050389, Willsmith, Wimt, Wise, Wissons, Wknight94, Wm, Wma108, Wmahan, Wolf202, Wolf206, Woohookitty, Workman, WorldlyWebster, Writtenright, Wshun, Wtracew, Wutwatwot, Wwwwangtao, X!, XJamRastafire, Xaosflux, Xchbla423, Xcomgs, Xenobog, Xezbeth, Xiggelee, Xinyujiang, Xmarquez, Xnuala, Xobxela, Xxpor, Xy7, YORKABE, Yahel Guhan, Yamamoto Ichiro, Yangsta, Yanksox, Yaron K., Yassens, Yath, YayGames, Yelyos, Youngin12345, Yoyochris924, Ysangkok, Yug, Ywong137, Zach Alexander, Zachlipton, Zahid Abdassabur, Zaphod Beeblebrox, Zazou, Zeldakix17, Zenohockey, Zeppelin4life, Zhy, Zigger, ZimZalaBim, Ziusudra, Zoe, Zoliblog, Zondor, Zoom92, Zoooonk, Zoz, Zpb52, ZsigE, Zsinj, Zzyzx11, ²¹², ·, 古 滑 阿 咸 , 5290 anonymous edits

Wiki (software) *Source*: http://en.wikipedia.org/w/index.php?oldid=309962896 *Contributors*: 16@r, 216.60.221.xxx, 62.82.226.xxx, 62.82.240.xxx, A. Parrot, AAAAA, Ahoerstemeier, Alansohn, AlissonSellaro, AmiDaniel, Analoguedragon, Andre Engels, Angela, Anthony, Asbestos, Ascánder, Asdfhjklq, Bartosz, Bergonom, Beta m, Bhadani, Bluezy, Bob Burton, Bobo192, Boly38, Bpt, Brettz9, Brion VIBBER, Brockert, Bryankennedy, CKBrown1000, Cactus.man, Camw, Catfoo, Chealer, Chocolateboy, Chrisjj, Christopher Mahan, CliffC, Cmkpl, ColourBurst, Conversion script, Cowabunga5587, DWizzy, DarTar, David Gerard, David Latapie, Davidgutschick, DcJohn, Deathphoenix, DennisDaniels, Dialog, Diberri, Dittaeva, Dori, Dsavalia, Dysprosia, Edward, Edward Vielmetti, Eloquence, Epbr123, Euicho, Everyking, EvilZak, FDuffy, Fmccown, FranckMartin, Francs2000, Fredrik, Fuzheado, Fvw, GiantSloth, Golbez, Gotyear, Grlloyd, Grunt, Guaka, Hadal, Hapsiainen, Hhielscher, Hick, Holizz, Htaccess, IMSoP, Imz, Indy, Infrogmation, Inter, Ivan423, J Kikuchi, JForget, JavaWoman, Jayk806, Jed S, Jnc, Jojit fb, JoseGonzalez66, Jrv, Kissall, Knallkopf, Korath, Kosebamse, Kukutz, Kungfuadam, Larsen, Leif, LiDaobing, Liao, Liftarn, Lunchboxhero, M2Ys4U, Mackeriv, Magnus Manske, Marclaporte, MartinHarper, Masukomi, MattisManzel, Mdmcginn, Mdsam2, Meelar, Merovingian, Michaelfavor, Mindmatrix, Minghong, Mjklin, Mkumarphp, Moroboshi, MrJones, Mrwojo, Neha85, Nirion, Norm, Novasource, Omeomi, Paranoid, Patrick, Persian Poet Gal, PeterThoeny, PierreAbbat, Pilotguy, PizzaofDoom, Planders, Pohta ce-am pohtit, Postdlf, RN, RaCha'ar, Red Director, Redeyed Treefrog, Rhobite, Richardcavell, RickK, Rob Zako, RockMFR, Rs2, Sagaciousuk, Sam Hocevar, Sandyc, Sango123, Sdfisher, Shanes, Shoaler, Sietse Snel, SimonP, Slipstream, SlowkingMan, SoWhy, Spinxa, Stephenb, Stevey7788, Susvolans, Swatjester, Sysy, Tarquin, Tbrethes, TeaDrinker, Techna1, Texture, Theleftorium, Thomas Veil, Thumperward, Timhowardriley, TittoAssini, TnS, Tomharrison, Tosha, Toussaint, TwoOneTwo, Uncle G, Unknown, Vadder, Vaneet18 malhotra, Virbhoj, Wackyvorlon, Wellithy, Wikipediarules2221, Worldtraveller, WriteRight1stTime, Yurik, Zazou, Zigger, 491 anonymous edits

Wikipedia *Source*: http://en.wikipedia.org/w/index.php?oldid=310441753 *Contributors*: (, (jarbarf), -) 2006, -- April, -Barry-, .1pp4VV4, .digamma, 02ashfords, 03webberg, 0T0, 0bvious, 0hn035!H4xx0r!, 0o64eva, 1(), 10galen, 11.74, 1123090118, 119, 11qwe, 11warnjames, 120381i, 12345blake, 123kuko321, 12theend21, 130.94.122.xxx, 15.67, 16@r, 172.135.153.xxx, 18.47, 1diesel, 1worddome, 2004-12-29T22:45Z, 216.126.89.xxx, 21655, 21th, 23@25, 24.144.84.178., 28675, 2bar, 321, 334a, 35493dl, 3friends, 3nih, 49ers14, 4r4, 5 ultra spek, 51015a, 5150pacer, 578, 5dsddddd, 5ko, 5thhour, 666, 7, 75th Trombone, 782349792834, 7fex5q2ek, 8gibbplace, 927, 98E, 99,999 bud, 99DBSIMLR, A Man For The Glen, A Nobody, A State Of Trance, A Train, A bit iffy, A new one, A-emet-son, A. Exeunt, A.Z., A104375, A1162199, A1kmm, AAA!, AAAAA, AB-me, ABCD, AC+793888, ACM, ADNghiem501, AGK, AHLU, ALL OF YOU ST, ALargeElk, AMK152, AOEU, AP1787, APUS, ARC Gritt, ASG1022, ASOTMKX, ATMarsden, ATerezi, Aaaaaaa7, Aakeem02, Aanhorn, Aarfdog, Aarkangel, Aarokid123, Aaron Lewicki, Aaron.peachey3, Aaru Bui, Abadone, Abc2, Abcdefgy2, Abecedare, Abeg92, Aberro, Abhic95, Abilityfun, Aborlan, Ac1983fan, Academic Challenger, Acaides, Acalamari, Accurizer, Acdc44, AceMyth, Acegikmo1, Aceleo, Acerperi, Aceshigh6, Acetic Acid, Acewolf359, Acroterion, Action.jackson, Actown, Adam Bishop, Adam1516, AdamJacobMuller, AdamSolomon, AdamWill, AdamantlyMike, Adambisset, Adambiswanger1, Adambro, Adamfinmo, Adamn, Adamv88, Adan Bishop, Adashiel, Adbaxter, Addit, Addshore, Adidaniteelf, AdjustShift, Adler723, Adolphus79, Ads77, Aeikozz, Aeon1006, Aeonoris, Aerion, Aerno, AfluentRider, Africanus, Afterwriting, Agent007ravi, AgentPeppermint, Agentcel, Aggie Jedi, Agjjy, Ah Liveto Domun, Ahall6, Ahanatamao'o, Ahmed.pervez, Ahoerstemeier, Ahunt, Aibogreens, Aidan00000, Aidepolcycne, Aillema, Ais523, Aitias, Ajay ijn, Ajmint, Ajsgeek, Akamad, Akanemoto, Akmak03, Aksent220, Aksi great, Aktalo, AlanAu, Alan Pascoe, AlanBarrett, Alaning, Alansohn, Alaverga, AlbanianMVP, Albinomonkey, Aldie, Ale jrb, AlefZet, Alekcandr, Aleksanteri, Alensha, Alex.muller, Alex.tan, Alex3212321, Alex42092, Alex456415451, Alex500000, Alex756, AlexBedard, AlexKrolewski, Alexandre linhares, Alexdellanzo, Alexey Petrov, Alexian5, AlexiusHoratius, Alexryan, Alexwg, Alexzanderhill, Alezander, Algumacoisaqq, Alhutch, Ali K, Ali@gwc.org.uk, Alias Flood, Alientraveller, Alienware220, Alihammoud, AlisonW, AlistairMcMillan, Alkivar, AllGloryToTheHypnotoad, Allstarecho, Alper Tolga, Alphachimp, Alphax, Alreajk, Als;dfkjd, Alsandair, Altenmann, Alterego, Altrocst, Alvinrune, Alza213, Amandajm, Amandude13, Amazon10x, Ambaal, Ambarish, Amberrock, Ambrose222, Ambuj.Saxena, Amcaja, Amcbride, Amcfreely, Amdrummer00, AmericanXplorer13, AmiDaniel, Amicon, Amir beckham, Ammar ammar, Ammar gerrard117, AmorimParga, Amos Han, Amren, Amritsingh9, An unattributed source, AnOddName, AnTi, Anand Karia, Anaraug, Ancheta Wis, Ande B., Andersmusician, Andfound815, Andman8, AndonicO, Andre Engels, AndreNatas, Andrea Parton, Andres, Andrevan, Andrew Levine, Andrew Parodi, Andrew Yong, Andrew73, Andrewericoleman, Andrewli121, Andrewlp1991, Andrewpmk, Andris, Android79, AndyM. Wang, Andy Marchbanks, Andy4you03, Andy6262, AndySimpson, Andyabides, Andypandy.UK, Andypham3000, Andysch, Anemte, Anescient, Anetode, Angade keithe, AngelAeris, AngelOfSadness, Angela, Angelaire, Angelic Enigma, Angeliswastaken, Angelo Saxon, Anger22, Angr, AngryParsley, Angusware, AniMate, Anilocra, Anirudh hungund, Anjo1131, Anna05, Annakitali, Anonymous Dissident, Anonymous anonymous, Anonymous editor, Another CommunismVandal, AnotherDeadPerson, Ans, Anskas, Antandrus, Ante450, Anthere, Anthony, Anthony Ivanoff, Anthony5429, Anthony717, Anti-Anonymex2, AntiMedia, AntiMediaW, AntiMediaWiki, Anticommunist, Antonielly, Antonin Sidaway, Antonio Lopez, Antonrojo, Antony1103, Anwar saadat, Appleboy, Aqair, Aqwis, Arakunem, Aranel, Arbeit Sockenpuppe, Arbitrary username, ArcT, Arcadie, Archanamiya, Archer3, Archer7, Archibald Mitternich, Arctic.gnome, Arcturus, Ardonik, ArenaRock, Aridd, ArielGold, Aristotle1990, Arite, Arkalochori, Arnon Chaffin, Arnos78, Arpingstone, Arqumhayat, Arrr matey, Arru, Arsenal lee4, Art LaPella, Artaxiad, Artemis10000, ArthritisCritic, Arthur Warrington Thomas, ArthurWeasley, Artyboy, Arvindn, Arwel Parry, Asasa, Asaspades9, Asbestos, Asc112, Asdfgh, Asdsdasd, Ashanc, Ashenai, Ashill, Ashton1983, Asianmang15, Asirota, Asparagus, AssistantX, Astro Chicken, Astro Turfing, AstroHurricane001, AstroNomer, Asyndeton, Athf1234, Athlete man11, Athyna, Atigersrock, Atlant, Atomicthumbs, Atroche, Atropos, Attilios, AuburnPilot, Audacity, Aude, Auos11, Austin512, Auuuu, Auzu, Ava me 182, Avador, Avala, Avantrosa, Avillia, Avnjay, Avraham, Awickert, Awolf002, AxG, AxelBoldt, Axeman89, Axl, Axpd, Axxxr, Aytakin, Ayudante, Az1568, AzaToth, Azer Red, Aziz090, AznPride88, Aznspazboi, Azrael Nightwalker, B, B&W AnimeFan, B1rd, B2drive, B9 hummingbird hovering, BCube, BECASC, BIG H, BJCenters, BLuNt- FoRcE, BMF81, BR9000, BUF4Life, BVM, BW,

Babajobu, Baca as, Bachrach44, BaconBailer, Bact, Badagnani, Badbats, Badger Badger Badger, Badgernet, Badjeros, Badland boyz, Baggins55, Bahameenballin, Baldnsexi69, Balkissoonsingh, Ballinsnowman, Balthazarduju, Banana04131, Bananakiddo, Bandalism2, Bandgeek221111, Bandit keith, Bandit495x, Bando26, Banes, Bang Bang Bigalow, Bannafish, Banson, BanyanTree, Barnaby dawson, BaronLarf, Bart133, Bartgenius, Bartzx3, Baseball007, Bashereyre, Basilanddrew, Bastique, Batmanand, Batmangreen, Bauersnarky, Bawolff, Bayerischermann, Baylink, BazookaJoe, Bazzajf, Bbatsell, Bbauer55, Bbpen, Bc84, Bcasterline, Bclhoiondk, Bcorr, Bcrwiki, Bdesham, Beachloghunter, Bear-of-the-Woods, Bear6253, BearblokeWiki, Bearly541, Beasley23803, BeastmasterGeneral, Beautiful Scars, Beefit uk, Beefbrain89, Beenagent, Behemoth01, Beidabaozi, Being99, Beland, Belgian man, Belginusanl, Bellmunch123, Ben Pearce, Ben Tillman, Ben.rice13, BenBenBen, BenP94, Benbread, Bencherlite, Benjwong, Benklop, Bennettchipper, Benno Briton, Benny21041995, Bennyandwill, Bennyb123456789, Beno1000, Bentong Isles, Bernburgerin, BernieFan51, Bertbradshaw, Betacommand, Betterworld, Bevo, Bewildebeast, Beyazid, Bf0189, Bfleisher, Bgittings, Bhadani, BhaiSaab, Bhamv, Bhrgvsridhar, Bhudson, Bi89753, Bibblyjord, Biblbroks, Bidgee, Big Bowski, Big Dipper Daddy, BigBoyTinMan, BigD527, Bigballer23, Bigbluefish, Bigcheesepie, Bigeasy, Biggspowd, Bigpappa, Bigscooper18, Bigtop, BikBagent, Bikram08, Bill Thayer, Bill37212, BillC, Billcampsey, Billinnowhere, Billybob68, Biot, Biscuit1258, Biscuitman56, Bishonen, Biwhite2, Bjwebb, Bkonrad, Black Omnimon, Black child, Black-Velvet, Blackdown Will, BlackestNight, Blackhawk440, Blackjack48, Blackjackgirl17, Blacklemon67, Blacksonicus, Blackspiderhead, Blade Leader, Blahdyblahdyblah, Blair P. Houghton, Blargman24, BlastOButter42, Blastinonyall, Blaylockjam10, Blenky119, Blob007, Blonde tiger, BloodRed Sandman, Blotto3, Blowof Light, Blu Aardvark, Blue bear sd, Blue boy0810, BlueBird, BlueCanary9999, BluePaladin, Blueangel90190, Bluecrabs, Blueduck silverduck, Bluefalcon07, Bluemoose, Bluezy, Bmgoau, Bmo54, Bmrbarre, Boatteeth, Bob Schaefer, Bob f it, Bob mcglargy, Bob, just Bob, Bob1, Bob200607, Bob657, Bob99938, BobBob, BobaKhan, Bobadeba, Bobafett12, Bobashotmace, Bobber2, Bobblehead, Bobblewik, Bobby Button, Bobbywand, BobbyBoulders22, Bobbysags, Bobdobbs1723, Bobet, Bobjane, Bobo192, Bodil, Boffy b, Bogdangiusca, Bogey97, Bogyman, Boijunk, Bok269, BokuAlec, Bolkoff, Bong water juggalo, Bongfresh, Bongwarrior, Bontenbal, Bonz1984, Boole, BoomBox Boom, Boothy443, Bootstoots, Booyabazooka, Booyahh1, BorgHunter, BorgQueen, Borgir91, Borisblue, Borislav, Borkface, Born2edit, Bornhj, Borski, Boudiccat, Boudiccat3, Bower69, Bowlerjpg, Bowlhover, BozMo, Bproud, Brad 014, Bradders9191, Bradeos Graphon, Bradleycook94, Bradshaw330, Bramlet Abercrombie, Brantford, Braskol, Bratsche, Brendan Moody, Brendenhull, Brettz9, Brian0918, Brianjd, Brianna11, Brianstew, Brighterorange, Brion VIBBER, Brisbanite, Brndnchpln, Brockd, Brockert, Broken Segue, BrokenSegue, Bruce89, Bryan Alba, Bryan Derksen, BryanG, Bryjwal13, Bsm15, Bstn9, Btgh1993, Btm, Bubb1es520, Bubbleboom, Bubblesmiles, Bububu, Bubzyz, Buccaneerande, Bucephalus, Buchanan-Hermit, Bucupedayu, Buddy Jesus, BuddyJesus, BuickCenturyDriver, Buickid, Bulla, Bulu4uu, Bunchofgrapes, BunnyMan54, Bunyipmurd, Buotte, Buquku, Burgundavia, Burner0718, Butros, Buttered Bread, Butwhatdoiknow, Bvlax2005, Bwithh, Bz2, C00w, C12H22O11, CAIRNSY90, CAPS LOCK, CBDunkerson, CJ, CJ King, CK2326, CLAUDistic, CLW, CRGreathouse, CSM-101, CSavel66, Cabhan, Caceo, Cactus.man, Cadmium, Caiaffa, Calandrella, Calder Pegden, Caledoni92, Calion, Caller-X, CallieSulake, Callipygian123, Callmemrshowoff, Callum101, CallumV, Calmypal, Caltas, Calton, Calvin 1998, CambridgeBayWeather, Camembert, Camillaherrmann, Camptown, Can't sleep, clown will eat me, Canadian-Bacon, CanadianCaesar, CanadianLinuxUser, Canderson7, Candy-Panda, Canjbez, Cannonstudent, Canterbury Tail, Capitain45678, Capncruch06, Capricorn42, Captain Disdain, Captain Zyrain, Captain-tucker, Carbinekilla, Carbonite, Carcharoth, CardinalDan, Cardsplayer4life, CarlHewitt, CarlWiki, Carlosguitar, Carterly, Cash202, Casius, Casper2k3, Cassano, Cassie bertram123, Cassowary, Catdude, Catgut, CatherineMunro, Catstail, Caulde, Causa sui, Caynsta, Cbdorsett, CdaMVvWgS, Cdangel, Cdaszenies, Cdc, Cdecece, Cdf333fad3a, Cdosoftei, Ce1984, CecilWard, CeciliaPang, Cedrus-Libani, Ceenan, Cehax, Celestianpower, Cenarium, Centrx, CesarB, Cfeet77, Cgingold, Cgsteezy145, Chairboy, Chairlunchdinner, Chal3s, Chameleon, Changing History, Chanting Fox, Charion, Charles Stewart, Charlesfahringer, CharlieRCD, Charliemeyers, CharlotteWebb, Charmcity2007, Charmii, CharonX, Chas licciardello, Chaser, Chcknwnm, Cheatcode2, Cheerfulguy, Cheese bacon, Cheese13, Cheesefurtle, Cheessey, Cheezus, Chensiyuan, CherryFlavoredAntacid, Chestnut string, Chewbm05, Chgojcs, Chic-ism, Chicken7, Chico rico, Chiefadmin, ChillyHikaru, Chillyhot8, Chinkydamouse, Chipmunk365, Chivista, Chmod007, Chochopk, Chocoforfriends, Chocolateboy, Chodorkovskiy, Cholling, Cholmes75, Chopchopwhitey, Chotchki, Chowbok, Chowells, Chrhardy, Chris 42, Chris 73, Chris Bainbridge, Chris Edgemon, Chris Roy, ChrisDHDR, ChrisGriswold, ChrisKennedy, ChrisLamb, ChrisMP1, ChrisO, Chrisbradford234, Chrishibbard7, Christian List, Christian Storm, Christopher Allan Donavan, Christopher Kraus, Christopher Mahan, Christopher Parham, Christopher Sundita, ChristopherB6616, ChristopherJones III, Chriswiki, Chronicler0, ChtFreak64, Chuck Marean, Chunkey, Chuq, Church of emacs, Cimon Avaro, Cinnamon, Circeus, Cirt, Citylover, Cj395, Cjustin, Cjwright79, Ck lostsword, Ckmn224, Clair de Lune, Clank787, Clarityfiend, Clarp, Classic Fan, Clawed, Clayzer, Cleared as filed, Clement Cherlin, ClericalError, Clilly, ClockworkSoul, CloudNine, Clout, Clyrenternal, Cma, Cmdrjameson, Cmmnism, Cnwb, Cobey13, CockSucker, CodeWeasel, Codex Sinaiticus, Codylolhi, Coelacan, Cognita, Cohesion, Cointyro, Cokoli, Colin Keigher, Collabi, Colleenthegreat, ColonelBroomstick, Coltsman444, ComKeen, Combat Wombat, Cometstyles, Cominoverdahill2, Commander, Commander Shepard, CommonsDelinker, CommunalConspiracy, CommunismVandal, Communistroadster, Compact105, Compass35, Computerjoe, Computor, Conchobhair, Conchuir, Coneslayer, Conjugacy, ConjurusRex, Connormom, Conor 1025, Conservatives are better than liberals, ContagiousTruth, Conti, Conversewearinghippie, Conversion script, Cookiemobsta, CoolBlue, Coolcole93, Coolhandscot, Coopadowny, CorbinSimpson, Core Networks GmbH, Coredesat, Cormaggio, Corneliusy, Cornerbock, Cotoco, Count Caspian, Cowman109, Cowpriest2, Cp111, Cpaulsinkhorn, Cpfanboy, Cptcellulose, Crab1, Crab182, Craig rae fuxake, CraigKeogh, CraigRNielsen, Craignielsen, Cramer crame, Crappy123, Crashaire, Crazy29, CrazyYankee, Crazycomputers, Crazymentalchris, Crazynas, Crazypersonbb, Crazytales, Crazyyoda1138, CreateEdit 000, Creenhurste, Creidieki, Crewsd, Crm2905, Crohnie, Cromag, Crosbie, Crossy26, Crum375, Crushthor, CryptoDerk, Crystallina, Cs che, Cuindless, Cup987, Curious1i, Curps, Curuinor, Cvaneg, Cvoz, Cxz, Cylzzle, CyanideSandwich, Cyber ninja, CyberSkull, Cybercat, Cybercobra, Cyberevil, Cyborg, Cyclonenim, Cyde, Cylonhunter, Cynicism addict, Cyp, Cyrius, Cyrusc, D greeney, D'Agosta, D-Rock, D6, DAFMM, DANNY AND KELLY MARTIN LIKE TO HAVE SEX WITH UNDERAGED BOYS!, DDL, DESiegel, DGJM, DHeyward, DJ Clayworth, DVD R W, DXBari, Da monster under your bed, Da wikipedia vandal, DaChief531, DaGizza, DaGrandPuba, Dachshundsinthehouse2, Dadevster, Dadscowgurl4eva, DagnyB, Dahveed323, Dakpowers, Dallman101, Damian Yerrick, Dan "The Beast" Severn, Dan D. Ric, Dan100, DanCupid, DanKeshet, DanMat6288, Dances with weebles, Dancrumb, Dandelions, Daniel, Daniel J. Leivick, Daniel Olsen, Daniel-1003, Daniel.Boldi, DanielCD, Danjewell, Danny, Dannycali, Dannywein, Danski14, Dantbass, Dante Alighieri, DanteSB, Dantheman0056, Danwingyding, Dar-Ape, Darcy Sabian, Darin-0, Dariusdeathbane, Dark Kyle, Dark Shikari, Dark spartan082, DarkDP, DarkHorizon, Darrenb16, Darth Panda, DarthVader, Das Ansehnlisch, Dasani, Dasu996, Datm, Daunrealist, Davadr, Dave6, DaveGorman, DaveJ7, Daveh4h, Davemcarlson, Daverocks, Davetheman44, Daveyboy16, Daveydweeb, David, David D Delta, David Gerard, David Johnson, David Levy, David Shankbone, David.Mestel, DavidLevinson, Davidcannon, Davidgauntlett, Davidgoldner18, Davidhorman, Davidm617617, Davidngl50, Davidsheiman, Davidstrauss, Davness, Davodd, Davud363000, Dawn Bard, Daz90, Dbenbenn, Dbtfz, Dburnsey433, Dcabrilo, Dcandeto, Dcflyer, Dcljr, Dcoetzee, Dcooper, Ddalez, DeadEyeArrow, Deadblob93, Deadcorpse, Deadflagblues, Deadmanwalking2006, DeanoF9, Death.to.smoochie, Deathboy911, Deathllama, Deathonblackwings, Deathpal, Deaytonist, Deboerjo, Decidedly so, Decimal10, Deckiller, Dedicated to learn, Dedman22, Deeptrivia, Def1pony, Defeated, Defenestrate, Deli nk, Delirium, Delldot, Delpino, Delsol312, Deltabeignet, Demondogsofwar, Demus Wiesbaden, Denalin, Dendodge, Denelson83, Denial, Dennis The Menace, Dennislee272727, DennyColt, Deovolenti, DerHexer, DerRichter, Derek Ross, Derontae23, DerrickOswald, Descendall, Deskana, Desmay, Detective 27, DevDawg27, DevastatorIIC, Devil1337, Dewet, Dewsta123, Dezidor, Dfire2010, Dforest, Dfrg.msc, Dgies, Dglynch, Dharmabum420, Dhawk37, Diagonalfish, Diana12345, Diberri, DickyRebooot, Diddyzelda, Die2014, Diego, Diego pmc, Digger3000, Digitalme, Digwuren, Dilbert307, Dillanlabagh, Dilldogg, Dillion1231, Dina, Dinokid, Dinorhino, Dionyziz, Dirc, Dirchlet, DirkvdM, Dirty bumsex man, Dirtydove4, Disastrophe, Disavian, Discodavid217, Discospinster, Diskid, Dispenser, Distance, Diversitygroup, DivineOmega, Dizzydopeweed, Djames, Djcastel, Dkndkn21, Dlohcierekim, Dlohcierekim's sock, Dmcc, Dmcohen, Dmn, Dmoss, Dnkidd, Do-a-zool, Dobbies, DobbyD, Doc glasgow, Docadut, Docbug, Dockingman, Doctor Awesome, Dods444, Dogman15, Dogsienyaw, Dom Kaos, Dominic, Dominic stevenson, Dominik92, Domthedude001, Donarreiskoffer, Donmiguel2, Donteditme, Doobloon, Doody09, DoomBW, Doomofhumans, Doomshifter, Doopokko, DopefishJustin, Doprendek, Dori, Dorini, Dothefandango, DoubleBlue, Dough4872, DougsTech, Dovi, Downtown dan seattle, Dpotter, Dr bab, Dr. Alan Sieve, Dr. Blofeld, Dr. H. Wilkins, DrBlevins, DrOxacropheles, DrQuincy, DrStrangelove95, Draconiator, Dragon Myth, Dragonball1986, DragonflySixtyseven, Drakodan, Dralwik, Drama freak, Drbaseball13, Dreaded Walrus, Dreamafter, Dreamword, Dreary101, Drewboy64, Dreyfus, Drilnoth, Drini, Drones in a box-411, DropDeadGorgias, Drum guy, Drumersrule, Drumguy8800, Drummerld1, Drwolffenstein, Ds555, Dschwen, Dsf7183, Dskills, Dsmith1987, Dstebbins, DtD90, Dthomsen8, Dtobias, DubaiTerminator, Dubba Dubba, Ducain, DuckyRoberta, Ducttapeguy, Dude11356, Duinemerwen, Duja, Duke of Geography, Dukee, Duketheredeemer, Dumbboy101, Duncharris, Dunemaire, Dungbringer, Dunlevyd, Dureo, DustFerret, Dustimagic, Dustin099, Dustindean, Dvdweng, Dwardini, Dwheeler, Dyamantese, Dylan620, Dysprosia, Dze27, E2m, EBG1234, ESkog, EWS23, Eaglizard, Eal, Earl Andrew, EastGermanAllStar, Eatmefortea, Ebarnes1621, Ebowdish, Eburge, Ec5618, Echo5Joker, Echoray, Ed Poor, Ed g2s, EdJohnston, Edcolins, EddieVanZant, Eddpayne, Eddy beerdrinks, Edgrmarriott, Editor437, Editschmedit, Edizzle8002, Edokter, Edratzer, Eduardo Sellan III, Edward, Edwy, Eeblefish, Eeeeee, Eeekster, Eep², Eequor, Eeyore5, Effeietsanders, Eggar, Eggyolk4, Eiler7, Eixo, Eje004, Ekmai, El C, El aprendelenguas, El barto8, El3m3ntsk8r24, ElTyrant, Elaich, Eleassar777, Eleizer, Elenseel, Eli Todd, Elian, EliasAlucard, Eliazar, ElinorD, Elipongo, Eliyahu S, Eljawa, Elkman, Elliottbrooks, Elliskev, Ellmist, Elm-39, Elmolover93, Elnoyola, Eloquence, Elpechos, Elvisguy46, Elwikipedista, Emanuele Saiu, Emersoni, Emijrp, Emilyxlovesxyou, Emirdengiz, Emocore, Empire-Loyalist, Emr1028, Emre D., Emufarmers, Emx, Encephalon, EncephalonSeven, Enchanter, Encyclopedist, Enforcer1, Engelos, EngineerScotty, EnglishEfternamn, Enjuewang, EnkyBurgess, Enochlau, Enter The Crypt, EnviroGranny, Enviroboy, Eoghanwilledit!hahaha, EonBlueApocalypse, Epbr123, Epoch Times, Epolk, Equazcion, Er199653, Eranb, Ereid01, Eric119, Eric76, EricV89, Ericoides, Ericva1992, Erik Zachte, Erin Haleray, Ernie 85, Errantminion, Erriiciii, Errina15, EscapingLife, Eskimo, Esprit15d, Essexmutant, Essjay,

Estebandoebolas, Esteffect, Estoy Aqui, Esurnir, Eszett, Eternalbeans, Ethan.hardman, Euchiasmus, EugeneZelenko, EurekaLott, EvanK0, Evb-wiki, EventHorizon, Evercat, Every name is taken12345, Everyking, Everykinq, Evil Monkey, Evil saltine, Evil00, EvilHom3r, EvilZak, EvocativeIntrigue, Excirial, Exert, Exeunt, Exodustheory, Expealidoceous, Explodicle, Extraordinary Machine, Ez910503, Ezhiki, Ezsaias, FDR, FML, FR Soliloquy, FRANCS2000 IS A CUNT, FREDDY, FT2, Fabiform, Fabio Longhorn, Fabricationary, Fact check, Factitious, Fagiolonero, Fagnostic, Fah007, Fakewikiman, Falconhurst1967, Falconleaf, Falling Man Productions, Fallout boy, Falphin, Fan-1967, Fang Aili, Fanger, Fapassier, Farmerchris, FatboyShrek, Father Ignatius, Fatty1234, Fatty8900, Fatyouto, Favouritesnail, Fawful66, FayssalF, Fayte, Fbv65edel, Fdp, Fear the hobbit, Feco, FedEx Pope, Feere Gorone, Feezo, Felipe Menegaz, Felix Folio Secundus, FelixDeSousa, Felixboy, Fenechboy, Fenice, Feqik, Ferbann, Ferkelparade, FermionGas, Ferrarigtr, Fethroesforia, Fetofs, Fiddleswith, Field kkg, Fieldday-sunday, Fifai, Figgles49, Filceolaire, Fildon, Filll, Filter1987, Fingers-of-Pyrex, Finlay McWalter, Fire wolf, FireDreams4, Fireball3332000, Firebert42, Firefoxman, Firehair12000, Firsfron, First draft of history, Fish and karate, Fishal, FisherQueen, Fitzgiggler, Fizron, Fjjf, Flagators1, Flameofpie, Flameviper, Flarn2005, Flash man999, Flcelloguy, Flightsim trekkie, Flint Marko, Flipskater876, Flockmeal, Floopik, Florentino floro, Florida4406, Floschneck, Flourgus, Flowerparty, Flowerpotman, Flubbit, FlufferA999, Fluteflute, Flux.books, Flyguy649, Flyingtoaster1337, Flyty5061, Fnfd, Fnordfinder, Folau111, Fonzy, Foobar, Foodman, Foodmarket, Foofighter1, Fook, Fooku, Forrestthealmighty, Francinne, Francis Irving, FrancoGG, Francs2000, Frank Anchor, FrankCostanza, Frap, Frazzydee, Freakmighty, Freakofnurture, Frecklefoot, FredegarBolger, Fredelige, Fredfred2, Fredrik, Free JoeM!!!!, Freerick, Frencheigh, Frenchman113, FreplySpang, FreplySpanq, FreshPineSent, Freyr, Friday, Frigo, Fritzlein, Frogger512, From.here.to.neverland, Frost000, Frozen Serge, Frymaster, Fschoenm, Ftyui135, Fudgegland, FuelWagon, Fukyaself, Fullerene, Fullertonart, Func, Fungus Mclatchey, Funky Llama, FunnyMan3595, Funnybunny, Funper, Fuzheado, FuzzyTatie, Fvw, Fxer, Fys, G Rose, G-Man, G. Campbell, GHe, GJenner, GMC09, GTBacchus, GW Simulations, Gabrielsimon, Gadfium, Gaff, Gagamagit, Gahusi, Gahzor, Gakusha, Galactor213, Galadh, Galanskov, Galaxiaad, Galoubet, Galwhaa, Gamagama, Gamaliel, Gamer1606, Gamma1847, Gangerli, GangstaEB, Ganiwueo, Gaohhaig, Garbyal, Gareth Owen, Garfield226, Garglebutt, Garik, Garion96, Garkalla, Garrett21, Gary Cziko, Gary King, Garzane, Gasolinedrinker, Gavinharris, Gavinsidhu, Gaylord the gay communism vandal, Gazpacho, Gbleem, Gboweswhitton, Gcziko, Gdo01, Gecafe, GeebsRilie, Geego, Geeman, General Eisenhower, Generaleskimo, Gengiskanhg, Geni, George The Dragon, George W. Ducky, GeorgeBills, GeorgeMoney, GeorgeMoney VandalProof, GeorgeStepanek, Georgia guy, Georgiopro, Geothermal, Germs-Bug, Gerrit, Getonyourfeet, Gettingtoit, Gftr, Ggb667, Ghettoboy9111, Ghhg, Ghingo, Gholam, Ghost109, Ghost901, Ghostbubbles, Ghosts&empties, Giggy, Gikuiiauw, GillianTipson, Gimboid13, Ginkgo100, Giorgi.alessio, Giovanna0, Girlskatermathus, Gjd001, GlassCobra, Glen, GlenDavis, Gmaxwell, Gnomeraver, GnuDoyng, Go for it!, Go on small dick block me!, Goatasaur, Godardesque, Godofkratos, Godrox3, Goeagles4321, Gogo Dodo, Gohn, Goin' Back to Houston Houston Houston., Gokoon, Golbez, Goldfinger644, Golfpro827, Gonnbe, Goodburger, GoodbyeBlueSky, Googl, Googoie, Goonerboy2007, Goplat, Gordon Freeman101, Got cheese4, Gotyear, Gowingsgo, Gr55tay, Gr8white, Grace Note, Gracefool, Gracenotes, GraemeL, Graham87, Grahampitt, Grammatical error, Grand Am, Grandad, Grande-Oracle, Grandexandi, Grease Monkey, Greater Userbox Mage, Green caterpillar, GreenHydrogen27, Greeney, Greenfan200, Greenofroogle, Greenpig123, Greenrd, Greeves, Greg Louis, Greg27uk, GregAsche, GregSon, Gregoli, GregorB, Gregorik, Gregorybeauchamp, Gretaisadog, Grey Knight 1ce, Gribachek, Grick, Griffin5, Griffith grad, Grifr006, Grika, Grin, Grinner, Grm wnr, Gronky, Grosscha, Grover cleveland, Grrrws, Grumphnoo, Grunt, Gscshoyru, GstrOSx, Guaca, Guaka, Guanaco, Guest9999, Guevara27, Guitarguy1996, Guitarheroguylol, Gumba gumba, GunnerMike89, Gunnycortez, Gurch, Gurchzilla, Gurubrahma, Guruclef, Gustavb, Gustaveio, Gustavobernhardt, Guthrie, Guttzu, Guy Harris, Guy M, Guy Peters, GuyKedem, Guycool28, Guyjohnston, Gwam, Gwbennett, Gwen570, Gwern, Gwernol, Gzdavidwong, Gzgianfreda, Gzornenplatz, H2g2bob, H@r@ld, HKT, HOHOMAN, Haakon, Habler 32, Habsfan1433, Hackysack93, Hadal, Hadrian89, HaeB, Haemo, Hagi1234, Haha169, Haham hanuka, Haipa Doragon, Halcatalyst, Hall Monitor, Hallam17, Hamedog, HammerHeadHuman, Hamster.dude, Hancock, HandGrenadePins, Handface, Handisnak, Hang gp28, Hao2lian, Haochi, HappyCamper, Happywaffle, Hapsala, Hapsiainen, Harej, Hargrimm, Harold Marry, HaroldRex, Haros, Harriv, Harro5, Harry, Harry., Harry491, Harryboyles, Harrywants, Hasamasa, Hatfield0835, Hatik, Haukurth, Havan, Hawkfan45, Hawstom, Hayden0604, Haydentomas, Hayford Peirce, Haynesjames, Hayzerthelayzer, Hazzard Thug, Hcheney, Hckydude1103, Hdante, Hdt83, HeadAsploded, Heah, Heaneypedia, Hebedebede, Hednrix444, Hee tee, Heegoop, Heeheehahahohoho, Heffers, HeikoEvermann, Heimstern, Hejooiu, Heliomance, HeliosUnit, Helixblue, Hellboy2hell, Hellcat fighter, Hellno2, Hello&Goodbye, Hello32020, Hellodonkey, Hellosalut, Hemanshu, Hendrixfan432, HenokY, Henry Flower, Henry58922, Henrygb, Hephaestos, Heqs, HereToHelp, Hermione1980, Heron, Hetar, Hey guys!!, Heysandyimsandy, Hg-fix, Hgf, Hhhhhh, HiEverybodyHiDoctorNick, Hibbajibba6969, Hibernian, Hiberno latin invasion, Hiddenidentity, High Hopes, High Plains Drifter, Highline, Hildanknight, HillbillyHomo, Hillsy92, Hinotori, HisSpaceResearch, Hmains, Hmmmm, Hn, Hockeydude7993, Hojimachong, Hokiado, Holek, HolloBath, Holy sauna, HomeSuggestion, Homerdonut666, Homunq, Honeycake, Hongshi, Hoodblazer1, HoodedMan, Hooduphodlum, Hooger, Hooo33ter, Hopefullyacceptable username, Horkana, Horlsg, Horologium, Hostile Hams, Hotchops8, Hotjock1, Houseman, Houseofhack, Howabout1, Hpaddict, Hslhfuh, Hsnetworks, Htnamus, Hu, Hudsonnc, Huinyu, Hules001, Hulmey, HumanFrailty, Humus sapiens, Hurricane111, Hurricanefreak777, Hurricanehink, Husky, Husond, Hut 8.5, Huvuxoa, Hvn0413, Hyad, Hygraed, I Am Not Willy On Wheels, I Ate Some Toast., I Spread Good News, I don't recognize "recognise", I just move too fast, I need a name, I'm a sawk, I-10, IAMTrust, IIVQ, IMSoP, IMvom, INyar, IRP, ISD, ISeeDeadPixels, ITV, Iafjo, Iamthebest4, Ian 2k3k, Ian13, Ianblair23, Ianhoyer, Iapetus, Ibagli, Ibapah, Icairns, Ice on mars not space, Icewedge, Iceyhot123, Idebomb, Idleguy, Idont Havaname, Ignatius09, IhavemorehairDOWNTHERE, Ihuxley, Iimbo Wales, Ikh, Ikuztan, Ilario, Iloveunicorns, Ilse@, Ilyanep, Imaglang, Impossible4, Impulse 360, In the beginning..., InShaneee, Inass, India25, Indiver, Inego, InfinityAndBeyond, Infoporfin, Infrogmation, Ingolfson, Inkington, Insanephantom, Insertusernamehere, Instinct, Inter, Interiot, IntfictExpert, Intheclub, Intimidated, InvisibleK, Inx272, IoanneB, Iojuge, Iothiania, Ioy, Ipgordon, Iphillip1, Ipigott, Irck, Iridescent, Irishguy, Irishmex rebel, IronChris, Ironiridis, Ironman0392, Isaac Rabinovitch, Isam, Isfisk, Isham.phantom, Isomorphic, Isopropyl, Itai, Italiacampione2006, Itastenice, Itel94, Itisfun, Itschris, Itsmine, Itsorin, Iuoogebo, Iusecapslock, Ixfd64, Ixtz, Izehar, Izno, J Di, J'raxis, J. Whales, J.J., J.delanoy, J1, J44xm, JAIME WALES, JCipriani, JDPhD, JForget, JHMM13, JHP, JImbo Wales, JNT724, JRM, JRR Trollkien, JTSu, JWSchmidt, JYolkowski, JaGa, JableTNigs, Jac16888, Jacek Kendysz, Jack, Jack Cox, Jack L, Jack Merridew, Jack324, Jackal ST, Jackdragon17, Jackjack210, Jackleyool, Jacks hacks, Jacob Menson, Jacob valliere, JacobshafferTOPEKA, Jacoplane, JadedSamurai, Jahangir99, Jahiegel, Jaime Wales, Jaimeglz, Jake Jerk, Jake Larsen, Jake Nettle, Jake Remington is snobby, Jake95, Jakebohler, Jakob Suckale, Jakshep2, Jambalaya, Jamed930, James Kemp, James Prude, JamesBeach, JamesMLane, JamesR, Jamesday, Jamesedwardsmith, Jameseyx, Jamesjbrownjr, Jamezp1, Jamie Bourne, Jamild, Jammerpunk1089, Jamyskis, Jan Hidders, Jane.fader, Janejellyroll, Janemba13, Janke, Janshiterator, Jaques O. Carvalho, Jaraalbe, Jaranda, Jared Hunt, Jared adams, JarlaxleArtemis, Jaroslavleff, JasonJack, Jasonater, Jatkins, Jauerback, Javert, Javier de la Cueva, Jaxl, Jay Gatsby, Jaydend, Jayen466, Jayjg, Jaymac407, Jayvalente, Jazjaz92, Jblatt, Jboyd, Jc iindyysgvxc, Jcw69, Jdavidb, Jdchamp31, Jdforrester, Jdrsmith, Jdsfhlkj, JeLuF, Jeandré du Toit, Jeansrock101, Jecowa, JediLofty, Jeff G., Jeff8765, Jeffcrowl, Jeffhoy, Jeffn8r, Jeffq, Jeffrey O. Gustafson, Jeffrey529, Jejnei, Jelligraze, Jello12, Jembay, Jensgb, Jeremy Visser, JeremyA, JeremyMcCracken, Jerky beef, Jeroen Coumans, Jerome 89, Jeronim, Jerrbear, Jerzy, Jesse2, JesseMueller, JesseW, JessicaSumac, Jetekus, Jetsfan28, Jew Aardvark will be at SolWestFri. July 28th!, Jew Aardvark: Pissing in the Kool-Aid since December 2005, Jewish Bacon, Jfdwolff, Jfkwentdown, Jfox433, Jgk009, Jh51681, Jhaagsma, Jian77, Jidanni, Jiddisch, Jigglyman, Jigo121, Jigster93, JillS123, Jim Gates, JimboD Wales, Jimbo Donal Wales, Jimbo VVales, Jimbo Wales, Jimbo Warez, Jimbo91uk, Jimbobsween, Jimbosgaylover, Jimi Boy, Jimmy D Wales, Jimmy Tagues, Jimmybutt, Jimregan, Jinnbo VVales, Jipcy, Jitterro, Jj137, Jjdukejj403, Jjjct, Jkelly, Jkl, Jklin, Jlomcc, Jmabel, Jmklooster, Jni, Jnich86, Jnothman, JoanneB, Joaodiogorp, Jobby12, Jobe6, Jocke666, Joe.aston, JoeBlogsDord, JoeBongard, JoeSmack, Joebeone, Joebobfenestre, Joel.anker, Joelholdsworth, Joelong, Joelpt, Joewigger, Joey0889, Joeyx22lm, Johann Wolfgang, John, John Carter, John Cumbers, John Fader, John Hubbard, John254, John910, JohnAFlynn, JohnAnderson, JohnCD, JohnOwens, JohnWittle, Johngillfan, Johnleemk, JohnofPhoenix, Johnowenlangham, Johnsk8er, Johnsmith1882, Johntex, Johshandlesmand332ffs, Joker1900, Jokestress, Jon Harald Søby, Jon Stockton, JonasRH, Jonathan321, JonathanFreed, Jonathanpops, Jongtu, Joniboy98, Jonik, Jonnyt1989, Jono1111, Jonr3, Jons63, Jookia, Jopxton, Jordan armstrong, Jormungander, JosebaAbaitua, Joseph Marks, Joseph Solis in Australia, Joseph.slater, Josephf, Josephus505, Joshbuddy, Joshhorvath, Joshl70, Joshua BishopRoby, Joshua Issac, JoshuaSpence, JoshuaZ, Joshuagross, Jossi, Journalist, Jouvenel, Joyous!, Jpatokal, JpbJersey, Jpgordon, Jr.steeler44, Jrdioko, Jredmond, Jrockley, JrsportsfanatikIII, Jrugordon, Jsalims8, Jsemmens, Jsiden, Jstaryuk, Jtal19, Jtkiefer, Jtneill, JuJube, Juddybuddy1981, Jufert, Juhustbe, Jules Merriam, JulianFT, Juliancolton, Julianos99, Julio Felipe Angelini, Jumbalya123, Jumbo Wales, Jumbuck, JungBuck, Junglecat, Jungwirthwillkillallrocks, Junkerboat, Junyor, Juppiter, Jurgenvd267, Jusjih, Just Another Dan, Just zis Guy, you know?, JustPhil, JustSomeKid, Justa Punk, JustinTyme, Juzeris, Jwanders, Jweiss11, Jwissick, Jwrosenzweig, Jwykes, K-UNIT, KAMiKAZOW, KD-G722, KD5TVI, KF, KFP, KJS77, KKC, KMcKenzie, KOMBA, KPH2293, KTo288, KURT ANGLE, KYPark, Kaabi, Kablammo, Kabuto Yakushi, Kadir12345, Kaganer, Kagekitsune, Kagome17, Kahvsi, Kaiba, Kaihsu, Kaisershatner, Kaizar, Kajasudhakarababu, Kalarn, Kalathalan, Kaldar, Kalteras, Kanata Kid, Kandar, Kane5187, Kane584, Kanon6917, Karada, Karimarie, Karl Dickman, Karlthegreat, Karmafist, Karol Langner, Kasei, Kasei-jin, Kasualty, Kasukei, Katefan0, Katimawan2005, Kay Körner 20.12.1983, Kazama3000, Kazikame, Kazikameuk, Kbdank71, Kbh3rd, Kdkatpir2, Kdogg2412, Ke4roh, Kecker, Keegan, Keelm, Keen000, Keenan Pepper, Keep10O, Keilana, Keitei, Kellap, KellyMartin, KenCat, Kenkoo1987, Kennet.mattfolk, Kennyisinvisible, Kent Wang, Keoki, Kermite, Kerotan, Kesac, Kesla, Kevin Breitenstein, Kevin S., KevinSaff, Kevin66, Kevinmooney, Kexpert, Keycard, Kghose, Kgm591, Khalid Mahmood, Khatru2, Khendon, Khoikhoi, Khukri, Kiat123, KickAir8P~, Kicking222, Kidburla, KiddySadurn, KiddySaturn, Kidwade, Kieff, Kierensfaroes1, Kikkid851, KileofDonegal, Kilfoyle, Kill, Killerman1, Killzone9999, Kilo-Lima, Kim.mason, Kimchi.sg, Kimmelaar, Kimvr, Kimyu12, KingBob324, King Dickie Roberta, King Jimbo, King Pong, King of Hearts, King oogy, KingNEGRO, KingTT, Kingdee53, Kingdomkey01, Kingingston, Kingkutz, Kingluey, Kingoomieiii, Kingthing49, Kingturtle, Kinneyboy90, Kinst, Kinu, Kirachinmoku, Kirbymaster28, Kirill Lokshin, Kis 0606004, KittenHuffer, Kiwi, Kizcaz, Kjaergaard, Kkkiiinnn, Klaser, Klenje, Klhs, Klington, Kmg90,

Kmhad, Knowledge Seeker, KnowledgeOfSelf, KnowledgeRequire, Knucmo2, Koavf,Kodster, KojiDude,Kokothebread, Kolfo,Kolkov,Kollision, Kong123, Konman72, Konob9, Konstable, Koolconstor, KorkyDay, Korny O'Near, Korossyl, Korp7, Kosebamse, Kotepho, Kotjze, Kovarik23, Koyaanis Qatsi, Kozuch, Kraigisreal, Krakatoa, Kratervideo, Krator, KratosY,Krauss, Krawehl, Kray, Krel, Krich, Kristen Eriksen, Krol:k,Krsont, Krzieman, Ksbhangu, Kslain, Kslays, Ktr101, Kudret abi, Kukini, Kungfuadam, Kunishman5000, Kuoraf,Kurtz69, Kuru, Kurykh, Kusunose, KuyaMike250, Kwamikagami, Kwekubo, Kwsn, Kwwiki,Kyle Barbour, Kylesmile, Kylu, Kyoko,KyotoKatana, Kyuubi-Kitsune, L33th4x0r, L33tminion, LCS2D,LGagnon, LOL, La goutte de pluie, LaMenta3, LabRat Abby,Labion Cave Beaver, Lacrimosus, Ladnav, LadyofShalott, Lafe, Laggedbehind, Lagragian, Lakhim, Lambiam, Lamrock, Lamy999, Land1234567890, LanguageMan, Lanjag Igloon, Lanoitarus, Lardz, Largematchboxfunguy, Larry Sanger, LarryGilbert, Larry_Sanger, Larryincinci, Lars Washington, Larsony, Latarontella, Latmere1, Lauraparkes, LavosBaconsForgotHisPassword,Lawrence Cohen, Laxplayer630, Lazaraf78, Lazybeef,Leahbbz, Leandra614, LeaveSleaves, Lectonar, Led Zeppelin Rules, Ledmonkey, Ledzeppelinjulian, Lee, Lee D, Lee Daniel Crocker, Lee010cooldude, Leegar84, Leeroy17, Legaleagle86, LegitimateAndEvenCompelling, Leithp, Leninlover, Lenoxus, Leo Collin, Leo The Clown, LeoNomis, LeoO3, Leon2323, Leon7, LeoniDb,Lephermessiah, Leranedo, Leroyinc, Let's Celebrate!, Lethe, Levineps, LexCorp, Lexor, Lgeorgel, Li-sung, Liam Skoda, Liamdaly620, Lick-the-pedia, Lickylick, Liek! I vandalised wikipedia!, Lifebaka, Liftarn, Light of Shadow,Lightdarkness, Lightdarkniss, Lighthead, Lightmouse, Lights, Ligulem, Lijealso, Lijil, Lildrumdude5000, Lillianjean, Lilnnw, Limasign, Limit point, Line, Linecircle, Ling.Nut, Linuxbeak, Linuxerist, Lioeh, Liquid entropy, Lisaab, Litefantastic, Little Darius Penguin, Little guru, Live and let Troll, LizardWizard, Llamallover, Llort, Llywrch, Loadmaster, Lobbie, Lobster hofster, Local604, Lockeandload, Locos epraix, Loft, Logan GBA, Logan89, LoganK, Lolalily216,Lolatjonny, Lolsat00rn, Lolwtf,Lolwtf2, Lomn, LonelyMarble, Longbitawilly, Longhair, Longhairmute, Longwalkshortpier, Loool,Loopy556, Lord Hero, Lord Nelson, Lord0z, LordLincoln8494, Lordbilby, Lordofsquad, Lorz1925, Loser guy 1151, Loste, Lostintherush, Lostwyvern, Louay 1996, Loue, Loughlin, Louis Waweru, Louiseb, Loup 9003, Lovepool2001, Lowellian, Loyd415,Lošmi,Lpress, Lquilter, Lstboarder, Luar, Lucasballard, Lucasbfr, Luckyherb, Luckypaper, Ludraman, Lugia lover09, Luigi1788, Luiscolorado, Luk, Lukeewing, Lukeisbest, Lulzworth, Lumbercutter, Lumos3, Luna Santin, Lunar Jesters, LunaticFringe, Lunchboxhero, Lupin, Lupizapi, Lupo, Lusciousmango, Lusical, Lyellin, Lyhana8, Lyokois Cool, M Johnson, M1ss1ontomars2k4, M3tal H3ad, MAJCRIMINAL, MBK004, MBisanz, MC Caveman, MC MasterChef, MDSantmyer, MEOW, MER-C, MG, MGTom, MONGO, MONSTER, Mabsjenbu123, Mac, MacGyverMagic, Macaddct1984, Macaddict1028, Machinewebuilt, Macintosh User, Mackan, Mackdaddy, Mackensen, Macro Shell, Macromill2002, Madchester, Maddebow, Madeline Gropecunt, Madhi65, Madieandemily, Madman, Maelnuneb, Maes Hughs, Maester mensch, Maestrosync, Magicallydajesus, Magneticflth, Magnus Manske, Mahalis, Mahanga, Mahay, Mahoogin v2, Mailer diablo, Mailer diablo, Mainevent69, Mais oui!, Majorly, Mak8907, Makatota, Malachirality, Malarc77, Malcolm, Malcolm Farmer, Malerin, Malevious, Malfoyl,Malhonen, Maliciousdude, Malinator, Malleus Fatuorum, Mallocks, Malo, Malyctenar, Mamawrites, Man of Kilkenny, Man vyi, ManChowda, Manchesterunited 666, Manfalk, Manfieldd, Mange01, MangeurDeCigogne, Manning Bartlett, Manning38, Manors, Manticore, Manx Monkey, Manzzzzzzzzzzzzzz, MarSch, Marasmusine, Maravan, Marblewonder, Marc-André Aßbrock, Marc44, Marcd30319, Marcika, Marcschulz, Marcus2, Margana, Marioland50, Mark, Mark Bergsma, Mark Dingemanse, Mark J, Mark Richards, Mark Yen, Mark7-2, MarkDonna, MarkGallagher, MarkS, MarkSutton, Markaci, Markcboylan, Marksgoals55, MarmadukePercy, Marshall123, Martarius, Martin-C, Martin451, MartinDK, MartinHarper, Martinp23, Martinwilke1980, Martpol, Marty660, Marudubshinki, Marvolo Gaunt, MarxWeep, Maryboo10, Masatran, MassimoAr, Massysett, Master Bater, Master Jay, Master of Puppets, Masterjamie, Masterofthegym, Masturcheef69, Matasenfave, Mateia, Matejpostolka, Materia hunter, Matilda, Matsteo, Matt 92, Matt Crypto, Matt Yeager, Matt59254, MattTM, Mattbrundage, Mattbuck, Matthew Woodcraft, Matthew0028, Matthewcl375, Mattman77, Mauriceparsons, Mauro Bieg, Maurog, Mav, MaxCosta, Maxamegalon2000, Maxamis21, Maximillion Pegasus, Maximus Rex, Maxos007, Maxtin, Mayarani500, Maywither, Mazzaman1997, Mb1000, Mbecker, Mbg6231, Mclamchop, Mcman777, Mcook1015, Mcpusc, Mcuringa, Mdebets, Mdh266, Mdowning3, MeEricYay, Meanhook, Measure, Meatyking, Medi01, Meelar, Meeples, MegaloManiac, Mehicdino, Mel Etitis, Melaen, Melongeed, Melsaran, MementoVivere, Memoo12, Memotype, Menchi, Meneth, Meno25, Mentifisto, Merkurix, Merotoker1, Merovingian, Merzul, Meshach, Mesosade, Message for Sakura Avalon, Metaeducation, MetalmanCaE, Metaspheres, Metasquares, Methnor, Mets501, MetsFan76, Mexcellent, Meximan93, Mgiganteus1, Mhking, Micahhainline, Michael Devore, Michael Greiner, Michael Hardy, Michael Shields, Michael Snow, Michael van den nieuwenhof, MichaelBillington, Michaelas10, Michaelbeckham, Michaelblory, Michaeldsuarez, Michaelman, Michalisphyl, Michbich, MickMacNee, Mickey Mickey You So Fine, You So Fine You Blow My Mind, Mickey, Mickeyjones, Mickybill, Mickyt91, Micmic28, MidMadWiki, Mighty Russia, MightyWarrior, Mihai, Mihoshi, Mikael Häggström, Mike Rosoft, Mike Serfas, Mike Storm, Mike3497, Mike6271, MikeBravo, MikeCapone, MikeGogulski, Mikep2008a, Mikewang, Mikezhao, Mil403, Milant, Milespianoforte, Mileycyrussoulja, MilkySmooooth, Milkyjoe2, Millionsandbillions, Millosh, Minavaan, MindSpillaqe, Mindspillage, Mineralè, Minesweeper, Mingcheese, Minneapolis Zack, Minta2, Minta3, Mintguy, Mira, Mirakouuui, Miranda, Mirodoc, Mirror Vax, Mirv, Misakichi, Miserlou, Miss Pippa, Mistah Juan, Mister Escapades, MisterWiki, Mistermandude, Misza13, Mitchello, Mithridates, Mitsuhirato, Mizuphd, Mjdmjdmjd, Mjpieters, Mk270, Mkdw, Mkreusch, Mkweise, Mls 91890, Mls 93 gurlie, Mm40, Mmmdonuts210, Mmx1, Mnemeson, Mnesfahani, Mo0, Moanna, Model Citizen, Modemac, Modulatum, Moe Epsilon, Moeson, Moi8642, Moink, Monbro, Moncrief, Mongo95, Monkeykiss, Monkeyllamaman, Monkman3, Monobi, Monotonehell, Monsieur Plump, Monsterxxl, Montrealais, MooTheCow2, Moon5, Moondyne, Moonraker69, Moop stick, Moopiefoof, Mooquackwooftweetmeow, Mooth.masher, Mor, Moraynolginge, Mordangal, Mordecai98, Moreschi, MorseCode, Mort Divine, Mortimeriroo, Morwen, Moshe Constantine Hassan Al-Silverburg, Mostlyharmless, Motameus, Motaros, Motherdp, Motorhead69, Moulder, Mountnbiker310, Mozzerati, Mr Adequate, Mr Hands, Mr WR, Mr ooj, Mr squirrel, Mr. Billion, Mr. Blake, Mr. Blonde 139, Mr. Joy, Mr. Lefty, Mr. Strong Bad, Mr. Wiki, Mr.Hesp, Mr.Unknown19, Mr.Z-man, Mr.bluntster, Mr.bonus, MrFish, MrMac, MrNintendo8794, Mrb0605, Mrbean667, Mrg3105, Mrhippekillerthe3rd, Mrholybrain, Mrmaroon25, Mrssow, Mrzaius, Ms2ger, Mschel, Msikma, Msimo, Mtbab, Mteorman, Mtgenito, Mts0405, Muchosucko, Muffin, Muggle38, Mulad, Mumble45, Munchkinguy, Murray Langton, Murraypaul, Mushroom, Musical Linguist, Musical Paddy, Mustanglover, Mutantchikin, Mved, Mwanner, Mwinslows, Mxn, My Cat inn, My expiry time is indefinite, MyNameIsNotBob, Myanw, Myglesias, MykReeve, Mynamesdrew, Myrtone86, Mysekurity, Mysidia, Mysterious BIG, MysteryDog, Mythbusterma, Mythology8, Mzajac, N8cantor, NAHID, NGerda, NMChico24, NOLAN!!!!!!!!, NSK, NSLE, NTDOY Fanboy, NYCJosh, NYScholar, Nach0king, Nadav1, Nadavspi, Nadegie, Nadyes, Nakon, Nand nand1, Nanobug, Naomib123, Narco, Narfbite, Narmanb, Naruto8912357085803, Nassim.sherif, Nat6138, Natalie Erin, Natgoo, Navy Blue, NawlinWiki, NazismIsntCool, NazismIsntCool, Nbeniwal, Ncma, Ndumbunsungu, Nealmcb, Necro.polis, Necrowarrio0, Nectarflowed, Ned Scott, Needlenose, Nehuf, Nekrostretch, NemoVon, Nemonoman, Nengli02, Nentuaby, Nenyedi, Neoelitism, Nephron, Nerd42, NerdyNSK, Nerdygurl, Nerull 777, Nerval, Nescio, NescioNomen, Nethgirb, Netscott, Netsnipe, Neumannkun, Neurolysis, Neurophyre, Neutralaccounting, Neutrality, Neutron65, Nevada, Never666, Neverquick, New article creator, NewButters, NewEnglandYankee, Newell13, Newnoise, Newtonmaia, Ngjrn, Nhaas34, Nhoj123, Niagakiw, NicAgent, Nicecheese556, NicholasMorg, Nicholasquekws, Nick, Nick Levine, Nick thawley, Nick012000, Nick125, NickBush24, Nickj, Nickkid218, Nickmattress, Nickshanks, Nickybutt, Nicowebster, Nicsa, Nielswik, Niestche is dead, Nigholith, Night Gyr, Night Stalker, NightDragon, Nightscream, Nigstol3mybik3, Nigy, Nihiltres, Nikos papadopoulos, Nil Einne, Nillanilla3ee, Nilpotent, Nils Grimsmo, Nimbulan, Ninja247, Ninnnu, Nintendude, Ninuor, Nippoo, NipsMcG, Niseiota, Nishkid64, Nixeagle, Njautobody, Njh@bandsman.co.uk, Njyoder, Nkids, Nnhorgan, No Guru, NoAccount, NoSeptember, Noir deluxe, Noit, Noitatic, Nol888, Noldoaran, Nomafuj, Non sense ha bitch, Nonforma, Nonplus, Noobletteowns, Noomo, Noor Qasmieh, Norm, Normxxx, Nosebud, Nosium von lerwick, Notheruser, Nothing444, Nothlit, Notjake13, Notthe9, Notyou7, Nova77, November05, Nsaa, Nsh, Nsigniacorp, Nskatrina, Nssbm117, Nswpheonix, Ntambwa, NubKnacker, NuclearWarfare, Nufy8, Nuggetboy, Nuiop729, Numair, Nunh-huh, Nunquam Dormio, NurMisur, Nutz000, Nv8200p, Nwyrkgiants8690, Nxtftrdirector, OCNative, OMFG! I vandalised wikipedia!, ONUnicorn, OSFockewolf, OSX, Oakleydoakley952, Oakster, Oat Kev, Obarskyr, Obi Wan 71, Obli, Ocee, Od Mishehu, Oden, Odengatan, Of, Off!, OffsBlink, Ohnoitsjamie, Okaj, Okiefromokla (old), Oklonia, Olaf Davis, Olathe, OldakQuill, Oldtuck, Oleg Alexandrov, Olismith07, Oliver Pereira, Olivier, Ollie Liddycoat, Olly150, OlofE, Olorin28, Olton Boulevard, OmarShavey, Omarsiddiqui728, Omegablackbelt, Omegatron, Omicronpersei8, Omphaloscope, Omt, On Wheezier Plot, Onceonthisisland, Onco p53, One, Oneshotpop, Ongas, OnionHorse, Onorem, Onslaught 789, Oo64eva, Ooglybooglyboo, Opabinia regalis, Open4D, Oppa62, Opple999, Optical Illusion, Optichan, OrbitOne, Oreoshane, Orioneight, Ortolan88, Oruj, Orzetto, Orzhovcrusader, Osfan914, Osidenate, Osizz, Oska, Oskar Sigvardsson, Osufan900, Otienomaji, Otolemur crassicaudatus, Otterathome, Otto heinemann vundafarks, OuroborosCobra, Overand, Overcow, Owain loft, OwenX, Owenhutds, Owenshahim, Oxf806, Oxycotton, Oxymoron83, Oyam5000, P0rked, P4k, PAK Man, PCWM, PDH, PEAR, PFHLai, PHDrillSergeant, PM Poon, PN123, PROFpipez, PS2pcGAMER, PSROXB, PZFUN, Pablo Agosto, Packers56789, Pacman5, Pacon, Pagingmrherman, Pahles, Pahoeho, Paine Ellsworth, Pakaran, Paladin2005, Palaeovia, Palpalpalpal, Pamri, Pants123, Papac, Papageorgio, Para, Paranomia, Parfitta, Paroxysm, Partapdua2, Parthava, Pascal666, Patar knight, Pathoschild, Patman, Patrick, Patrick4444, Patriotfootball, Pats1222, Pats21, Patsfan 1254, Patstuart, Paul August, Paul Hayward, Paul20070, Paulie2499, Paulley, Pavel Vozenilek, Paxsimius, Pbroks13, Pcb21, Pchancharl, Pcollison, Pcpcpc, Pd THOR, Pediaedit88, Pedro, PedroPVZ, Pegasus1138, Pegsi, Pelizzoli22, Pelvis Thrust, Pendotigers, Pengo, Penis stalker, Penubag, Penwhale, Pep1863, Pepsidrinka, Peregrine Fisher, Perididdle, Peripitus, Perl, Perl guy, Perscriptionmario, Persian Poet Gal, Person594, Peruvianllama, Pete walker, Pete y1520@hotmail.com, PeteVerdon, PeteX, Peteforsyth, Peter, Peter Campbell, Peter Ellis, Peter McGinley, Peter paul, Peter zhao, PeterSymonds, Pethr, PetosGreatos, Petros417, Petruza, Pevarnj, Peyna, Pfalstad, Pg2114, Pgan002, Pgillman, Pgk, Pgk`, Pgripp, Pharos, Phase Theory, Pherring, Phi beta, Phil Sandifer, PhilHibbs, PhilKnight, Phileas, Philip Baird Shearer, PhilipO, Phillejay, PhillieLWillie, Phillipowenobj, Philthecow, Phoebe, Phoenix713, PhotoBox, Photographerguy, Phædrus, Picaroon, Pick up a penguin, Pierco, Piezo wezo, Pifactorial, Pifro, Pigfluff, Piggydangerzeerip, Pigmietheclub, Pigsonthewing, Pikachu444, Pikminlover, Pilotguy, Pimadude, PinchasC, Pineapple30, Pinkadelica, Piotrus, Pious7, Pixel ;-), Pixelface, Pixiesfan37, Pizzachicken, Pizzapocket51, Placebic ecstasy, Plaid Rainbows, PlasmaDragon, PlasticMan, PlatinumX, Platonides, Platypusdara, Plausible to deny,

Tiyuiyutn, Tjbktjb, Tjkooker, Tjkooker3.0, Tkachuky, Tkgd2007, Tkteun, Tlcothran, Tlustulimu, Tmopkisn, Tnds, Toast-modern, Toast563, Tobias Conradi, Tobias Escher, Toby Bartels, Tobyw87, Toffer, Tokigun, Tokinwalrus, Toklar, Tokral, Tollbooth5578, Tom, Tom davies, Tom-, TomPhil, TomPreuss, TomasBat, Tomayres, Tombomp, Tomcckk, Tomdaly4321, Tomgally, Tomi Undergallows, Tomlillis, Tomlinsond, Tomlovesyankees, Tommer man, Tommytocker, Tommytommytommy, Tomomac23, Tomos, Tomwalden, Tomwashere, Tone, Tony Fox, Tony1, Tony45844, TonyAfro, TonyClarke, TonySt, Tooto, Topbanana, TopherXXX, Torch1992, Torlak, Tormor, Torrie, Tortanick, Totaka, Totnesmartin, Toytoy, Tpbradbury, Tragicomedian, Trapolator, Traroth, Trausten2, Travelbird, Treborbassett, Tree Biting Conspiracy, Tregoweth, TrevX9, Trevdna, Trevor MacInnis, Trevyn, Trezatium, Tricooon, Trilobite, Trinite, Trip95, Triskaideka, Triwbe, Trntrznr04, Trojansfan5, TroyReid, Trulexicon, Trusilver, Truth is relative, understanding is limited, TruthAboutTobacco, Tryggvia, Trypa, Ttfan12311, Ttony21, Ttttttttttttttttttttttttttttttttttttttttttt, Tualha, Tubyboulin, Tucker 2323, Tuckerson, Tud123, Turbovoxel, Turmeric3, Turnerjer, Turtleboy267, Tuspm, Tuvic, Tv-hog, Tv316, TwakTwik, Twas Now, Tweedy, Tweetweehead, Twilsonb, Twinkiethekid, Twipie, Twisty96, Twri, Tygar, Tyler128974, TylerMad8, Tylerhammond1, Tyrant5413, Tyro55555, Tyu, U.S.A.U.S.A.U.S.A., UBeR, UNHchabo, UROOJ, USAOwnz, UberMan5000, UberScienceNerd, Ucanlookitup, Uchiha4evr, Ucucha, Udonknome, Ufwuct, Ugen64, Ugotservedbyme, Ulflarsen, Ultimus, Ulysseus, Umapathy, Uncle Dick, Uncle G, Unclebif4, Unclebulgaria, UndZiggy, Underage, UnicornTapestry, UninvitedCompany, Unit, Unknown User, Unschool, Until It Sleeps, Untouch wwe, Uogl, Uris, Urmom123, Urzu100, Usa 2 aus792, Usarock, Uscfootball27, User name one, Usermtt6928, Usnavy13, Utopianheaven, Utroko, Uturnaroun, Uyo, Uyonirahagien, V.I. Lenin, V10, VDWI, VG Cats Tipe 2, VMS Mosaic, VSquared, Valentinian, Valeriaha, Valkov, Vandalqq, Vanished user, Vaoverland, Varactyl, Vargenau, Vary, Vbdrummer0, Vbs, Veinteyuno, Velthalos, VengeancePrime, Ventura, Venullian, Veraff, Verdigras13, Verrai, Versageek, Versus22, Veteranjay, Vghgv, Vicarious, Vicfirth, Vicipéidtá cumannachas, Vickbain, VidGameFreak, VigilancePrime, Vikingstad, Vildricianus, Vilerage, Vinay412, Violetriga, ViolinGirl, Viridian, Virxold, VisionThing, Vkem, Vlad788, Vlmastra, Vmart, Vodremere, Voice of All, Voice of All (MTG), Voidxor, Volney, Voltosx, Voodoochild93, Vovkav, Voyagerfan5761, Voytekthe Polish Biker, Vranak, Vslashg, Vwmike7, Võrolang, WAS 4.250, WGee, WHLfan, WIC, WJetChao, WLAfightsforFreedom, WLAmemeber, WLAwarrior, WMD, WPjcm, WSABFCBuddy, WTD, Wacky z, WackyWiiZ, Wafulz, Waggers, Wagonkeys, Walers, Walkerma, Walkiped, Walkmic, Walowick, Walter, WaltonOne, Wangi, Wapcaplet, Warfwar3, Wariott, Warofdreams, Waronide, Wartzina, Wassupg, Waterpolo379, Wattsini1, Watx5, Wavelength, Wayavas1337, Wayward, WazzaMan, Wazzup970, Wcquidditch, Weak e pedia, Web129, Weefolk29, Weinerheadshaboom, Weirdo92, Weirsy284, Wellithy, WendelL, Wenenen, Werdawurld, Werdna, Weremovingman, Werideatdusk33, Wesener, Wesleycool12, West Brom 4ever, Weston sagle, Weyes, WhackaWhackaWoo, Whale plane, Whassits, What!?Why?Who?, Whatcanuexpect, Whateverdontmatter, Where, Whimperkitten, WhisperToMe, Whit Wordsworth, White Cat, WhiteCat, WhiteOak2006, Whiteboywonder, Whitecloth, Whitefire45108, Who, Whomp, Whosme, Whouk, WhyBeNormal, Whyareall2, Whyt74, Whytokay, Wiarthurhu, Wickethewok, Wiggar, Wiiguy5, Wik, Wiki Sux, Wiki alf, WikiLaurent, WikiLeon, WikiReaper, WikiSlasher, Wikiacc, Wikibofh, Wikiboss, Wikichanger1, Wikider, Wikidogia, Wikihater09, Wikihelper9002006, WikiIlrsc, Wikikone, Wikiman232, Wikinator07, Wikinerdsarelosers, Wikipediascape, Wikipedia Admin, Wikipedia Sans Communism, Wikipedia brown, Wikipedia este comunism, Wikipedia is Communism, Wikipedia is inaccurate, Wikipedia is אا!, Wikipediajest komunizm, Wikipedialà chủ nghĩa cộng sản, Wikipedia on kommunismi, Wikipedia är kommunismo, Wikipediaè comunismo, Wikipediaé comunismo, Wikipedia.InaccurateByDesign, Wikipedia.blows, WikipediaAdmin, WikipediaHotDog, Wikipediaeditor2, Wikipediaexpert, Wikipedian231, WikipedianMarlith, Wikipediarules2221, Wikipedical, Wikisuper, Wikiwikiwikiwiki wiki, WikkyHorse, Wildnox, Wildthing61476, Will Beback, Will Hunting, Willblew, WilliamHenry Gates, WilliamKF, Willisis2, Willking1979, WillowW, Willy 0.01, Willy Wonka's Chocolate Factory on Wheels, Willy on Wheels 2CV, Willypie, Wilsongod, Wim, Wimt, Win118neo, Windowsvistafan, Windyboi, Wine glum, Wing Ninja, Wingo, Winhunter, Winklerteen, Winterus, Wisc06, Wisc409, Wissahickon, Witty lama, Wizardman, Wknight94, Wm, Wmahan, Wmgallagher, WoW, Woggly, Wolblade, Wolfkeeper, Wolfmankurd, Woods-house, Woody, Woohookitty, WordsExpert, Worldtraveller, Wormblood, Worthawholebean, Woshinidema, Wossi, Wrestlingdude1, Wrexhamliverpoolfan, Wuhwuzdat, Wuzzie, Wykliffe, X Tron 13, XAll Out Adamx, XDanielx, XFactorInfinity, XIIIStruggle, XJamRastafire, XP, XRedcomet, XX-turntablejunky-Xx, XXWRAITHXx, Xaos, Xaosflux, Xbadwolfx, Xblahx, Xcentaur, Xdenizen, Xed, Xenavion, Xeno, XenonFreek, Xeysz, Xezbeth, Xiahou, Xkeeper, Xnux, Xowfmp, Xp54321, Xplicitrulz, Xproject, Xryanwhitelawx, Xsoundx, Xtc 2701, Xtrasimplicity, Xuxieixid, Xuy, Xwassac, Xxpor, Xxsoccerstud01xx, Xxthelegacyxx, Xy7, Y0u, Yacht, Yahel Guhan, Yahi, Yakbutter27, Yamamoto Ichiro, Yamara, Yamla, Yanksox, Ybbor, Yeaboiitskurt, Yeago, Yeawoow, YellowMonkey, Yelyos, Yfcuwviiw, Yid63, Ymrg5, Yoare, Yohoroho, Yokojorge, Yom, Yonatan, Yonghokim, Yonnyladuck, YoudownwithTCP, Young dfler, Youremyjuliet, Yourtruthormine?66, Youssefsan, Youtubewatcher, Yowwow, Yoyomonster, Ysangkok, Yubersoz, Yug, Yuje, Yuliyag, Yurmum, Yurmum5, Yworo, Yzzug, Z4diamond, Z5, Zabek, Zacber, Zachwoo, Zagalejo, Zain engineer, ZakRipper, Zakprit, Zanchawdry, Zanimum, Zantastik, Zanter, Zanyzacky, Zaphod Beeblebrox, Zaydana, Zcmini, Zelky, Zen444, Zenohockey, Zephalis, Zephyr21, Zephyr2k, Zerak-Tul, Zero R, ZeroUm, ZeroxMd, Zeus000, Zezimassasin, Zgames, Zigger, Ziggur, Ziggurat, Ziggyzack99, ZimZalaBim, Zingi, Zman2000, Zmaz0ox, Zmehlo, Zntrip, Zoe, Zoidburg, Zolfers, Zomgwowzers, Zondor, Zone46, Zoohouse, Zootm, Zorbak123, Zoz, Zpb52, Zschernicky, Zsero, Zsinj, Zurishaddai, Zweng, Zwmalone, Zxcv101, Zyclone, ZydecoRogue, Zyqwux, Zzuuzz, Zzyzx11, Zé do Telhado, ^demon,
———, Ævar ArnfjörðBjarmason, Über Nerd 2000, ŒΣ ´®† ¥πø˜ , Βικιπαίδεια είναι κομουνισμός, Википедия будет коммунизм, Вікіпедіяє комунізм, Методије, Уикипедия е комунизъм, ШIILLY OИ ШHEELS, Яippawallet, ויקיפדיה, קומוניזם, ول ى ڪ دیواوی اصولپ تراکی الست اش, বিকিপিডিয়াইঘ贺 ウ ィ キ ペ デ ィ ア は 共 産 主 義 で あ る, 中国人, 위키 백과는 공산주의 이다, 9406 anonymous edits

WikiWikiWeb *Source*: http://en.wikipedia.org/w/index.php?oldid=306062372 *Contributors*: -- April, 16@r, 2004-12-29T22:45Z, AdamZivner, Adambiswanger1, Addshore, AdelaMae, Adoniscik, Adw2000, Aj00200, Alansohn, Ale jrb, Alphachimp, Amphytrite, Anokomoonlight, Avraham, Benhoyt, Blathnaid, Bloodstruckdrum, BodyTag, CharlesC, ChrizC, Cirt, Cometstyles, Conversionscript, Crenner, Cybercobra, DXBari, DanMS, David Gerard, Dirkbb, Discospinster, Doug Bell, Dummmmmmy, DurinsBane87, Earle Martin, Ekspiulo, Eloquence, FlyEmiratesArsenal, GHe, Gaurav, Gnewf, Godzig, Gracenotes, Graham87, Greeves, Gurubrahma, Habj, Hairchrm, IanOsgood, Ipatrol, Ixfd64, Jarhed, Jatkins, Jclemens, JeremyA, JulesH, Kurt.campbell, Lambyuk, Largematchboxfunguy, Lee Daniel Crocker, Maniadis, Manning Bartlett, Marc Mongenet, Martial75, Mav, Metoule, Mike Segal, Mmmmmmmeeeeeee, Murftown, Musical Linguist, Myrtone86, Oblivious, Onw4life, OwenX, Ozgod, Pax85, Peteforsyth, Pharos, Pogi mongster, Random832, RaviC, RedWolf, Redeyed Treefrog, Reisio, Revised, Rhindle The Red, RickDeNatale, Rmhermen, Robofish, RockMFR, Ronaldomundo, Sammygseir, Schzmo, Scrier, ShakataGaNai, Snarius, Sopoforic, Sparksm4, Spcc-jrob7021, Springnuts, SqueakBox, Steven Walling, TakuyaMurata, TantalumTelluride, ThePolemistis, Thetorpedodog, TidyCat, Toussaint, Voretus, Wayward, Xezbeth, Zzuuzz, 188 anonymous edits

History of wikis *Source*: http://en.wikipedia.org/w/index.php?oldid=310356686 *Contributors*: Amire80, Andrewrox, Anirvan, Barek, Bevinbell, Bongwarrior, ChrisCork, Cirt, Cormaggio, DeadEyeArrow, Deconstructhis, Dreaded Walrus, Earle Martin, Elassint, Emily024, EngineerScotty, Enviroboy, EoNy, HaeB, Hmle2007, Hut 8.5, Jgreen, Jmbalzan, Kingof Hearts, Lars Washington, Mandarax, Math321, Ninja247, O, Philip Baird Shearer, Plastikspork, Reagle, Red Act, Redeyed Treefrog, Rjwilmsi, Rwwww, Sbootth, Scagnoli, Stephan Leeds, Tarinth, Tiptoety, Toussaint, Travis Evans, Twas Now, Visor, Vlad, 33 anonymous edits

Memory Alpha *Source*: http://en.wikipedia.org/w/index.php?oldid=310442290 *Contributors*: Aervanath, Agamemnon2, Alkivar, Alphachimp, Andrew Levine, Angela, Atlan, Azertus, Baddabing, Bdoserror, Benjiboi, Betacommand, BorgHunter, Bp0, Bramlet Abercrombie, BurnDownBabylon, CaptainMike, Carlosguitar, Cburnett, Cheechie Chung, Chriscf, CigarFanatic, Circeus, Civlov, Coccyx Bloccyx, Colonel Warden, CommonsDelinker, ComputerSherpa, Coredesat, Crumb01, Cryptic, CyberSkull, DXRAW, DarkHorizon, Darkildor, Davecampbell, Davidstrauss, Deskana, Downwards, Dragonfiend, Dvp7, EEMIV, Edison, Eloquence, ElvisThePrince, Eniac turing, Enzo Aquarius, Epaphroditus Ph. M., Eternal Equinox, Etoile, Fivebytwo, Flcelloguy, Fraterm, Fredrik, Furrykef, Gaius Cornelius, Gdo01, Gelma, GeorgeMoney, Gmaxwell, Gmcfoley, Guaka, Gurch, Gvsualan, Harry Doddema, Horkana, Ixfd64, J Darnley, Jasca Ducato, Jayunderscorezero, Jclemens, Jibbajabba, JoaoRicardo, John Broughton, JohnnyPez, Josh a z, Karada, King of Hearts, Kizor, Lawrence Cohen, Lee J Haywood, Leif, LeyteWolfer, Ligulem, Llwrch, Locke Cole, Lucamauri, Lunchboxhero, MBisanz, MakeRocketGoNow, Marskell, Mattbuck, Matthew, Mboverload, Memory, Mightyfastpig, Minderbinder, MinutiaeMan, Mourn, Mulad, Musical Linguist, Mütze, Narco, Nat, Natalie Erin, NawlinWiki, Night Gyr, Nihiltres, NorthernThunder, Notowikia, Nualran, OGoncho, Oldag07, Particlepeople, Paul Erik, Pd THOR, PhilHibbs, Piotrus, Plasticdog, Platypus222, Plicease, Plkrtn, PuzzletChung, Quadell, Rbraunwa, Rehevkor, Renegade54, Rich Farmbrough, Rjwilmsi, Robert G, Ruud Koot, Savidan, Scapler, Sceptre, Schrei, Seth Ilys, SillyDan, Singularity, Skomorokh, Slomox, Sochwa, SqueakBox, Star TrekMan, Stephen Bain, TenPoundHammer, The Wookieepedian, TheDataMonster, TheRedPenOfDoom, Thumperward, ThylekShran, Tim Thomasons Temporary Username, Timwi, Tony Sidaway, Tothwolf, Trlkly, Tschravic, Vedek Dukat, Wiendietry, Wizardman, Yelgrun, Zidel333, ^demon, 59 anonymousedits

Comparison of wiki farms *Source*: http://en.wikipedia.org/w/index.php?oldid=310422900 *Contributors*: 16@r, 2004-12-29T22:45Z, 2005, AaronRoe, Academblip, Acidburn24m, Akve, AkvoD3, Alexfusco5, AndrewTReynolds, Anomo, Ansell, Applesareyummy, Argento, Arkrishna, ArnoldReinhold, Bill3000, Bjmspangler, Bkeairns, Boud, Brainkeeper, BrentLaabs, Bsoft, BuickCenturyDriver, Cacycle, Camerajohn, Captain-tucker, Caracho, Cganske, Charitwo, Cherry blossom tree, ChildofMidnight, CiaranG, Ciciban, Cmelbye, Cobu, Coccyx Bloccyx, Ctiefel, Cybercobra, Dantman, Dave rep, David Edgar, Davidovic, Deltabeignet, Discombobulator, Dm, Dreaded Walrus, DreamGuy, Dweekly, Epolk, Etouch, Excirial, Extraordinary, Fish and karate, Flatlyimpressed, Freakofnurture, Ftiercel, Gail, Galoubet, Gardar Rurak, GateKeeperX, George100, GeorgeLouis, Gerdami, Geschichte, Gioto, Gogo Dodo, GoodNoise, GraemeL, Green Ambush, GreenReaper, Greeneto, Gscshoyru, Guldeldar, Guyact, Hanoi Girl, HelloAnnyong, Helmuti pdorf,

Helpingstudents, Hemo, Hhielscher, Hu12, I, Podius, Ian Moody, IanManka, Ikip, IIterates, JLaTondre, Jack Phoenix, Jacroe, JamesR, JanCK, Jbyers, Jeandré du Toit, Jeb, Jessicakem, Jjupiter100, Johnleemk, Julescubtree, JzG, Kappa, Kbfseattle, Kernigh, Khalid hassani, Koreanegosegos, Leon2323, Leuce, Liempt, Linuxerist, Lloydbudd, Lobster101, Logixoul, Lumenos, MBisanz, Manticore, Marclaporte, Martin451, Maryluke, Mat86, Matthew, MattisManzel, Maurreen, Mhenry07, Michael Hardy, MichaelFrey, MichaelJanich, MichaelQSchmidt, Michaeldsuarez, Mightyfastpig, Mikael Häggström, Minghong, Missdipsy, MisterSheik, Mjparry716, Moonpool66, Muthu4all, Nealmcb, Nyashinsky, OlavN, OrangeDog, Ose, Oyejorge, Paranomia, Patrick, Perfecto, Peripitus, Peter, Piotrus, Pjacobi, Pklipp, Pointe LaRoche, Prodego, Promethean, Quatloo, Qxz, R, Rabmag, Rakd, Rcannon100, Rdpniners, Renmiri, Rinotallsox, Rjwilmsi, RobKohr, Ronz, Ryan Roos, SMcCandlish, SPQRobin, Sam Odio (dinarprofits.com), SamOdio, Samer.hc, Scarian, SchfiftyThree, Sean Heron, Shreevatsa, Simonkoldyk, Smiddle, Sreed888, Starwed, Steel, Steven Walling, Su-steve, Sujmishra, Taidawang, Tanthalas39, Tastemyhouse, Tbrethes, Techna1, Teex, Tgattis, The Moneycruncher, The wub, Thegn, Thumperward, ThurnerRupert, Timeshifter, Tizio, Tokek, Tomik99, Toussaint, Turk17, Unionhawk, Vdavisson, Vipul, Voyagerfan5761, WPjcm, WastlDaGammla, Wickethewok, Wikid77, WingZero, Wolfgang1018, Xavidp, Xoposhiy, Yaron K., Zondor, ^demon, 252 anonymousedits

Wikitravel *Source*: http://en.wikipedia.org/w/index.php?oldid=309227216 *Contributors*: 119, 17Drew, Agateller, Aitias, Angela, Anthony, Ash, Ashishbhatnagar72, Belovedfreak, Bewareofdog, BlankVerse, Bookofjude, Boothy443, Booyabazooka, Borgx, Brandon, Brightside88, CCMcluster, Cacahuate, Cadby WaydellBainbrydge, Canaen, Chris j wood, Chrisbak, Cjensen, Danlev, Deemans, Delirium, Dfrg.msc, Discospinster, Doris060602, Dysprosia, El C, Ellmist, Emrrans, Esprit15d, EvanProdromou, Finlay McWalter, Gentgeen, Giorgio, Gronky, Guaka, Guyjohnston, Hawaiian717, Hu12, Hypermiler, Infrogmation, It Is Me Here, J1729, JYOuyang, JamesMLane, Jamesday, Jaranda, Jatkins, Jefftrent, Jensre, Jojit fb, Jonath.in Stokes, Joseph Solis in Australia, JosephBarillari, Joyous!, Jpatokal, Jpstivala, Keithonearth, Kevin Saff, Kimyu12, Korg, LOL, Lbs6380, Lou.weird, LoveWikis, Lunchboxhero, MattFrost, Maximus Rex, Mikepjones, Mingwangx, Mion, Mulleflupp, Mxn, Naufana, NawlinWiki, Night Gyr, Nihiltres, Numbo3, Omegatron, One, Oroso, Oxymoron83, Pacific Coast Highway, Paul A, Peterfitzgerald, Phirazo, Piddle, Pmsyyz, Podzemnik, PrivateWiddle, Priyanhere, Quuxplusone, Raul654, Ravikiran r, RegentsPark, Rmrfstar, RolandUnger, Rossami, RoyBoy, RyanGerbil10, SGBailey, Saibod, Sander Säde, Sango123, Sapphire, Scarian, Schneelocke, Schutz, Sentineneve, Sillyfolkboy, Sin-man, Steven Walling, Sverdrup, Tetraminoe, The wub, Tom, Uncle G, Versageek, Väsk, WorldlyWebster, Worldtraveller, Xeno, Yann, Zeno Gantner, Zzuuzz, 137 anonymous edits

World66 *Source*: http://en.wikipedia.org/w/index.php?oldid=174286585 *Contributors*: Angela, Bogdangiusca, Bookofjude, Booyabazooka, Clarin, CompRhetoric, Davidcannon, Donarreiskoffer, Giorgio, Gommax, Guaka, Joseph Solis in Australia, Jpatokal, Lunchboxhero, MonteChristof, New Bully on the Block, Nzd, Olivier, Rob-nick, RoyBoy, RyanGerbil10, Scriberius, Sietse Snel, Sverdrup, Telso, UnitedStatesian, Vegaswikian, Versageek, Wereon, Wizzard2k, 20 anonymous edits

Susning.nu *Source*: http://en.wikipedia.org/w/index.php?oldid=296138249 *Contributors*: 16@r, 172, 2004-12-29T22:45Z, Buncronan, Camptown, Carlossuarez46, Chmod007, David Martland, Diegogrez, Docu, DragonflySixtyseven, Eloquence, Fred J, Fredrik, Jack Merridew, Jon Harald Søby, Joseph Solis in Australia, Liftarn, LilHelpa, Lunchboxhero, Mais oui!, Mikez, MisterWiki, MykReeve, NeoChaosX, Oolong, Otterathome, Pavel Vozenilek, Quiddity, RockMFR, Ruhrjung, RunOrDie, Scapler, Solkoll, Sverdrup, Thue, Tomas e, Tomi, Twkratte, VeryVerily, Vovkav, WhisperToMe, Wmahan, 8 anonymous edits

WikiSym *Source*: http://en.wikipedia.org/w/index.php?oldid=305248457 *Contributors*: Angela, BD2412, BrandonCsSanders, Chuck SMITH, DarTar, Dirk Riehle, Ketiltrout, Liberlogos, Lord Voldemort, Margana, MarkBernstein, Mgaved, MikeGasser, Miym, Morten Blaabjerg, Ooo222, Phoebe, Piotrus, Plasticup, Poor Yorick, ProductBox, Rjwilmsi, Robofish, StaticGull, Tedernst, Yamamoto Ichiro, Yanksox, Zanimum, 7 anonymous edits

Wikimania *Source*: http://en.wikipedia.org/w/index.php?oldid=309015277 *Contributors*: 16@r, 21655, AaronSw, Abtvctkto61, Aleenf1, Alexsh, Alison, Ambuj.Saxena, Anetode, Angela, Anmolsinghmehroke, Anonymous Dissident, Antandrus, Armando12, ArnoldReinhold, Astrowob, Austin Hair, Avillia, Avraham, AxelBoldt, BabuBhatt, Barcex, BeautifulFlying, BenFrantzDale, Bensin, BhaiSaab, BillC, BillWilliamson55, Billydee313, Bobo192, BorgHunter, Brazil4Linux, Briaboru, BrockF5, Buchanan-Hermit, BusterD, Can't sleep, clown will eat me, Caseforyou, Cbrown1023, Cescoby, Cfp, Chochopk, Ciaran UK, Cipherswarm, Clorisee, CobaltBlue, CoolKid1993, Crucis, Cyde, DXRAW, Dalgspleh, Danellicus, Daqu, Dawhitfield, Deathawk, Delirium, DennyColt, Derek.munneke, Disavian, Djmckee1, Dl2000, Donarreiskoffer, DrMichaelEdelstein, Dragfyre, Dreadstar, Drork, Dungodung, EVula, Edward, ElinorD, Elonka, FR Soliloquy, Flrn, Fredrik, FreedomisforALL, FreelanceWizard, Fuzheado, Gaius Cornelius, Geni, Gerrybader19, Go Green Go White, Golbez, GreenReaper, Greenman, Gronky, Gruznov, Guaka, Gökhan, HOHOMAN, Hankhimmler, HenkvD, HisSpaceResearch, Holycharly, Hyad, Icairns, Iceshark7, IhavemorehairDOWNTHERE, Ike9898, It Is Me Here, Jacoplane, Japanese Searobin, Jersey Devil, Jimbosgaylover, Koavf, Kozuch, Kpalion, Kpjas, Largematchboxfunguy, Lishkee, Littlebtc, Loginnow, Longhair, Luna Santin, MER-C, MYISTHEBIGGESTINTHEWORLD, Malo, Marcoscramer, Marudubshinki, MattJubb, Maximaximax, MayaSimFan, Mctpyt, MdReisman, Merovingian, Meursault2004, Mido, Mikael Häggström, Mike Halterman, Milkbreath, Miranda, Moley15, Moondyne, Mopelia, Morwen, Mysekurity, Nae'blis, NawlinWiki, NedFlanders, Nevinho, Newnoise, NicholasTurnbull, OlEnglish, OsamaK, Penubag, Pgk, Philipemarlow, Phoebe, Piotrus, Pomte, PseudoSudo, Purplefeltangel, Quatloo, Qxz, RaseaC, Rdsmith4, Rekrutacja, Richard001, Rmrfstar, RollyGem, Romaine, Rui Silva, Ryan, SACUE, SPQRobin, Sam Li, Samjohnson, Sanbeg, Sarouk7, Satori Son, Schnob Reider, Schzmo, Sciurinæ, Seasurfer, Securiger, Seth Ilys, Sethant, Shalom Yechiel, Shanes, Shimgray, Sikon, Simon Shek, SimonLyall, SimonP, Singularity, Sj, Skillywilly, Skinnyweed, Speakhandsforme, Sparka, Steel, Stelio, Tascha96, Tedernst, The Giant Puffin, The Rambling Man, The411guy, TheEgyptian, TheNewPhobia, Theodoranian, Thingg, This deserves inclusion, Vlad, VolatileChemical, WAS 4.250, WJBscribe, WLAfightsforFreedom, WLAmemeber, WLAwarrior, Waldir, Walkerma, WeFightTheSystem, Whereismycat, WhisperToMe, Wiki alf, WikipedianMarlith, Wimt, Wisl, Wossi, Yaron K., Yuanchosaan, Zanimum, 73 anonymous edits

Wikimedia Foundation *Source*: http://en.wikipedia.org/w/index.php?oldid=310251122 *Contributors*: 16@r, 2004-12-29T22:45Z, 23skidoo, 2bar, 4hicksjam, 6u56u, A Softer Answer, A bit iffy, A-giau, AGK, ALC Washington, AP1787, ATeppup, Abigor, Ac1983fan, Acroterion, Aeon1006, Ahoerstemeier, Ahonc, Al tally, Alansohn, AlbertR, Alerante, Alex756, Alexander Iwaschkin, Alison, AlisonW, Allstarecho, Alphachimp, Amgine, AmiDaniel, Andiharve, Andrejj, Andy Marchbanks, Andycjp, Angela, Animum, Anonymous Dissident, Anonymouse123, Antandrus, Anthere, Anthony, Antonio Lopez, Aphaia, Aquillion, ArielGold, Armandeh, Arthursimms, ArttuS's Sp, Asbestos, Asmeurer, Astuishin, Ataricodfish, Athaenara, Atlant, Atlantima, Auroranorth, AussieLegend, Aviara, Avraham, AzaToth, B, BackMaun, Badbats, BanyanTree, Bastique, Bawolff, Bdesham, Bearian, Beginacct, Behaafarid, Belginusanl, Bibihihi, Biggins, Bjelleklang, Bladestorm, Blakegripling ph, Bloodstruckdrum, Bobet, Bobo192, Bongwarrior, BradPatrick, Braindrain0000, Bramlet Abercrombie, BraneJ, Breinstein Q' Kurja, Brian0918, Brion VIBBER, Bubba hotep, Burgundavia, CWY2190, Calandrella, CambridgeBayWeather, Can't sleep, clown will eat me, Canadian-Bacon, CanadianLinuxUser, Capricorn42, Captain Wikify, Carolyn-WMF, Caue.cm.rego, Cbrown1023, Cenarium, Centrx, Cescoby, Chanlyn, CharlotteWebb, Chrislk02, Christian List, Christianrocker90, Christopher Kraus, Chuck Marean, Cirt, CitationMonger, Clmbrmike, Closedmouth, CloudNine, Combat Wombat, Cometstyles, CommonsDelinker, Conti, Cool3, Coolcaesar, Cormaggio, Corvus cornix, Couchpotato99, Crazycomputers, Crystallina, Curps, Cwlq, Cwoyte, DBZROCKS, DJ Clayworth, Dakolli, Damicatz, Daniel, Daranz, Dark Shikari, Davewild, David Gerard, David in DC, David.Mestel, Davidcannon, Dcljr, DeadEyeArrow, Delldot, Dementedd, Dendodge, DennyColt, Densock, DerHexer, DickRodgersPwns, Discospinster, Doc glasgow, Don't fear the reaper, Dookama, Dorftrottel, Downchuck, Draeco, Dragunova, Draugen, Dreadstar, Drilnoth, East718, Eep², Effeietsanders, Eggd3, Eight Oh-Six, Elian, ElinorD, Ellmist, Eloquence, Elwikipedista, Enchanter, Eracnil, Erielhonan, Escape Orbit, Esperant, Eurleif, Eurobas, Evercat, Evice, Explodicle, FCYTravis, FT2, Falcon8765, Fandyllic, Fantasy, FastReverter, FatBastardInk, Fawcett5, Ferkelparade, Ffransoo, Fish and karate, Fleetflame, Flexxx, FloNight, Fonzy, FrancoGG, Frap, Fredrik, FreplySpang, Friday, FromFoamsToWaves, Ftahanlangit, Fvw, Fyyer, GChriss, Gadfium, Gail, Galoubet, Ganfon, Gangsta c, Gary King, Garybrimley, Gavia immer, Gbchaosmaster, Gbleem, Geni, Ggtuhifuhgd, Gogo Dodo, Googoie, Goplat, GraemeL, Grandfather Clock, Gravitan, GreaterWikiholic, Greenrd, Greeves, GregAsche, Grendelkhan, Grin, Gronky, Gtg204y, Gstricky, Guaka, Guanaco, Gudeldar, Guillom, Gurch, Gutzky, Gwern, H2g2bob, Haakon, HappyDog, Harej, Harro5, Hashar, Hdt83, Heritage Lens, Hetar, Hiding, Hijklmn, Hmrox, Hshhh, I´m not really here, Hu12, Humblefool, Husky, Hut 8.5, Hyad, IMSoP, IRP, Icez, Ijmoha, Ilikevandalismtowikipeida, Illyria05, Incnis Mrsi, Indon, InkSplotch, Iridescent, Ironprot, Isb1009, Iuio, Iyamyas07, J'raxis, J.delanoy, JForget, JRM, JWSchmidt, JackJohn23, Jahiegel, Jake Wartenberg, Jannex, Jappoz, Jaranda, JasonM, JayHenry, Jdforrester, Jeff G., Jeff0987654321, Jeffrey Mall, Jehochman, Jennavecia, JeremyA, Jeronim, Jiang, Jiddisch, Jim VC3, Jimbo Wales, Jimfbleak, Jimpartame, Jmiotto, Jmlk17, JoanneB, John Broughton, John Reaves, John254, Johnleemk, Jojit fb, Jon Harald Søby, Joseph Solis in Australia, Joshdboz, Jossi, Jredmond, Jriggsy, Jrockley, Jtico, JulesH, Julian Mendez, Jumbo Snails, Justmeherenow, Jéské Couriano, Kanodin, Karl Dickman, Kasuro, Kbdank71, Kenb215, Kenwarren, Kesac, Khatru2, KingBoy EB, Kitia, Konstable, Korg, Koweja, Kozuch, Kuldip1, Kungfuadam, Kurt Jansson, Kurykh, Kylu, LOL, Lalala95, Lambiam, Leebo, Leon2323, Lethalgaming, Lethe, Levine2112, Lightmouse, Lightsup55, Lir, LittleDan, LittleJedi, Looxix, Luckas Blade, Ludvikus, Luk, Lulzhansolo, Luna Santin, Lunchboxhero, Lycurgus, Lzur, MBGpower, MBK004, MBisanz, MER-C, MPerel, MZMcBride, Mac, Mackensen, Madman, Mahomet, Majorly, Manop, Marcika, Mark, Markaci, Marshall Williams2, Martarius, MartinHarper, Martynrosney, Mas Ahmad, Master Bigode, Master of Puppets, Matt Yeager, Mav, Maverick Leonhart, Max Rex, MaxSem, Maximus Rex, Mb1000, Mbimmler, Mboverload, Mccready, Meco, Meeso, Melburnian, Menchi, Mentifisto, Merovingian, Methnor, Meursault2004, Mightyms, Mikael Häggström, Mike Halterman, Mike R, Mindspillage, Mirv, Mistercow, Mormegil, Mr.Z-man, MrRadioGuy,

Mrmiscellanious, Msikma, Msimo, Mtmelendez, Muchosucko, Mulad, Mxn, Mygerardromance, NYScholar, Naerii, Nakon, Nanabozho, Naryathegreat, Nathanael Bar-Aur L., NawlinWiki, Nemo bis, Newyorkbrad, Nick, Nick1915, NickBush24, Nicopedia, Nightscream, Nintendude, Nirvana2013, Niteowlneils, Nixeagle, No Guru, Notafish, NuclearWarfare, Nuiop, O^O, Oddity-, OhanaUnited, Omegatron, Omniplex, Onco p53, One, Ortonmc, Ottre, OwenX, Oxydo, Pacino's Insanity, Pakaran, Paranomia, Paroxysm, Parsecboy, Patchouli, Patrick, Paul A, Pavel Vozenilek, PeepP, Penubag, PeterSymonds, Pevernagie, Pfan70, Phaedriel, Phil Sandifer, Philip Trueman, Philipemarlow, Piano non troppo, Picaroon, Platonides, Plauz, Plrk, Pmsyyz, Poderi, PokeYourHeadOff, Polimerek, Prodego, Psy guy, Pyrospirit, Qst, QuackGuru, Quackers the duck, Quackslikeaduck, Qxz, REX, RG2, RN, RScheiber, Ral315, Ramir, Random832, Randomblue, Ranveig, Raven in Orbit, Rdsmith4, Red super, Retired username, RexNL, Rich Farmbrough, Risker, Rjd0060, Rjensen, Rjwilmsi, Rmhermen, RobH, Robchurch, Robert K S, Robofish, Robth, RockMFR, Rodrigo.T.Argenton, Ronburgundy67, Ross Rhodes, Rotem Dan, Royalguard11, Rumblemunky, SPQRobin, SPUI, SUL, Sakurambo, Sam Korn, Sam Li, Samuel Erau, Sattvic2780, Scepia, Sceptre, SchfiftyThree, Schmiddy, SchnitzelMannGreek, Scido, Scienceinc., Sdr, Secret, SelfQ, Seraphimblade, Sesshomaru, Seth Finkelstein, Seth Ilys, Sfmammamia, Shanel, Shanes, ShiningEyes, Shlomke, Shoemaker's Holiday, Showbrown ljnkjbn, Sikon, Silsor, Simeon, SimonP, Siroxo, Sj, Skomorokh, Smee, Smkatz, Soapy44, Somebody in the WWW, Sons of the Profits, Spangineer, Specter01010, SpeedyGonsales, Spellcast is a homosexual infected with AIDS., Spinxa, Splash, SqueakBox, Steel, Stephenb, Stewartadcock, Studude23, Suruena, Susvolans, Suzannejb, Swatjester, TD Jackson, Tacoelf30, Tacoelf6, Taggard, TakuyaMurata, Talonxx89, Tangotango, Tawker, Terence, Terrible Corvax, TerryE, TexasAndroid, Texcarson, Texture, The Eternal Highjacker, The Iraq, The Mad Echidna, TheCatalyst31, TheDJ, TheKMan, TheParanoidOne, Thekohser, Theresa knott, Thewayforward, Thinboy00, Threeafterthree, Thryduulf, TigerShark, Tim Q. Wells, Timwi, Titoxd, Tobias Conradi, Toddst1, Tony1, Tree Biting Conspiracy, Tregoweth, Trixt, Trondtr, Turlo Lomon, TylerJarHead, UberScienceNerd, Uncle G, UninvitedCompany, Username1, V111P, Vagemulo, Violetriga, Voiceof All, W.F. Siu, WAS 4.250, WJetChao, WODUP, WaWa12, Wangi, Wcquidditch, Weyes, Wiki alf, WikiBone, Wikiacc, Wikidemon, Wikinerd, Wikixosa, Will Beback, Wknight94, Wmahan, Wolfram, Wotwot, Www.wikinerds.org, XDanielx, Xnatedawgx, Yeeshenhao, Yom, Yonatan, Yonidebest, Youandme, Youssefsan, Yuyu, Zanimum, Zenohockey, Zhen Lin, Zondor, ·, Ævar Arnfjörð Bjarmason, Кулмер, 726 anonymous edits

Comparison of wiki software *Source*: http://en.wikipedia.org/w/index.php?oldid=310122940 *Contributors*: 16@r, 5ko, AaronRoe, Adscott32, Agent X2, Ahoerstemeier, Akavel, Akve, Alex Schröder, Alexfusco5, AlistairMcMillan, Altonbr, Aluvus, Andrewmasri, Andy120290, Angela, Antonrojo, Ariel Zamir, Aron.gombas, Aronzak, Artichoker, Aunant, AuntySue, Barrytallis, BenWilson, Beta m, Blanchette, BlueLED, BobDively, Brainkeeper, BrentLaabs, Brian R Hunter, Brianko, Brockert, BruceRD, Capricorn42, Catfoo, Cganske, Cgranade, ChaosControl, Charles Gaudette, Chase me ladies, I'm the Cavalry, Chealer, Chiefsequoya, ChrisO, Cmstester, Colonies Chris, Computer Guru, Cumeo89, Cœur, DStoykov, DamianParker, Dandv, DarTar, David Andel, DeirdreGerhardt, Dennys, Deodar, Destx, Dfrankow, Dmccreary, Doug W, Dsavalia, Dtdennis, Dweekly, Dxtrous, Dyl, EAman, Earle Martin, Ed W. Cogburn, EdwinInTampa, Eloquence, Enviroboy, Eric.dane, Evie em, Family Guy Guy, Firepol, Flaurijssens, For the love of Pi!, Fpaiano, Fplay, Francinne, Frank Shearar, Frap, Freewol, GNrailfan, Galoubet, Gary King, Gasperj, Geeklizzard, Georgeryp, Geschichte, Gotyear, Gpky, Greeneto, Greenman, GreyCat, Grlloyd, Gronky, Gudeldar, Harmon13, Herbythyme, Hertzsprung, Hgupta, Hhielscher, Hooloovoo, IanOsgood, Igelkott, Ikip, Imjustmatthew, Imlepid, InsufficientData, JLaTondre, Janto, Jarothbart, Jayk806, Jbyers, Jimmyp29, Jjardon, Jlbrainard, John Broughton, JonathanRoes, Joonga, Joshua4, Josquin, Jouke, Jphaffe, Julio.maranhao, Jvdrean, JzG, Karl Meier, KevinLawver, Kitanin, Kostmo, KramarDanIkabu, Larstobi, Lcarsdata, Leevanjackson, LeonardoGregianin, Lethe, Lightmouse, Logixoul, MER-C, Mahanga, Manning Bartlett, Marclaporte, Marky1124, Martin.Budden, Maryluke, Mbell, Meduz, Mendel, Mevac, MichaelBillington, Michaelfavor, Mikael Häggström, MikhailKolesnikov, Mindmatrix, Minghong, Misovec, Moa3333, Monkbel, Mpo, Mproud, Mrwojo, Mtitlan, Mwiseley, Mwtoews, Mxhunter, MySchizoBuddy, Namkyux, Narendra Sisodiya, Nelsonchris, NeutralPoint, Nidonocu, Nosilleg, Octane, OlavN, Oyejorge, PGSONIC, PatriceNeff, Patrick, Pattermeister, PavloShevelo, Peak, PeterThoeny, Pjacobi, Pmsyyz, Prowlx, Psarmstr, R3m0t, Ramorum, Rdpniners, Redjar, Reedy, ReiniUrban, Remuel, Ren Sydrick, Rich Farmbrough, Ricks99, Rjwilmsi, Robchurch, Ronz, Rpardee@gmail.com, Rschmertz, RxS, SF007, Sebastian Wallroth, Sebras, Sergiu.dumitriu, Shmooth, Silvertrough, Simon12, SimonRyan, SkyWalker, Slambo, Snesfm, Sowen, Stas Davydov, Steel, SteffenPoulsen, Stephan Leeds, StephenWaterbury, Steppres, Stewartadcock, Sutch, Sysy, Tdanard, Telepark, Tfejos, Thiamshui, Thomas.mortagne, ThreeBlindMice, Thryduulf, Tintazul, TnS, Tobias Conradi, Tomik99, Torc2, Toussaint, TowerDragon, Treelovinhippie, Trödel, Tyler Stransky, Ubermuppet, Unforgettableid, Uzume, Vargenau, VasilievVV, Walkie, Weiyu.csie, Wickethewok, Wikinaut, WikishAS, Wikitank, Williamanthony, WissenVeredeln, Wrh2, XDanielx, Xavidp, Yardi, Yoann, YorkBW, Youngoat, Zigger, Zpally, Zven, ^demon, Ævar Arnfjörð Bjarmason, 560 anonymous edits

Content management system *Source*: http://en.wikipedia.org/w/index.php?oldid=310010241 *Contributors*: 16x9, Abelsp@netdirect.net, Academic Challenger, Aelfnig, Ahoerstemeier, Ahuskay, Ajavalera, Aksi great, AlanUS, Ale jrb, Aleenf1, Alerante, Ali K, Allen3, Alphax, Amalas, Amd628, Anaines0210, Anamanfan, Anandcpr, AndersGM, AndrewWatt, Andrewpmk, AndriuZ, Andvd, Andypandy.UK, Angela, Anoopa, Antandrus, Antiadminleague, Aoi, Ap, Apexprim8, Arancaytar, Aranel, Arisbourg, Asbestos, Astrophil, Athaenara, AxelBoldt, Ayla, Babajobu, Badr, Beetstra, Beezhive, Bhadani, Big Smooth, Bmdmedia, Bn, Bobet, Bonadea, Bornhj, Brendathomas, Brian Money, Brucevdk, Bubba hotep, Butros, C.rowlatt, Clreland, Callisto`, Callumh93, CambridgeBayWeather, Can't sleep, clown will eat me, Capellan, Capricorn42, Carl McCall, Ceas webmaster, Celestianpower, Charlesfahringer, Chet Gray, Chris 73, Chris is me, Chrisvnicholson, Chuckrussell, Chzz, Cianpeco, CiaranG, Cipher nemo, Clandestino usr, Closedmouth, Cmormina, Cms-8, Cmscritic, Conscious, Craigb81, Crazycomputers, Crenner, CristianoMacaluso, CygnusPius, Cynical, D2s, DDeckert, DMacks, Danakil, Dancter, DarkArctic, David.Mestel, Davidjamesgill, Davidm fr, Davidp, DeadEyeArrow, Debendranandi, Delldot, Deltabeignet, DemonX, Den fjättrade ankan, DennisDaniels, DerHexer, Derek Ross, Descendall, Desert lizard, Dgeiser13, Dim-com, Discospinster, Dkcreatto, Dna4salE, Dnyanraj, Dogsgomoo, Drakeja, Dreftymac, Dthomsen8, Dungodung, EEMIV, ESkog, EastAttica2311, Edmz, Edunet, Eglim, El C, El T, Eliz81, Elmao, Elonka, Elvislam, Emurphy42, ErichCervantez, Erkan Yilmaz, Espanyol orabi, Everyking, Ewolfram, F.smirnoff, FJPB, Falcofire, Faradayplank, Femto, Fleminra, Flexportal, Flockmeal, Fluffykryptonite, Folletto, Fred Bradstadt, Fredrick day, Frehley, Furrykef, Fusesite, Fuzheado, GTwest, Gene s, Geneffects, Geologyguy, Gifford Watkins, Giraffedata, Glenn, Godzig, Gonzalovazquez, GraemeL, Greyskinnedboy, Groogle, Gujamin, Gurch, Guyzero, Gwernol, Ham Pastrami, Harshadoak, Hcgtv, Heath007, HendyMusic, Herbythyme, Heron, Hexagon1, Hideyuki, Hirzel, Hongooi, Hootus, Hu12, Huawuan, Huji, Huon, Hyperweb, IRP, Iced Kola, Inimino, Interiot, IronD, Istartfires, Ixfd64, J.delanoy, JHMM13, Jacj, JanHart, Janadore, Jason Potter, Jatkins, Javert, JavierMC, Jay, Jcleath, Jeffrey O. Gustafson, Jesna, Jezmck, Jkeene, Jni, Joeblakesley, John Fader, John Nixon, John254, John259, Johnhannawin, Johnleemk, JonHarder, Jonathan Drain, Jonglee372, Joseph Dwayne, Joshsteiner, Jpbowen, Jrgetsin, Julia Rossi, Justin Eiler, Jwissick, JzG, KD5TVI, KeithChee, Kerim Friedman, Kff, Khaledelmansoury, Khalidhassani, Khym Chanur, Kloot, KnowledgeOfSelf, Knutux, Koffer, Kozuch, Krich, Kthemank, Kubko X, Kungming2, Kuru, L.sogabe, LakeHMM, Lakhim, Lasilyt, Laura SIMMONS, Lauratto, LeGreg, LeeHunter, Leif, Lembda99, Lightcube, LindsayH, Linforest, Linkspamremover, Linuxerist, LiquidFire, Longhair, Lootzyne21, Lootzynewiki, Loren.wilton, Luca.digaspero, Lucamauri, Lucky6.9, Lurgid, Luís Felipe Braga, Lvr, Lycurgus, M7, MER-C, MSchmahl, MacTed, MalcolmGorman, Mandarax, Mange01, MansonP, Margin1522, Markish99, Marknew, Martinvie, Mauro Bieg, Maury Markowitz, Maximus Rex, Mcswell, Mdd4696, Meeples, Melsaran, Menchi, Meno25, Mentifisto, Mglaser, Michael Hardy, Mido, Mikecook, Miker@sundialservices.com, Mind21 98, Minghong, MisterCharlie, Mjquin id, Mmichalak, Moreschi, Mrglass22, Mshecket, Mulad, Mushroom, Mxn, Myanw, Mydogategodshat, Mydoggnarley, Naveedmemon, NawlinWiki, Neilc, Neutrality, Nevst, Nickj, Niteowlneils, Nitya Dharma, Noldoaran, Nosforit, NovaDog, Novasource, Nufm, Nurelm, Nurg, Ohnoitsjamie, Oicumayberight, Oldsoul, Oli Filth, Optakeover, P3net, Panchhee, PaperConfessional, Partyboi59, Pathomasjtj, Patrick, Paulino Michelazzo, Pavel Vozenilek, Pavillion, Peachey88, Pello, Persian Poet Gal, Person1988, Petrias, Pgk, PhantomS, Pharos, PhilipO, PhilipR, Phmagnabosco, Piano non troppo, Piroroadkill, Plrk, PowerFlower, Poweroid, Prabhakardatla, Pradzee123, Prestonmcconkie, ProxyUser, Publishing, Pvinci, Qef, Qirex, Quendus, QuickFox, Quoth, RG2, RadioKirk, RainbowOfLight, Ramir, Random contributor, Rasmus Faber, Raven4x4x, RazorICE, Rdsmith4, Red Winged Duck, RedWolf, Reedy, Retired username, RexNL, ReynoldLeming, Ric man, Richss, Rio517, Rje, Rkiesler, Robert K S, Roberta F., Robomaeyhem, RodC, Rodii, Romanm, Ron Ritzman, Ronz, Roux, Rthrash, Rugops, Runeberge, Rvcms, Ryunnn, S.K., S2d jamesr, SMC, Saanvik, Saibod, Salsa Shark, Sam Hocevar, Sam Korn, Scarian, Schmalfungus, Scofield1, Scott A Herbert, Seajay1979, Seajay19792, Seantheman444, Sebleblanc, Seglea, Senator Palpatine, Sergeant85, Shadowjams, Shanes, Shaun mcgrath, Sheiko, Sheldon Rampton, Shell Kinney, Sherbrooke, Shoeofdeath, Silverninja, Silvestre Zabala, Simeon, Sindri, Skalman, Slakr, Slark, Sleepyhead81, Slham1972, Snoutholder, Snoyes, SpaceFlight89, Spider8, SpuriousQ, SqueakBox, Stephen Gilbert, Stevekennett, Sumit81garg, Suruena, Sweet2, Sworthy, Synchronism, Syphonbyte, TakingUpSpace, TakuyaMurata, Tallbonez, Talrias, Tannin, Tanvir Ahmmed, Tarquin, TastyPoutine, Tbyrne, TeaDrinker, Teacup, Tedickey, The Anome, The Rambling Man, The wub, TheRanger, Thecmsforum, Thenextlevel2k7, This user has left wikipedia, ThorstenNY, Timo Honkasalo, Timwienk, TnS, Tobias Bergemann, Todd, Tolsen718, Tomharrison, TonyW, Tonyf12, Topher67, Tpappas, Tregoweth, Trudesign, Trusilver, Tyraios, UMwoodr0, Ugur Basak, Ukexpat, Unteer, V111P, Vagon, Vantrick, VegaDark, Venache, Versageek, VictorAnyakin, Vietsmall, VinceB, Viriditas, Vivio Testarossa, Waldir, Waninge, WeißNix, Whkoh, Wiki Raja, Wikiaccount1, Wikiaccount2, Wikidmoz, Wiknerd, Willking1979, Wimt, Wookipedian, WorldlyWebster, Xinconnu, Xy7, Yelyos, Yummytork, Zadcat, Zeerus, Zivi03, Zuwiki, Zzuuzz, 1841 anonymous edits

List of wikis *Source*: http://en.wikipedia.org/w/index.php?oldid=309958471 *Contributors*: 09jeljoh, 2004-12-29T22:45Z, =ppy, AaronSw, Acidburn24m, AdamAtlas, AdmiralTreyDavid, Adrian64, Affv, Ahy1, Alanlastufka, Alensha, Alex3001, Alexander Vince, Alexei Kojenov, Alexius08, Aliencam, Allemannster, Almighty Rajah, Almond123, AlphaTwo, Alphador, Alsocal, AltiusBimm, Alxndr, American Eagle, Americanfreedom, Amgine, Amiad1984,

AmyNelson, Anetode, Angela, Angr, Ankhet, Anomo,Antelope9999, Anthony Ivanoff,Antorjal, Arbustoo, Arcturus, Arien Elensar, ArnoldReinhold, Articleworld, Artimalone, Artur Nowak, Ashtead Tutor, Atlantima, Atuuschaaw, Ausir, Axmann8,Ayanoa,Babajobu, Bahonesi, Bammerwiki, Banjolin, Barnsdirect, Bartolah, Bartosz, Barystone66, Basketball110, Bdeetz, Bencherlite, Bentendo24, Benwa, Bestlyriccollection, Betenner, Beyond silence, BigBoyToys, Bigbluefish, Bill37212, BillWSmithJr,BioYu-Gi!, Bitbit, Bizarre223, Bjones,Blueteaw, Bogdangiusca, Bonás, Brainz42, Bramlet Abercrombie, Branddobbe, Brettz9, BrianAldridge, Briefer, Brockert, Bruguiea, Brusselsshrek, Brutal Enigma, Bunny-chan,Caleb 236, Camo-crazed, CanisRufus, Carnildo, Catgut, Cazcazcaz, Cdnrav4x4, Ceburnbluekn1, Celticfan383, Cenarium, Cet utilisateur, Chachu207, Chanlyn,Chase me ladies, I'm the Cavalry, Chaser, Chealer, Chinflaps, Chocolateboy, Chris Iz Cali,Chris Mason,Chriswaterguy, Cjbeckwith,Clashfrankcastle, Cleared as filed, Cmdrjameson, Cmgibson,ColdCase, ColinIam,Companyman75, Computerwiki, Concordia, ConnorJack, Conor Kenny,Conti, Cooper678, Corpx, Corvus cornix, Crazybobbles, Crisses, Cryptic,Csandb, Curps, Curtbeckmann, CyberSkull,Cyberguru, CygnusTM,Cygnusia, DABANANAMUFFIN, DJ Clayworth, DS1953, Da404lewzer, Daniel slomka, Dansiman, Dark Shikari, DaveGorman, Davejenk1ns, David Johnson, DavidCary, Davidboots, Davidcannon, Davodd, Dbachmann, Deadkid dk, Deathphoenix, Decboy, Decstuff, Defunkt, DeletedUser00, Demoeconomist, DenisDiderot, Depressed Marvin, Derekwwww,Dersaidin, Derumi, Desalvionjr, DieWeisseRose, Dilbert, Dimitrisandlefty, Dirk gently, Discospinster, Dismas, Diza, Djf2014, Dkristoffersson, Dog79jtb, Donarreiskoffer, DragonChi, DragonWR12LB, Drini, DrunkenSmurf, Drwolffenstein, Dubrie, Dudleybus, Dugwiki,EJVargas, East718, Ebookads, Echalone, EdJohnston, EditingMachine, Edsmilde, Eduardo Sellan III, Efloean, Ekem, Ekmai, El Otro, Elliotgoodrich, Ellisjudd, Elwikipedista, Englishgirls, Enzo Aquarius, Epbr123, Epdp14, Eric the Rexman,Ericoides, Esanchez7587, Eshatologist, Eskeptik, Eugene van der Pijll, Evil Eye, Evisruc, Exlex,Fajji, Fang 23, Fanofdemocracy, Fastily, FatBoyGettingSlimmer,Fayenatic london, Fish and karate, Fishpaste4000, Fiziker, Flood6, Fram, FreplySpang, FurryiamIAM,Fusion7, Fyboo, GG Crono, GTBacchus, Galaxy001, Gary Morgan, GeorgeStepanek, Georgehoar, Gerph, Gerritklaschke, Gible, Gilliam, Goobergunch, Gormenghastly, Gothbag, Gotyear, GrabBrain, Graham87, Grand loser, Grandmasterka, GreenReaper, Greenrd, Gsingh, Guanaco, Gunfun, Gwyndon,H4lo, HK22,Halo, HamillianActor, HappyUser, Hapsiainen, Hardvice, Harisingh, Harry Wood,Haseldon, Hellokitty86,HenryGale, Herostratus, Hierophantasmagoria, Hipocrite, HomerSimpson08, Husond, Hyarion, I LIVE IN A HAT, IDerfy, IMSoP, ISD, IWhisky, IanManka,Ianrispin, Icewedge, Ickalanda, Igorberger, IlGreven,ImDero, Improbcat, InShaneee, IndigoGenius, Interesdom, Interiot, Interrobang², Invader Poonchy, Ioeth, Ipstenu, Irishdog123, Irishguy, Irsnex, Ivasara, J'raxis, JFromm,JRA WestyQld2, Jabrwocky7, Jacoplane, Jaina222, James.S, JamesBWatson, Jamesy, Jamie, JarlaxleArtemis, Jasper1066, JavierMC,Jaybomb, Jblogg, Jbyers, Jeffrey Smith, Jeltz, Jennypei, Jeodesic, Jerics99, JetLover, JethroX, Jetman, Jim Bough, Jimkloss, Jimmy R, Jjb9e, Jjfootballer92, Jlerner, Jmark13, Jmcgowan, Joe Beaudoin Jr., JoeMoron2000, John Abbe, John Fader, JohnJLothian, Johnmarkh, Jonobennett, Jonverve, Joshua368, JoshuaZ, Joskirps, Jossi, Judson, JulieC,Justchillinyo, JzG, K1Bond007, Karonaway, Kate Flanagan, Kathleen.wright5, Kawana, Kazvorpal,Keensdesign, Keilana, Keitei, Kenchew, Kevincroy, KikosPapadopoulos, Kimchi.sg, King of Hearts, KingKoopr, Kkcologne, Klptyzm, Koavf,Krimpet, Krisallnutt, Kv9, La Pianista, Lanma726,Larry laptop, Lazyquasar, LemmieCookie,Leon math, Leon2323, Levin2007, Lifeartist, LilHelpa, Lockesdonkey, Logos36, Longhair, Longshot14, Lorensen, Loudsox,Lowfly, LtNOWIS, Lumenos, M Alan Kazlev, MBurbank, MCG,MER-C,Ma Swingle, Macukali, Mahemoff, Maheshkumaryadav, Mamyles, Manjolin, Mark Richards, Mark87, MarkGallagher, MarkJaroski, Marklar951, MasterA113, Matthew83, Matticus78, Maximus Rex,Mayfoev, Mdotley,MeltBanana, Merovingian, Metroid composite, Miami Volts, Michael Johnson, Michael Suess, Midoladido,Mikael Häggström, Mike Foker, Mike Payne, Mikebar, Minghong, Minor Contributer, Mithridates, Mixd,Mjrmtg, Mongolmax, Mortiska, Motmajor, MrRadioGuy, Mrmanjpns, Mtw7777, Mukashi, Multimedia Mike, Mushroom, MykeFahrenheit, Myseagull, Mysekurity, Mysticwarloc, NSK,Nabla, Nae'blis, Nahue, Nanenj, Nankai, Nat Booth, Ncusa367, Neurophyre, NicholasTurnbull, Nick R, Nifboy, Niteowlneils, Northgrove, NorwegianMarcus, Number36, Nunquam Dormio,Oboeboy, OddityEG,Okiefromokla, OlavN, Old Right, OldRight,One, Optional1, Ordosingularis, Osama bin dipesh, Otolemur crassicaudatus, Otterathome, Pairadox,Paradoxos,Patrickjoel, Pattyjuggles, Pcarbonn, Pearle, Perl, PeterT, PeterThoeny, Pgaffney09,Phauly, Philosopher06, Pintman, PlasmaDragon, Plrk, Poccil, Poobaloo, Porlob, Ppoi307, Prentice5, Pseudo Intellectual, Pstudier, Pyrospirit, Python eggs, Pz.Az.04Maus,Qlahue, Quadratus, Quarl,Quarqalaq, R9tgokunks, RHaworth, Raiku Samiyaza, Rajeshontheweb, RandyJohnston, Ransus, Rapigan, Ratchet 957, Rberr4, Rbifan,Realist2, Red marquis, Redeyed Treefrog, Reggiecasual, Reinyday, ReneeFountain, Renmiri, Rettetast, Rexhammock,Ribonucleic, Ripalda, Rjwilmsi, Rkmlai, RobKohr, RoboAction, Robofish, RockOfVictory, Rod57, Rodii, Rodtrent, Rory096, Rossami, Rovo79,Rpshetty, RuneArmor, Rursus, Ryangibsonstewart, SColombo,Sacca, SakotGrimshine, Salix alba, Sallicio, SallyForth123, Salty!, Samboy, Samtheboy, Samuel Blanning, Santasslay27, SarekOfVulcan,Sasha l, Sc147, Scapler, Scarecroe, Scetoaux, SeanMD80,Searchmaven, Seedat, Seiche, Serendipodous, Sertmann, SevenMass, Sgilbertwiki, Shamaz, Shanak, Shannara Fan, Siam, SilkCow JamBuses, Silver Edge, Simeonb, Simoes, Sith Penguin Lord, Sj, Sk5893, Sklocke, Skomorokh, Skosuri, Skwee, Skysmith, Slmader, Small business, Smalljim,Smeggysmeg, Snoutholder, Sockr44e, Someoneinmyheadbutit'snotme, Spellcast, Splash, Sprigot, Spud Gun, SteffenPoulsen, Steinsky, Steve is King, Stevemcelwee, Steven Walling, Stevietheman, Stfoley21,Stifle, Strait, Sturgeonman, Stux, Super Sam, SuperDude115, SuperN, Suso, SweetMelissaGT, Szyslak, Tagishsimon, Taidawang, Tannerduke, Tawker, Techfan, Techtonik, Teratornis, Texaswebscout, Thatother1dude, The Rogue Penguin, The Thing, The wub, The.thing, TheEvilBlueberryCouncil,TheListUpdater, TheThingy, Thehotelambush, Thereverseengineers, Thewism, Thivierr, Thomas Blomberg, Timneu22, Timothy 2066, Tom Morris, Totovoto, Toussaint, Tpbradbury, Tregoweth, Trlkly,TryntonShines, Turnstep, Txomin, Tyagi, Tysto, UberScienceNerd, Ukexpat, UnitedStatesian, Utopiah, VeniVidiVici007, Vereinigen, Victorgrigas, Vorash, Vovkav,Vsmith, WAvegetarian, WJBscribe, WLU, WPjcm,Wadleym, Walabio, Wannawiki, Wavelength, Webdrops, Wendell, Weyes, Whiner01, Whizkid120, Whoisjohngalt, Wickethewok, WikiFan04, WikiPasy.pl, Wikiair, Wikifaq, Wikipepedia, Wikiph, Wikispecs, Wizzard2k, Xanadu1, Xavidp, Xevious, Xezbeth, Yarnalgo, Yaron K., Ybelov, Yeahyeahyeah, Yserarau, Zanimum, Zepheriah, Zfang, Zimnx,Zippokovich,Zippy, Zondor, Zorgrian, Zouavman Le Zouave, Zpally, Zzz345zzz, حلمﺍ, 1103 anonymous edits

Mass collaboration *Source*: http://en.wikipedia.org/w/index.php?oldid=304372557 *Contributors*: Chendy, Danellicus, EdBever, Firsfron, Gurch, HisSpaceResearch, Iridescent, John Vandenberg, Kozuch, Macroethicist, Mark Elliott, Mikko Pohjola, MrOllie, Ph.eyes, Philwiki,Primequbit, Psantora, Qwfp, ResidueOfDesign, Robofish, RyanGerbil10, Stacionari, Surfsup00, Toussaint, 15 anonymous edits

Universal edit button *Source*: http://en.wikipedia.org/w/index.php?oldid=309275422 *Contributors*: AdeMiami, AndrewHowse, AndyDingley, Animeronin, DarTar, Equazcion, Evosoho,Fish and karate, Ipatrol, Mabdul, OrangeDog, Sandstein, Shinyplasticbag, Skomorokh, Steven Walling, Superm401, The New Mikemoral, Thumperward, 18 anonymous edits

Image Sources, Licenses and Contributors

Image:HNL Wiki Wiki Bus.jpg *Source*: http://en.wikipedia.org/w/index.php?title=File:HNL_Wiki_Wiki_Bus.jpg *License*: Creative Commons Attribution-Sharealike 2.0 *Contributors*: Andrew Laing

Image:History comparison example.png *Source*: http://en.wikipedia.org/w/index.php?title=File:History_comparison_example.png *License*: unknown *Contributors*: User:J.smith

File:Wikipedia-logo-en-big.png *Source*: http://en.wikipedia.org/w/index.php?title=File:Wikipedia-logo-en-big.png *License*: logo *Contributors*: Chininazu12, Dbenbenn, Eloquence, Jossifresco, LivingGodGroup, Quibik, Str4nd, WAvegetarian, Waldir, 8 anonymous edits

File:Www.wikipedia.org screenshot.png *Source*: http://en.wikipedia.org/w/index.php?title=File:Www.wikipedia.org_screenshot.png *License*: logo *Contributors*: 555, CatherineMunro, Chuck Marean, Danny B., Dbenbenn, Deadstar, Dsmurat, Er Komandante, Eusebius, Froztbyte, GaynaJones, Gurch, Haha169, Herbythyme, I Love Pi, J.delanoy, J.smith, Juliancolton, Kanonkas, Kelvinc, Krofesyonel, LX, Learnsales, Leon2323, Lockal, Mahahahaneapneap, Mandavi, Mike.lifeguard, Mxn, Nard the Bard, Prince Kassad, Rocket000, Sertion, Stratford490, Thehelpfulone, Tiptoety, Vanderdecken, VolodymyrF, WikiSlasher, Yarnalgo, 40 anonymous edits

File:ImageNupedia.png *Source*: http://en.wikipedia.org/w/index.php?title=File:ImageNupedia.png *License*: logo *Contributors*: IDosh

File:EnglishWikipediaArticleCountGraph linear.png *Source*: http://en.wikipedia.org/w/index.php?title=File:EnglishWikipediaArticleCountGraph_linear.png *License*: Creative Commons Attribution-Sharealike 2.5 *Contributors*: User:Seattle Skier, User:TakuyaMurata

File:Wiki feel stupid v2.ogv *Source*: http://en.wikipedia.org/w/index.php?title=File:Wiki_feel_stupid_v2.ogv *License*: unknown *Contributors*: Bolt Peters

File:History comparison example.png *Source*: http://en.wikipedia.org/w/index.php?title=File:History_comparison_example.png *License*: unknown *Contributors*: User:J.smith

File:John Seigenthaler Sr. speaking.jpg *Source*: http://en.wikipedia.org/w/index.php?title=File:John_Seigenthaler_Sr._speaking.jpg *License*: Creative Commons Attribution-Sharealike 2.0 *Contributors*: Photo by Curtis Palmer

File:WIkimania-2006 010.jpg *Source*: http://en.wikipedia.org/w/index.php?title=File:WIkimania-2006_010.jpg *License*: Creative Commons Attribution-Sharealike 2.0 *Contributors*: alex roshuk

File:Wikimedia Foundation RGBlogo with text.svg *Source*: http://en.wikipedia.org/w/index.php?title=File:Wikimedia_Foundation_RGB_logo_with_text.svg *License*: logo *Contributors*: User:DarkEvil, User:SkyBon

File:Wikimedia-servers-2009-04-05.svg *Source*: http://en.wikipedia.org/w/index.php?title=File:Wikimedia-servers-2009-04-05.svg *License*: Creative Commons Attribution-Sharealike 3.0 *Contributors*: self-made

File:PercentWikipediasGraph.png *Source*: http://en.wikipedia.org/w/index.php?title=File:PercentWikipediasGraph.png *License*: unknown *Contributors*: User:Seattle Skier

File:English Wikipedia contributors by country.svg *Source*: http://en.wikipedia.org/w/index.php?title=File:English_Wikipedia_contributors_by_country.svg *License*: GNU Free Documentation License *Contributors*: User:16@r, User:Superm401

Image:Time Between Edits Graph.Jul05-Present.png *Source*: http://en.wikipedia.org/w/index.php?title=File:Time_Between_Edits_Graph_Jul05-Present.png *License*: Public Domain *Contributors*: User:Katalaveno

File:White Nerdy YOU SUCK cropped.jpg *Source*: http://en.wikipedia.org/w/index.php?title=File:White_Nerdy_YOU_SUCK_cropped.jpg *License*: unknown *Contributors*: Original uploader was Damian Yerrick at en.wikipedia Later version(s) were uploaded by Pd THOR at en.wikipedia.

File:Onion wikipedia.jpg *Source*: http://en.wikipedia.org/w/index.php?title=File:Onion_wikipedia.jpg *License*: unknown *Contributors*: Edokter, Guest9999, Melesse, Mwtoews, Skier Dude, TakuyaMurata, 1 anonymous edits

File:Webcomic xkcd - Wikipedian protester.png *Source*: http://en.wikipedia.org/w/index.php?title=File:Webcomic_xkcd_-_Wikipedian_protester.png *License*: Creative Commons Attribution 2.5 *Contributors*: Randall Munroe ()

File:Quadriga-verleihung-rr-02.jpg *Source*: http://en.wikipedia.org/w/index.php?title=File:Quadriga-verleihung-rr-02.jpg *License*: unknown *Contributors*: User:Ralf Roletschek

Image:Memory Alpha Logo.png *Source*: http://en.wikipedia.org/w/index.php?title=File:Memory_Alpha_Logo.png *License*: Creative Commons Attribution 2.5 *Contributors*: Kristian Trigwell

Image:wikitravel.png *Source*: http://en.wikipedia.org/w/index.php?title=File:Wikitravel.png *License*: unknown *Contributors*: Duesentrieb, IMSoP, John Biancato, Jpatokal, Nico-dk, Rikouman

File:Susning.nus logo.png *Source*: http://en.wikipedia.org/w/index.php?title=File:Susning.nus_logo.png *License*: unknown *Contributors*: User:LA2

File:Wikisym-logo.jpg *Source*: http://en.wikipedia.org/w/index.php?title=File:Wikisym-logo.jpg *License*: logo *Contributors*: DarTar

File:Wikimania.svg *Source*: http://en.wikipedia.org/w/index.php?title=File:Wikimania.svg *License*: GNU Free Documentation License *Contributors*: User:Kaganer

Image:Flag of Germany.svg *Source*: http://en.wikipedia.org/w/index.php?title=File:Flag_of_Germany.svg *License*: Public Domain *Contributors*: User:Pumbaa80

Image:Flag of the United States.svg *Source*: http://en.wikipedia.org/w/index.php?title=File:Flag_of_the_United_States.svg *License*: Public Domain *Contributors*: User:Dbenbenn, User:Indolences, User:Jacobolus, User:Technion, User:Zscout370

Image:Flag of the Republic of China.svg *Source*: http://en.wikipedia.org/w/index.php?title=File:Flag_of_the_Republic_of_China.svg *License*: Public Domain *Contributors*: 555, Bestalex, Bigmorr, Denelson83, Ed veg, Gzdavidwong, Herbythyme, Isletakee, Kakoui, Kallerna, Kibinsky, Mattes, Mizunoryu, Neq00, Nickpo, Nightstallion, Odder, Pymouss, R.O.C, Reisio, Reuvenk, Rkt2312, Rocket000, Runningfridgesrule, Samwingkit, Shizhao, Sk, Tabasco, Vzb83, Wrightbus, Zscout370, 72 anonymous edits

Image:Flag of Egypt.svg *Source*: http://en.wikipedia.org/w/index.php?title=File:Flag_of_Egypt.svg *License*: unknown *Contributors*: 16@r, Alnokta, ArséniureDeGallium, BomBom, Denelson83, Dinsdagskind, Duesentrieb, F l a n k e r, Flad, Foroa, Herbythyme, Homolupus, Iamunknown, Klemen Kocjancic, Kookaburra, Lumijaguaari, Mattes, Moroboshi, Neq00, Nightstallion, OsamaK, Reisio, Rimshot, ThomasPusch, Thyes, Vonvon, Wikiborg, Wikimedia is Communism, Überraschungsbilder, 26 anonymous edits

Image:Flag of Argentina.svg *Source*: http://en.wikipedia.org/w/index.php?title=File:Flag_of_Argentina.svg *License*: Public Domain *Contributors*: User:Dbenbenn

Image:Flag of Poland.svg *Source*: http://en.wikipedia.org/w/index.php?title=File:Flag_of_Poland.svg *License*: Public Domain *Contributors*: User:Mareklug, User:Wanted

File:Wikimania globalvoicespanel.jpg *Source*: http://en.wikipedia.org/w/index.php?title=File:Wikimania_globalvoicespanel.jpg *License*: unknown *Contributors*: User:Elya

File:WM2006 0018.jpg *Source*: http://en.wikipedia.org/w/index.php?title=File:WM2006_0018.jpg *License*: unknown *Contributors*: Gus Freedman

File:CHTnWikimania2007.JPG *Source*: http://en.wikipedia.org/w/index.php?title=File:CHTnWikimania2007.JPG *License*: unknown *Contributors*: User:KaurJmeb

File:Wikimania Alexandria 2008-Banner.jpg *Source*: http://en.wikipedia.org/w/index.php?title=File:Wikimania_Alexandria_2008-Banner.jpg *License*: unknown *Contributors*: Mohamed elShamy

License

LaVergne, TN USA
22 January 2010
170909LV00002B/6/P

9 781742 441665